Lincoln Revisited

THE LINCOLN FORUM

Lincoln Revisited

New Insights from the Lincoln Forum

EDITED BY

John Y. Simon, Harold Holzer,
AND
Dawn Vogel

FORDHAM UNIVERSITY PRESS
New York • 2007

LIBRARY OF CONGRESS CATALOGING-IN-PUBLICATION DATA

Lincoln revisited : new insights from the Lincoln Forum / edited by John Y. Simon,
Harold Holzer, and Dawn Vogel.

p. cm.

Essays originally delivered as Lincoln Forum lectures between 2003 and 2005.
Includes bibliographical references.

ISBN-13: 978-0-8232-2736-5 (cloth : alk. paper)
ISBN-10: 0-8232-2736-7 (cloth : alk. paper)

1. Lincoln, Abraham, 1809–1865.   2. Lincoln, Abraham, 1809–1865—Political and
social views.   3. Lincoln, Abraham, 1809–1865—Military leadership.
4. Presidents—United States—Biography.   5. United States—History—Civil War,
1861–1865.   6. United States—Politics and government—Civil War,
1861–1865.   I. Simon, John Y.   II. Holzer, Harold.   III. Vogel, Dawn.
IV. Lincoln Forum.

E457.8L747   2007
973.7092—dc22
2007012989

Printed in the United States of America
09 08 07   5 4 3 2 1
FIRST EDITION

Contents

Acknowledgments

THE LINCOLN FORUM is grateful to its hundreds of members for their support, encouragement, input, and energy. No symposium could be managed without their help and enthusiasm, and for ten years the Forum has boasted an abundance of both.

Ours is a volunteer organization, with one exception: our highly professional administrator, Annette Westerby. The members of the executive committee of the Forum—Frank J. Williams, chairman; Harold Holzer, vice chairman; Charles Platt, our late founding treasurer; and John Y. Simon—all express our thanks to Annette for the brilliant job she does planning and managing these annual events.

Virginia Williams, Edith Holzer, Linda Platt, and Harriet Simon all offer their own immeasurable support to the committee and the editors. And Kay Lawyer and the staff of the Holiday Inn Gettysburg Battlefield welcome our group each year with unfailing hospitality and efficiency.

Finally, we thank our friends at Fordham University Press for their support for this series of books. Robert Oppedisano has been a source of inspiration for us, and Loomis Mayer has guided two of these books into print with his usual high level of competence. We are always proud to partner with Fordham in the effort to share Lincoln Forum scholarship with the broad public.

Introduction

FOR TEN CONSECUTIVE YEARS, Lincoln scholars and Civil War historians from around the country—together with a growing, and increasingly appreciative, public—have gathered in Gettysburg, Pennsylvania each November 16–18 for an annual event called The Lincoln Forum symposium.

Scheduled to coincide with the anniversary week of the Gettysburg Address, and to lead directly into local events that take place in the village each year to commemorate Abraham Lincoln's greatest rhetorical triumph, the Forum offers history students of all ages, and from all regions, the opportunity to share camaraderie, banquets, battlefield tours, and, most of all, of course, good current scholarship. The scholarship is offered at morning and afternoon lectures, after-dinner talks, and lively panel discussions by the finest Lincoln experts of our time.

But "of necessity," as Lincoln himself might have put it, attendance at these symposia is limited by the available space at our headquarters hotel, which sits only a mile or so from the spot, inside the still-haunting Soldiers' National Cemetery, where the sixteenth president spoke on November 19, 1863. For the benefit of the hundreds of Lincoln Forum members who cannot attend all of these events all the time, the organization has been dedicated to work that appears, happily, to be not only unfinished, but perennial: the publication of book-length collections of the essays that have been delivered at the symposia. In this way, the scholarship can be shared with all of its members, and an even wider audience of Lincoln students. This is the third—and by far the longest, and strongest—of these volumes.

It appears at a time—just a few years short of the bicentennial of Abraham Lincoln's birth—when Lincoln scholarship appears to be as robust and provocative as at any time since his death in 1865. Major, recent Lincoln books have earned both critical praise and lofty places on national best-seller lists. Television biographies, however controversial, have scored surprisingly high ratings, feature films are in the works, and new books are being published, republished, announced, and contemplated at an astonishing rate—with no end in sight, and no apparent diminution of reader interest. True, Abraham Lincoln recently "lost" a televised "Who's The Greatest American" phone-in election to Ronald Reagan—the victim, most likely, of an unwinnable contest between the silent old photographs of the nineteenth century and the vivid televised images of the twentieth. But Lincoln remains first in the hearts of his countrymen, and of professional historians, in survey after survey of the reputations of American presidents.

Astonishingly, his omnipresence in the culture does little to stifle interest or debate. Rather, Lincoln continues to inspire new generations of historians to tackle, in new ways, this most written-about story in our history. And more often than not, notwithstanding the occasional detour toward the lurid and sensational, they find something new and worthwhile to say.

The essays in this book represent a wide variety of such recent and important contributions to the literature of the Lincoln field.

All were originally delivered as Lincoln Forum lectures between 2003 and 2005, and the editors hope they retain their freshness and immediacy. Most required very little editing, and preserve the unique literary style of each writer. The range of subjects is broad: their authors came to the Forum either to tackle entirely new and uncharted scholarly territory, to preview important new books, or to offer new perspectives on projects that they had recently published. This mix of approaches—prospective and retrospective alike—proves nothing short of exhilarating.

Here, for example, historians Michael Vorenberg, Matthew Pinsker, Ronald C. White, Jr., Jean Edward Smith, William C. Harris, and Edward Steers, Jr., reconsider their own recent work: on freedom, Lincoln's private life, presidential oratory, Lincoln as commander in chief, Lincoln as diplomat, and Lincoln as victim of presidential assassination, respectively.

Military historians Craig Symonds and John Marszalek weigh in on the president's leadership of his army and navy. Lincoln Forum chairman Frank J. Williams, who serves as Chief Justice of the Rhode Island Supreme Court, examines the still-timely subject of civil liberties in wartime. And poet/biographer Daniel Mark Epstein considers the influence Walt Whitman exerted on Lincoln, and vice versa. Offering a taste of scholarship to come, acclaimed veteran historians Garry Wills and William Lee Miller offer exciting previews of forthcoming work, while fine young scholars Lucas Morel and Joseph Fornieri examine Lincoln's political and religious faith.

Finally, two of the three editors of this volume provide chapters as well. It is our hope that we were able to apply to ourselves the same high standards that we, and all the members of The Lincoln Forum, so routinely expect of others.

Harold Holzer

Lincoln Revisited

CHAPTER 1

Lincoln's Political Faith in the Peoria Address

Joseph R. Fornieri

"LITTLE BY LITTLE, BUT STEADILY AS MAN'S MARCH TO THE grave, we have been giving up the OLD for the NEW faith"—so proclaimed Abraham Lincoln on October 16, 1854, at Peoria, Illinois.[1] What did Lincoln mean by this provocative statement? Just what was the "OLD" faith? And what was the "NEW" faith? What were the American people giving up?

It is my purpose to explore Lincoln's political faith in the Peoria Address as an ultimate moral justification of American public life, one that combines the moral and religious teachings of the Bible with the Founders' republicanism. It is my contention that the Peoria Address was the most mature and profound expression of Lincoln's political thought to date in 1854, and that its rich teaching on the moral foundations of American popular government has been overshadowed by scholarly attention given to earlier works like the Lyceum Address of 1838, and to subsequent works like the Second Inaugural Address of 1865. Though scholars have acknowledged its greatness, there has been no comprehensive treatment of the Peoria Address as exemplary of Lincoln's integration of religion and politics.[2] I seek to remedy this gap in the voluminous Lincoln literature.

Let us first consider what a political faith is. Even a cursory reading of Lincoln's speeches and writings will reveal that his interpretation of American democracy was thoroughly imbued by the Judeo-Christian worldview revealed in the Bible. It is well known that he was an avid reader of Scripture, and that he sought to apply its wisdom to politics, explaining that "the good old maxims of the Bible are applicable, and truly applicable to human affairs, . . ."[3] Noteworthy in this regard was Lincoln's penchant for describing the first principles of American republicanism in terms of a sacred creed. Indeed, Lincoln often spoke of America's "political faith," its "Ancient faith," the "Old Faith," "the early faith of the republic," a "political religion," "the national faith," and "those sacred principles enunciated" by the Founding Fathers. All of these terms denote a union of religion and politics—a participation of the secular in the sacred. Lincoln's related effort to articulate, defend and affirm the legitimacy of American self-government against the threat posed to it by the "new faith" of slavery led him to probe the moral foundations of political order. Among the many reasons Lincoln is of enduring significance is his rare ability to provide an ultimate moral justification of American public life. This vindication of the founding principles of the American Democratic Republic is what is meant by his political faith.

The term "political faith" was coined originally by Thomas Jefferson in his First Inaugural Address where he described the core principles of American republicanism as the "creed of our *political faith*—the text of civil instruction—the touchstone by which to try the services of those we trust; and should we wander from them in moments of error or alarm, let us hasten to retrace our steps and to regain the road which alone leads to peace, liberty, and safety."[4] Lincoln forthrightly acknowledged his political debt to the Author of the Declaration when he identified "the principles of Jefferson" as "the definitions and axioms of free society."[5] Consequently, Lincoln interpreted his mission to preserve the Union as an endeavor "to save the principles of Jefferson from total overthrow in this nation."[6] Saving the principles meant reinvigorating the political faith or "ancient faith" of the Founders. As reported by the *Illinois Journal* on October 5, 1854, Lincoln candidly revealed his political vocation to uphold the "political faith":

> Taking up the anti-slavery ordinance of 1787, that had been applied to all the North-west Territory, Mr. Lincoln presented that act of the fathers of our republic, the vindicators of our liberty, and the framers of our government, as the *best* exposition of their views of slavery as an institution. It was also a most striking commentary of their *political faith*, and showed how the views of those political sages, to whom we owe liberty, government, and all, comported with the new-fangled doctrines of popular rights, invented in these degenerate latter days to cloak the spread of slavery.[7]

Indeed, Lincoln's remarks at Springfield help shed light on his articulation of the "old faith" and "ancient faith" in the Peoria Address, which was delivered twelve days later.

Lincoln envisioned the Declaration of Independence as a moral covenant that articulated the first principles of the regime's political faith. The self-evident truths of the Declaration were sacred and therefore worthy of reverence insofar as they constituted a rational expression of humankind's participation in the divine law that governs the universe. In effect, Lincoln interpreted the Declaration as a declaration of the precepts of natural law.[8] Throughout his public life, he consistently maintained that the moral legitimacy of human laws must be measured in terms of their conformity to a transcendent normative standard—that is, a universal rule and measure of "how things ought to be." This standard was calibrated by God's moral universe, promulgated by the Declaration, and known through the cooperation of both human reason and divine revelation in the Bible. According to Lincoln, human rights were antecedent to government because they came from the hand of the Creator. Natural rights were not the gift of government, but of God. Metaphorically, Lincoln's political faith may be viewed as a "yardstick" to judge the moral progress or decline of the country. Similarly, Jefferson described this political faith as the "text of our civil instruction" and "the touchstone by which to try the services of those we trust."

It must be emphasized that Lincoln's political faith was not formulated as an abstract doctrine, but as a concrete, historical response to rival interpretations of American public life vying for the nation's soul. The struggle over slavery in the mid-nineteenth century raised ultimate questions about the meaning and destiny of the Union. Both sides invoked the *same God*, the *same Bible*, and the *same Constitution* to vindicate their particular interpretation of the American regime.

The struggle over slavery was at the same time a struggle over competing interpretations of Christianity and the Bible. Southern Divines like Frederick Ross appealed to Romans 13 in support of their claim that "Slavery was ordained of God." This, by the way, was the title of Ross's book on proslavery theology, a work that Lincoln repudiated.[9] In the North, abolitionists like William Lloyd Garrison declared that there could be "no Union with slaveholders," reviling the Constitution as "a covenant with death, and an agreement with hell." Even Stephen A. Douglas, certainly no abolitionist and one who decried the mixing of religion and politics, exploited the Bible in defense of popular sovereignty. As will be seen, during the Peoria Address, Douglas interrupted Lincoln as claiming that popular sovereignty was prefigured in the Garden of Eden where God offered Adam and Eve the Freedom of Choice to eat from the tree of knowledge. Douglas further exploited the Bible to defend the moral relativism of popular sovereignty, invoking

Matthew 7:1, "judge not lest ye be judged" as a divine prohibition against making any judgment about slavery's inherent goodness or evil. It is in this context that Lincoln's political faith emerges as a response to rival accounts of American order.

Because Lincoln's moral justification of American public life combined the moral and religious teachings of the Bible with the Founders' republican tradition of self-government, it may be described as biblical republicanism. I contend further that Lincoln's political faith was constituted by *the mutual influence and the philosophic harmony* between these traditions. For Lincoln, the moral precepts of God's revelation in the Bible were confirmed by natural, unassisted reason, and vice versa. The teachings of the Bible were made publicly authoritative through the common language of reason. Consequently, one may speak of The Three R's of Lincoln's political faith: reason, revelation, and republicanism. The complementary insights of these traditions reinforced one another in affirming the moral legitimacy of American democracy.[10]

The immediate context of the Peoria Address was in response to Douglas who toured Illinois in September of 1854 defending the Kansas-Nebraska Act, passed the same year, and trumpeting his doctrine of popular sovereignty. The ostensible subject of the speech was the repeal of the Missouri Compromise of 1820 by the Kansas-Nebraska Act. This event polarized sectional conflict with increasing vigor, and it marked an important turning point in Lincoln's public life and the life of the nation. After 1854, Lincoln would focus his energies against the tangible threat of slavery's extension. From this point onward, he would consistently appeal to the Declaration as the moral covenant of American republicanism. To be sure, Lincoln's response at Peoria was motivated by the danger that slavery extension posed to the Union's perpetuity at home, and to the nation's moral credibility abroad. He thus called for a restoration of "the national faith" based upon the principles of the Declaration of Independence.[11]

Throughout the Peoria Address, Lincoln quoted the Bible directly and extensively, drawing upon its moral teachings, and its rich
allegorical symbolism to vindicate republican government. It should
be noted that in the mid-nineteenth century, Lincoln's audience
would have recognized his myriad references to the Bible. The King
James Bible was widely read at the time and its authority was taken
for granted. Throughout the eighteenth and mid-nineteenth centuries, the Bible was viewed as a comprehensive guide to both private
and public life. Indeed, John Adams once praised the Good Book
for its political wisdom, stating that, "The Bible contains the most
profound. philosophy, the most perfect morality, and the most re-
fined policy, that was ever was conceived upon earth. It is the most
republican book in the world."[12] Significantly, Adams envisioned the
moral teachings of the Bible as confirming republican government
in a manner similar to Lincoln.

Let us now consider more specifically how the Peoria Address
exemplifies Lincoln's political faith. We begin with the many references Lincoln makes to a political creed in the speech. He uses the
terms "national faith," "ancient faith," and "old faith" synonymously
on five different occasions. Remarkably, Lincoln's sole passing reference in the Lyceum Address to a "political religion" has received
more attention than his myriad references to the ancient faith in the
Peoria Address. The references to the ancient faith in the Peoria
Address denote more than a mere instrumental use of religion to
buttress the rule of law, as in Lincoln's Lyceum Address. By contrast,
the Peoria Address provides a more vivid expression of Lincoln's
political faith, one that involves a more fully developed articulation
of the natural law teaching of the Declaration of Independence.

As noted, Lincoln viewed the Declaration as an American Deca-
logue, which promulgated America's republican creed. The self-
evident truth of human equality and its correlative principle of consent were the principal articles of this faith. At a climactic moment

in the middle of the Peoria Address, Lincoln quoted the Declaration's celebrated prologue—"We hold these truths to be self-evident: that all men are created equal. . . ." By doing this, Lincoln was, in effect, bearing witness to the self-evident truth of equality as the "central idea" of the regime.

Lincoln's interpretation of the self-evident truth of equality relied upon the biblical teaching that all persons are created in the image of God, thereby possessing a unique rational and moral dignity among created beings. This unique rational and moral dignity constitutes the basis of our common humanity. And it suggests that manifest differences among human beings are differences in degree, not in kind. Such differences do not alter our fundamental essence as members of the same human family. Despite variances in ability, all human beings, given their composite nature as both rational and sentient beings, occupy the middle station in the hierarchy of being between God and the beasts.[13] Thus, to debase a human being from the rank of a man to the rank of an animal was to degrade the inherent dignity of one created in the likeness of God. Popular sovereignty was "perfectly logical," argued Lincoln, "if there is no difference between hogs and Negroes." Affirming the equal humanity of the African-American at Peoria, Lincoln blamed Douglas for having "no very vivid impression that the negro is a human; and consequently [having] no idea that there can be any moral question in legislating about him."[14]

In Lincoln's political faith, consent of the governed is the moral corollary of equality. Because the principle of consent acknowledges the equal dignity of each human being, it is the only just principle of governance. Popular sovereignty, in Lincoln's view, constituted a spurious interpretation of self-government because it denied the principle of consent to an entire class of human beings. Distinguishing between the new faith of popular sovereignty and the ancient faith of the Founders, Lincoln stated:

The doctrine of self-government is right—absolutely and eternally right—but it has no just application, as here attempted. Or perhaps I should rather say that whether it has such just application depends upon whether a negro is *not* or *is* a man. If he is *not* a man, why in that case, he who *is* a man may, as a matter of self-government, do just as he pleases with him. But if the negro *is* a man, is not to that extent, a total destruction of self-government, to say that he too shall not govern *himself*? When the white man governs himself that is self-government; but when he governs himself, and also governs *another* man [without that other's consent], that is *more* than self-government—that is despotism. If the negro is a *man*, why then my ancient faith teaches me that "all men are created equal"; and that there can be no moral right in connection with one man's making a slave of another.[15]

After affirming the equal humanity of the African-American, Lincoln then declared, "no man is good enough to govern another man, *without that other's consent*. I say this is the leading principle—the sheet anchor of American republicanism."[16] Lincoln's statement that "no man is *good enough* to govern another without that other's consent" implies the Christian teaching of original sin. In Lincoln's political faith, the equal depravity of mankind is just as relevant to democracy as the equal dignity of mankind. Lincoln's further statement that "Slavery is founded in the selfishness of man's nature—opposition to it, is [in?] his love of justice. These principles are an eternal antagonism" also reflects the teaching of original sin and the cosmic struggle between good and evil.[17]

Though Lincoln believed that we are entitled to equal rights based on our equal humanity as rational, moral and free beings, he also believed that we are equally fallible and prone to selfishness. Lincoln would have accepted Lord Acton's famous aphorism that

"Power tends to corrupt and absolute power corrupts absolutely." That is to say, no matter how virtuous, no fallible human being can be entrusted with absolute power over another—as in the case of slavery or Divine Right. Given the common defect of our human nature, no one is entitled to a godlike superiority over his fellows. To claim such a superiority of kind would be tantamount to elevating oneself above the rest of humanity, thereby exempting one from the same moral laws that apply to everyone else—the very principle behind the Divine Right of Kings. Thus, Lincoln explained that the "master . . . governs by a set of rules altogether different from those which he prescribes for himself." Indeed, this statement in the Peoria Address is an expression of the Golden Rule in Matthew 7:12: "Do unto others as you would have them do unto you."

At Peoria, Lincoln characterized popular sovereignty as a novel faith that threatened to supersede the old faith of the Founders. Lurking beneath popular sovereignty's moral neutrality over slavery was a thinly disguised contempt for the African-American's humanity and a covert zeal for the spread of the institution. Lincoln repudiated Douglas's purported moral indifference to the monstrous injustice of slavery in these terms:

> This *declared* indifference, but as I must think, covert *real* zeal for the spread of slavery, I can not but hate. I hate it because of the monstrous injustice of slavery itself. I hate it because it deprives our republican example of its just influence in the world—enables the enemies of free institutions, with plausibility, to taunt us as hypocrites—causes the real friends of freedom to doubt our sincerity, and especially because it forces so many really good men amongst ourselves into an open war with the very fundamental principles of civil liberty—criticizing the Declaration of Independence, and insisting that there is no right principle of action but *self-interest*.[18]

To leave no doubt in the mind of his audience, Lincoln used the strong language of "hate" to convey his feelings towards slavery. He argued that no responsible citizen, let alone a decent human being, could be indifferent to the monstrous injustice of slavery. He profoundly discerned that popular sovereignty was more than just a libertarian doctrine, guaranteeing settlers the freedom to choose. In addition, it carried with it the positive implication that one could enslave another as a matter of moral right, provided it was in one's self-interest to do so. Popular sovereignty debased the political faith of the nation by exalting self-interest of the white majority as a legitimate principle of governance regardless of any higher moral considerations. As noted, Lincoln saw popular sovereignty as nothing more than an excuse to justify the selfishness of human nature. In effect, it amounted to the principle of might makes right. And for Lincoln it was absurd to claim a moral right to do wrong.

While Lincoln regarded statesmanship as necessarily a moral endeavor, Douglas attempted to divorce ethics and politics. According to Douglas, the public invocation of moral absolutes not only limited freedom of choice, but it also intensified political conflict. Douglas believed that the removal of vexing moral questions from national politics would diminish sectional conflict. His solution involved the subordination of morality to the democratic process and the will of the majority. The logic of popular sovereignty implied that nothing was good or evil per se, but merely relative to the subjective interests of territorial majorities: the decision to choose freedom or slavery was a matter of subjective taste comparable to the decision to plant either corn or tobacco.

In response to Douglas's professed moral relativism, Lincoln stigmatized slavery as "a monstrous injustice" and a "GREAT evil." And to emphasize this point, he capitalized each letter of the adjective *great* in his written speech. Affirming a moral universe in which God's law cannot be silenced, Lincoln exclaimed, "the great mass of mankind . . . consider slavery a great moral wrong; and their feelings against it, is not evanescent, but eternal. It lies at the very foundation of their sense of justice; and it cannot be trifled with. It is a great and durable element of popular action, and, I think, no statesman can safely disregard it."[19] Here Lincoln reveals his vision of true statesmanship as guiding public opinion and public policies towards legitimate moral ends. To treat slavery as a matter of moral indifference was to trivialize a great evil. To emphasize this point, Lincoln devoted the second half of the Peoria Address to a consideration of whether or not the "avowed principle" of slavery extension was "intrinsically right." Throughout his speech, he demanded that subsequent public policy on the question of slavery should be governed by the moral recognition of its inherent evil.

Indeed, at Peoria, Lincoln defined the struggle over slavery as a struggle over the moral foundations of republican government. Highlighting the clash between the ancient faith of the Declaration and the new faith of popular sovereignty, he proclaimed:

> Little by little, but steadily as man's march to the grave, we have been giving up the OLD for the NEW faith. Near eighty years ago we began by declaring that all men are created equal; but now from that beginning we have run down to the other declaration, that for SOME men to enslave OTHERS is a "sacred right of self-government." These principles can not stand together. They are as opposite as God and mammon; and whoever holds to the one, must despise the other.[20]

Lincoln's characterization of the slavery debate as ultimately a contest between two incompatible moral principles in his Peoria Address of 1854 prefigures the same message in his House Divided Speech of 1858.

Notably, Lincoln's reference above to God and Mammon paraphrases Matthew 6:24: "No one can serve two masters: for either he will hate the one, and love the other; or else he will hold to the one, and despise the other. Ye cannot serve God and mammon." Lincoln's allusion to mammon—an Aramaic word meaning wealth or property—was entirely consistent with his interpretation of slavery as rooted in the pride and selfishness of human nature.

The Peoria Address also relied upon a biblical view of conscience as found in Jeremiah 31:33: "I will put my law in their inward parts, and write it in their hearts." Like Jeremiah, Lincoln presumed that God had endowed human beings with an inherent capacity to apprehend good and evil. Reminding his audience that the inner voice of conscience could not be muted, Lincoln defiantly challenged Douglas to "repeal the Missouri compromise—repeal all compromises—repeal the declaration of independence—repeal all past history, you still can not repeal human nature. It still will be the abundance of man's heart, that slavery extension is wrong; and out of the abundance of his heart, his mouth will continue to speak."[21] The final sentence is a verbatim quote from Luke 6:45. Here, Lincoln pricks the nation's conscience by reiterating the Bible's teaching that the dignity and depravity of man proceeded from the same source—the human heart.

However, the most powerful appeal to conscience in the Peoria Address—and perhaps in American history—occurs when Lincoln rhetorically asks slaveholders a series of questions about their own actions, thereby prompting his listeners to an intuitive apprehension of slavery's evil. Lincoln rhetorically asked Southerners why they had stigmatized the slave trade as piracy. Why did they shun the slave trader as a vile human being, not allowing their children to play with his children? And why did they emancipate their slaves at vast pecuniary sacrifice? In each case, Lincoln noted that "SOMETHING" had operated on the minds and hearts of Southern people. This something was, in fact, the inner voice of conscience, which grasped the evil of slavery and the African-American's equal humanity despite sophistic arguments to the contrary. To emphasize this point, Lincoln capitalized each letter of the word *something* in his written speech. "What is that SOME-THING?" Lincoln asked. "Is there any mistaking it? In all these cases it is your sense of justice, and human sympathy, continually telling you, that the poor negro has some natural right to himself—that those who deny it, and make merchandise of him, deserve kickings, contempt and death."[22] Through his appeal to conscience at Peoria, Lincoln compelled people of good will—both Northerners and Southerners—to acknowledge the evil of slavery through their own speech and deed. Not the incendiary, self-righteous rhetoric of the abolitionists, but rather the internal moral contradictions of slaveholders themselves, provided the most powerful indictment against slavery.

As noted at the beginning of this essay, both sides of the slavery debate appealed to the Bible. To be sure, Douglas toted the weight of the Good Book to justify his new faith of popular sovereignty. Douglas, who was present at Peoria, interrupted Lincoln, claiming that the principle of popular sovereignty could be traced to the Garden of Eden where God had placed good and evil before man, bidding him to choose one or the other. For Douglas, good and evil in the Garden of Eden was analogous to slavery and freedom in the territories—a matter of choice.

Lincoln's impromptu response once again demonstrates his superior command of Scripture. Whereas Douglas incorrectly read the story from Genesis as an affirmation of man's autonomy to decide for himself what was good and evil, Lincoln correctly saw the injunction against eating the fruit as a moral imperative, imposing a binding duty and obligation upon Adam and Eve. Lincoln scornfully answered Douglas by retorting, "God did not place good and evil before man, telling him to make his choice. On the contrary, he did tell him there was one tree, of the fruit of which, he should not eat, upon the pain of certain death."[23] If taken to its logical conclusion, Douglas's reading of the Bible would obliterate any firm basis for moral judgments by making them entirely relative to personal choice.

Lincoln's relentless pursuit of the moral foundations of self-government at Peoria led him to identify the principle of popular sovereignty with the Divine Right of Kings: by Divine Right, he explained, "the King is to do just as he pleases with his white subjects, being responsible to God alone. By [popular sovereignty] the white man is to do just as he pleases with his black slaves, being responsible to God alone."[24] The American embrace of the principle of Divine Right in the form of popular sovereignty represented a backsliding that was comparable to the Israelites abandoning their monotheism in exchange for the pagan idols of Egypt and Mesopotamia.

Lincoln's use of biblical symbolism in the Peoria Address culminates with an invocation of the Seventh Chapter of the Book of Revelations. This section of Revelations describes the redemption of the Christian community through the purification of their white baptismal robes with the blood of the lamb. With this context in mind, we can better appreciate the force of Lincoln's biblical rhetoric in the Peoria Address when he declared,

> Our republican robe is soiled, and trailed in the dust. Let us repurify it. Let us turn and wash it white, in the spirit, if not the blood, of the Revolution. Let us turn slavery from its claims of "moral right," back upon its existing legal rights, and its argument of "necessity." Let us return it to the position our fathers gave it; and there let it rest in peace. Let us re-adopt the Declaration of Independence, and with it, the practices, and policy, which harmonize with it. Let north and south—let all Americans—let all lovers of liberty every-where—join in the great and good work. If we do this, we shall not only have saved the Union; but we shall have so

saved it, as to make, and to keep it, forever worthy of the saving.[25]

Just as the Christians' white robe had been tainted by sin but redeemed through the blood of Christ, so the nation's republican robe had been stained by the sin of slavery but could be washed clean through the blood of the Revolution, which symbolically represented the political faith of the Founders—the spirit of 1776. Only a return to this simple faith in the purity of its principles would ensure the nation's safe passage through the coming "fiery trial" of Civil War. Lincoln's demand in the statement above that all "practices" and "policy" must be harmonized with the principles of the Declaration also reflects his natural law understanding of the document as a universal rule and measure, an objective standard, to judge human actions.

The Peoria Address is also notable in its clear expression of Lincoln's moral vision of the Union. In the quotation above, Lincoln emphasizes that the Union must be "worthy of the saving." In his view, the Union was only worth saving in light of the principles for which it stood—that is, the sacred principles of the Declaration. Those who accuse Lincoln of being a political opportunist fail to see the inseparable connection in his mind between preserving the Union and upholding the regime's political faith.

Lincoln's moral vision of the Union in the Peoria Address ends with a quotation from the Magnificat in Luke 1:48. The preservation of the American experiment, in the purity of its principles, would cause "succeeding millions of free happy people, the world over, [to] rise up, and call us blessed, to the latest generations."[26] This interpretation of American destiny relies on a notion of mission whose origin can be traced to the Puritan's calling to establish "a city upon a hill" (Matthew 5:14). Like the Puritan forebears, Lincoln believed that America had a mission—a divine calling, to play a role of worldwide significance in the unfolding drama of God's

Providence—namely, to serve as a standard bearer of democracy to the world. In his words, "the monstrous injustice of slavery . . . deprived our republican example of its just influence in the world."

In sum, Lincoln's integration of biblical symbolism, republican tradition and natural reason at Peoria to provide an ultimate moral justification of American public life constitutes the most mature expression of his political faith to date, one that fully articulates a natural law understanding of the Declaration as the foundation of the American experiment. But what relevance does Lincoln's political faith have for us today? Though we have become a more secular culture from the time of Lincoln, the issue of religion in American public life remains. The debate over the Ten Commandments in Alabama, "under God" in the Pledge of Allegiance, and the reemergence of Just War Theory are just a few examples.

I believe that Lincoln's political faith presents challenges to both sides of the church-state debate: On the one hand, it challenges those who seek to drive religion out of the public sphere, and on the other, it challenges those sectarians who would seek to apply the principles of the Bible literally to politics without prudential mediation. Lincoln's affirmation of the mysterious character of the Divine Will, his political moderation, his aversion to self-righteousness, and his ironic criticism of those—both North and South—who exploited the Bible to justify utopian and wicked policies should give pause to those who claim a special dispensation from God. Those who would invoke the Bible in politics should follow Lincoln's example by translating its moral teachings into the common language of the public square: reason. Lincoln's reply to a "Group of Chicago Christians of All Denominations" who presented him with a memorial urging immediate emancipation displays his practical wisdom in applying the moral precepts of the Bible to politics:

> The subject presented in the memorial is one upon which I
> have thought much for weeks past, and I may even say for

months. I am approached with the most opposite opinions and advice, and that by religious men, who are equally certain that they represent the Divine will. I am sure that either the one or the other class is mistaken in that belief, and perhaps in some respects both. I hope it will not be irreverent for me to say that if it is probable that God would reveal his will to others, on a point so connected with my duty, it might be supposed he would reveal it directly to me; for, unless I am more deceived in myself than I often am, it is my earnest desire to know the will of Providence in this matter. *And if I can learn what it is I will do it!* These are not, however, the days of miracles, and I suppose it will be granted that I am not to expect a direct revelation. I must study the plain physical facts of the case, ascertain what is possible and learn what appears to be wise and right. The subject is difficult, and good men do not agree.[27]

While the first principles of equality and liberty in the American regime were derived, in part, from faith-based traditions, the Founders themselves emphasized that these principles were universal and rationally accessible to all human beings regardless of their religious creed. And to those who insist upon driving the sacred out of the public square, it should be remembered that Jefferson, the very person who coined the term "separation of church and state," also coined the term "political faith" in his First Inaugural Address. While the separation of church and state has ensured unprecedented religious liberty in this country and should be maintained, it should also be noted that the Founders never intended to deny religion a voice in the public square.[28] Contrasting the public role of religion in France and America, Alexis de Tocqueville—the French political philosopher who came to America during the Age of Jackson to study democracy—noted: "In France I had seen the spirits of religion and freedom almost always marching in opposite directions. In America I found them intimately linked together in joint reign over the same land."[29] The contemporary debate over the display of religious symbols in French public schools should serve as a reminder of the threat that a rigid secularism may pose to the "free exercise" of religion in the United States. In driving the sacred out of the public square, we inevitably drive out Lincoln—the foremost representative of our political faith. It should not be forgotten that the term "under God" in our Pledge originated from the Gettysburg Address; that the first national Day of Thanksgiving to God was officially established by Lincoln; that the motto "in God we trust" appearing on our coins was authorized by Lincoln; and that the Declaration of Independence—the document viewed by Lincoln as our nation's moral covenant—contains four references to a Supreme Being. Indeed, the attempt to remove two hundred years of nondenominational references to God, a Supreme Being, and an ultimate order in public life, inevitably strikes at the very moral legitimacy of our regime—at least as that regime was understood by Lincoln and the Founders. Whatever their personal beliefs, the Founders maintained that either a hostility or indifference to religion would sap republican government of the moral vitality that sustained it.[30]

At the dawn of the twenty-first century, we are confronted by new threats to human dignity and to our national destiny—biotechnology and the war on terrorism to name a few. In responding to these challenges, we would do well to ponder Lincoln's political faith as a guide, as a moral compass to point us in the right direction. The Lincoln Forum's annual gatherings at Gettysburg bear witness to the political faith that Lincoln lived by—and died for.

CHAPTER 2

Lincoln's Political Religion and Religious Politics

Lucas E. Morel

IN HIS FIRST DEBATE WITH SENATOR STEPHEN DOUGLAS, Abraham Lincoln observed, "In this and like communities, public sentiment is everything. With public sentiment, nothing can fail; without it nothing can succeed. Consequently he who moulds public sentiment, goes deeper than he who enacts statutes or pronounces decisions. He makes statutes and decisions possible or impossible to be executed."[1] Lincoln saw the important role that public opinion played in a republic. He therefore highlighted the influence and therewith the responsibility that molders of public opinion have, and used the bully pulpit to teach Americans about the requirements of self-government. And so a symposium focusing in part on Lincoln as "Communicator in Chief" is, to borrow from Lincoln, "altogether fitting and proper."

One reason for Lincoln's continued resonance with the American people is the religious imagery with which he addressed the

A version of this essay appears in Mark J. Rozell and Gleaves Whitney, eds., *Religion and the American Presidency: The Evolving American Presidency* (New York: Palgrave Macmillan, 2007).

nation's most pressing concerns. Just imagine the Gettysburg Address or the Second Inaugural Address without their biblical references and cadences. To do so would be to strip those timeless documents of their most memorable phrases, if not their most telling reflections on American self-government. In fact, the great orator Frederick Douglass said of Lincoln's Second Inaugural Address that it "sounded more like a sermon than like a state paper," and told Lincoln it was "a sacred effort."[2]

Lincoln's understanding of the requirements of republican government led him to direct religious sentiment toward responsible democracy or self-government. As a successful republic requires a moral or self-controlled people, he believed the religious impulse of society could help moderate the excesses of passion and self-interest in the community. As a means of achieving this social order, Lincoln promoted "support of the Constitution" and "reverence for the laws" to become what he called "the *political religion* of the nation."[3] Lincoln believed that the perpetuation of the free government established by the American Revolution depended on this almost sacred law-abidingness,[4] and he called on both politician and preacher to promote this "political religion."

But if this were the only expression of Lincoln's understanding of the relationship between religion and republican government, one would be hard-pressed to understand him to be, in Elton Trueblood's phrase, "the theologian of American anguish."[5] True, in his Gettysburg and Second Inaugural Addresses, he drew upon the religious sentiments of the American people to cultivate a civil religion in addition to his strictly "political" religion of reverent obedience to the laws.[6] But while the political uses of religion seem to predominate in Lincoln's politics, he never forgot that religion existed for a higher purpose than supporting government. Lincoln, in other words, did not confuse the political utility of religion with religion's true aim: to connect people to God, not to their government.

Lincoln noted, however, that religion was not all sweetness and light for America. He concerned himself as well with the detrimental effect that religious extremists could have on free government, as exhibited by some moral reform movements that promoted temperance and abolition. Some of these reform societies tended to approach their causes with a self-righteousness that allowed little room for discussion and hence posed a threat to the deliberative processes of self-government.[7] In them he saw a religious character that could lead to excesses adverse to constitutional government: namely, theocratic absolutism, which would undermine a regime based on public deliberation as opposed to a theological litmus test. The dependence of self-government on public morality, influenced by the virtues *and* vices of revealed religion, presented Lincoln with a political burden intrinsic to free government. Lincoln's genius was displayed in his preaching and practice of a political religion and religious politics that preserved the respective domains of both government and religion.

What is Lincoln's "religious politics"? Anyone the least familiar with Lincoln's speeches and writings, especially those of his presidential years, knows that his political formulations were the most theological the nation has ever witnessed. From his 1838 Lyceum Address to his 1865 Second Inaugural Address, Lincoln quoted or alluded to the Bible with a familiarity and profundity that rivaled the preachers of his day.[8] This has led much of the debate over Lincoln and religion to center on his own faith (or lack thereof), with scholars and laymen alike arguing for and against Lincoln's Christianity in a way that has virtually eclipsed what I think Lincoln would have seen as a more important issue regarding his contribution to American political thought and practice: namely, how did he think religion should inform politics? What did Lincoln say and do in the political arena about religion that teaches us its proper role in the American regime? And how did Lincoln's political use of religion indicate the proper extent of religion's influence on political affairs? Curiously enough, and to his credit, Lincoln's religious politics spells out not only the limits of religious involvement in politics, but also the limits of political involvement with religion! For a comprehensive treatment of these issues, I refer you to my book *Lincoln's Sacred Effort*, but for the purposes of this essay, I will focus on a few examples of "Lincoln's political religion and religious politics" to illustrate what he thought was a prudent connection between politics and religion.

As early as 1838, at the Young Men's Lyceum of Springfield, Lincoln addressed a problem the United States faced as its revolutionary war veterans passed this earth, leaving no living memory to help perpetuate the grand American experiment in self-government. Lincoln saw this as a major weakening of the republic, and believed only a "political religion" of reverence for the laws and the Constitution could prevent mob rule from giving rise to a "towering genius" who sought to gratify his thirst for fame "at the expense of emancipating slaves, or enslaving freemen."[9] Lincoln proclaims:

> Let reverence for the laws, be breathed by every American mother, to the lisping babe, that prattles on her lap—let it be taught in schools, in seminaries, and in colleges;—let it be written in Primmers, spelling books, and in Almanacs;—let it be preached from the pulpit, proclaimed in legislative halls, and enforced in courts of justice. And, in short, let it become the *political religion* of the nation; and let the old and the young, the rich and the poor, the grave and the gay, of all sexes and tongues, and colors and conditions, sacrifice unceasingly upon its altars.[10]

His religious examples—"reverence," "seminaries," "preached from the pulpit," and "sacrifice unceasingly upon its altars"—and exhortative tone rouse the listener to the seriousness of his cause, a seriousness evoked earlier by calls to one's patriotism and ancestry and now complemented by the aura of religion. Religion, here, serves the republic as the handmaiden of government in the latter's effort to ensure obedience to its laws—an obedience conducive of not only civil but religious liberty.[11]

Lincoln's reference to "the pulpit" heads a list that calls for the gospel of law-abidingness also to be "proclaimed in legislative halls, and enforced in courts of justice." But why does he omit its proclamation from the seat of the executive, the one branch of government missing from his list? Lincoln appears to replace the executive seat with "the pulpit." Regarding "reverence for the laws," the sentence reads: "let it be preached from the pulpit, proclaimed in legislative halls, and enforced in courts of justice."[12] The conspicuous substitution of the preacher for the governor or president leads one to wonder about Lincoln's intention. Is he implying that a governor or president would overstep his authority by preaching the gospel of law-abidingness? This cannot be, because an implicit call for strict separation of church and state would as well exclude the legislature and judiciary Lincoln mentions. Conversely, an overly scrupulous adherence to a separation of church and state would exclude the preaching of Lincoln's "political" religion from "the pulpit." In fact, Lincoln the legislator preached this gospel of law-abidingness in the Baptist Church of Springfield![13]

A review of the immediate context of his listing of the preacher with the legislator and judge shows that Lincoln cites almost every significant influence on a citizen growing up in America:

> Let reverence for the laws, be breathed by every American mother, to the lisping babe, that prattles on her lap—let it be taught in schools, in seminaries, and in colleges;—let it be written in Primmers, spelling books, and in Almanacs;—let it be preached from the pulpit, proclaimed in legislative halls, and enforced in courts of justice.

Starting with the family, moving through the educational system, and concluding with the church and government (with the exception of the executive department), Lincoln shows his primary concern to enlist every possible influence on Americans to the cause of law-abidingness. Here he imitates Moses, who exhorted the Israelites to meditate continually on the commandments: "And these words, which I command thee this day, shall be in thine heart: And thou shalt teach them diligently unto thy children, and shalt talk of them when thou sittest in thine house, and when thou walkest by the way, and when thou liest down, and when thou risest up" (Deut. 6:6–7). Lincoln clearly uses "the pulpit" to symbolize the influence of the church, while he includes the legislature and judiciary to represent the general influence of government.

But why include two of three branches of government and leave out the third? Why not leave the judiciary out, or better still, include the executive as well? A secondary consideration for Lincoln's omission of the executive comes from the concluding sentence of this paragraph, which immediately follows the sentence about preaching reverence for the laws from the pulpit: "And, in short, let it become the *political religion* of the nation; and let the old and the young, the rich and the poor, the grave and the gay, of all sexes and tongues, and colors and conditions, sacrifice unceasingly upon its altars." By calling strict obedience to the laws a political "religion," Lincoln emphasizes the seriousness of his advice and, therefore, the importance of spreading this message in the same manner that a preacher spreads the word of God. Perhaps the executive department is present under the guise of "the pulpit," implying that a religious aspect must be donned by the chief administrator of government—the executive, one uniquely situated among the branches of government to speak with one voice. As the political leader and chief law enforcer of the community, and thus one called to promote law-abidingness, the executive must adopt the mode of a preacher to enlist the community as fellow believers. In short, while explicitly referring to "the pulpit," and thereby invoking the aid of churches against mob violence, Lincoln's listing of the preacher at the head of his otherwise "governmental" list serves as an equivocal reference to the work of the executive in the cause of American salvation from the sin of mob violence. If a republic needs a "political" religion to survive, as Lincoln makes clear, its executive must become its "political" preacher.

Lincoln's explicit call for the community's religious leaders and institutions to help promote the "political religion" of law-abiding-ness brings the first reference to the church's influence on the perpetuation of free government: preaching that strict obedience to the government and laws pleases God. Although the church is not a political institution, Lincoln enlists its support in a way consistent with its own teaching. For example, 1 Peter 2:13–14 states: "Submit yourselves to every ordinance of man for the Lord's sake: whether it be to the king, as supreme; Or unto governors, as unto them that are sent by him for the punishment of evil-doers, and for the praise of them that do well."

Lincoln's "political religion," ironically enough, has little if anything to do with religion proper. To be sure, he calls upon "seminaries" and "pulpits" to spread the message of political salvation through civil obedience. Lincoln even speaks of "altars" upon which the people are to "sacrifice unceasingly" as part of their obedience to all of the laws. His political religion, however, is more politics than religion.[14] The only direct connection to religion is the commitment it requires of each citizen. One could as well phrase it "political zeal" or "political faith," the former emphasizing the passion and the latter the trust of the public. The phrase chosen by Lincoln, "political religion," represents both the passion and trust necessary to ensure the perpetuation of the American regime.

With respect to political zeal, one might wonder why Lincoln would make such an appeal, for he has already shown the danger of community zeal when manifested in the form of vigilante pursuit of justice. "Mobocracy," a zeal for the immediate gratification of a community's desire for justice, leads ultimately to the public's disregard for the laws and government. Lincoln appealed earlier, though, to the passions of his listeners by calling to mind the efforts of their forebears in establishing their present blessings, an appeal that vivifies an otherwise uninspiring call to mere civil obedience. One must involve the emotions of a community in order to move them to follow even the most rational advice: to wit, "let every man remember that to violate the law, is to trample on the blood of his father." Even though Lincoln counsels that the passionate excesses of a self-governing community will cause their downfall, he is careful not to exclude passion altogether, for it serves to support the regime when linked to the laws and the Constitution.[15] Furthermore, Lincoln follows the paragraph containing the phrase "political religion" with one describing it as "a state of feeling." To engender this "feeling" is his present project, albeit one argued meticulously on the ground of reason, which is seen most clearly when he closes the address with an ode to reason: "Passion has helped us; but can do so no more. It will in future be our enemy. Reason, cold, calculating, unimpassioned reason, must furnish all the materials for our future support and defence."[16]

Aside from "political religion" and, more generally, the political utility of religion, Lincoln's political practice also points to political respect for religion. This may have been driven, in part, from his own growing appreciation of religion in his own life. For example, in the summer of 1864, Lincoln invited his long-time friend, Joshua F. Speed, to spend the night at his retreat at Soldiers' Home, just three miles north of the White House. Speed wrote of his stay at Soldiers' Home years later, and it gives perhaps the clearest indication of Lincoln's religious faith late in life:

> As I entered the room, near night, he was sitting near a window intently reading his Bible. Approaching him I said,

"I am glad to see you so profitably engaged." "Yes" said he, "I am profitably engaged." "Well," said I, "If you have recovered from your skepticism, I am sorry to say that I have not." Looking me earnestly in the face, and placing his hand on my shoulder, he said, "You are wrong Speed, take all of this book upon reason that you can, and the balance on faith, and you will live and die a happier and better man."[17]

Speed notes that Lincoln had come a long way from his early days of religious "skepticism."[18] This famous recollection of Lincoln's dearest friend reveals an appreciation of religion that transcends its mere usefulness to the government. For Lincoln, religion *qua* religion had a purpose far beyond that of simply supporting the government: It existed to fulfill a divine purpose between an individual and God and ought not to be viewed solely in light of its political utility. Because religion's reason for being stands independent of political necessity, Lincoln made sure to enlist its services to the regime without subverting its own reason for being. He saw to it that government, while he was at the helm, accommodated religion as the citizenry saw to its higher end.

This understanding of religion's ambivalent support of the state has only recently been revived in scholarly circles.[19] For example, historian Mark Y. Hanley argues that "Protestant spiritual discourse, anchored by religious jeremiads and regular sermons, . . . placed faith's temporal benefits on a fulcrum that gave weighted advantage to a transcendent spirituality beyond the Commonwealth." In other words, while some religious leaders saw a close affinity of purpose between Christianity and the American republic, others presented "faith's capacity to improve society as a subordinate aim" to its highest priority: pointing men and women toward "a spiritual destiny beyond the commonwealth."[20]

A telling example of Lincoln's respect for revealed religion, especially as a principal influence on society, is his 1846 "Handbill

Replying to Charges of Infidelity." In his run for Congress in 1846, Lincoln campaigned against the well-known Methodist circuit rider Peter Cartwright. Friends told Lincoln that Cartwright "was whispering the charge of infidelity" against him,[21] suggesting that Lincoln held unorthodox views about religion. Lincoln, therefore, responded with a handbill explaining his understanding of the controversy.

As the July 31, 1846, handbill contains the most direct expression of Lincoln's view of religion and public life, at least to that point in his life, we quote it in its entirety:

> *To the Voters of the Seventh Congressional District.*
> FELLOW CITIZENS:
>
> A charge having got into circulation in some of the neighborhoods of this District, in substance that I am an open scoffer at Christianity, I have by the advice of some friends concluded to notice the subject in this form. That I am not a member of any Christian Church, is true; but I have never denied the truth of the Scriptures; and I have never spoken with intentional disrespect of religion in general, or of any denomination of Christians in particular. It is true that in early life I was inclined to believe in what I understand is called the "Doctrine of Necessity"—that is, that the human mind is impelled to action, or held in rest by some power, over which the mind itself has no control; and I have sometimes (with one, two or three, but never publicly) tried to maintain this opinion in argument. The habit of arguing thus however, I have, entirely left off for more than five years. And I add here, I have always understood this same opinion to be held by several of the Christian denominations. The foregoing, is the whole truth, briefly stated, in relation to myself, upon this subject.

I do not think I could myself, be brought to support a man for office, whom I knew to be an open enemy of, and scoffer at, religion. Leaving the higher matter of eternal consequences, between him and his Maker, I still do not think any man has the right thus to insult the feelings, and injure the morals, of the community in which he may live. If, then, I was guilty of such conduct, I should blame no man who should condemn me for it; but I do blame those, whoever they may be, who falsely put such a charge in circulation against me.[22]

Lincoln admits that he is not a member of any Christian church. As a state legislator, Lincoln did not attend church services regularly. Soon after he moved to Springfield, the new state capital, he wrote to Mary Owens, "I've never been to church yet, nor probably shall not be soon. I stay away because I am conscious I should not know how to behave myself."[23] In the midst of the Civil War he would confess, "I have often wished that I was a more devout man than I am."[24] His closest friend, Speed, also recalled Lincoln's personal struggle of faith during his early years in Springfield: "When I knew him, in early life, he was a skeptic." Speed added, however, that Lincoln "was very cautious never to give expression to any thought or sentiment that would grate harshly upon a Christian's ear."[25] The exoneration implicit in his handbill—"I have never denied the truth of the Scriptures"—lies with his belief that infidelity or lack of faith lies primarily in one's view of the Holy Scriptures and not with membership at a particular church congregation.

Most important, Lincoln wishes to address the political relevance of a candidate's religious beliefs and practice. He adds that he never spoke "with intentional disrespect" of religion or any particular denomination. His concern not to show disrespect toward the faith of others can be seen in his draft of a speech comparing

Thomas Jefferson and Zachary Taylor (the Whig presidential candidate in 1848) on the presidential veto power: "They are more alike than the accounts of the crucifixion, as given by any two of the evangelists—more alike, or at least as much alike, as any two accounts of the inscription, written and erected by Pilate at that time."[26] In his only term as congressman, Lincoln omitted the biblical reference in his final draft. He knew enough not to stir up controversy over apparent inconsistencies in the Bible.

Some have been troubled by Lincoln's reticence in the 1846 handbill to profess anything specific about his religious beliefs.[27] To be sure, Lincoln had little time for religious doctrines and sectarian institutions derived from the Holy Scriptures by fallible human minds[28] and was careful not to misrepresent himself religiously on the stump. But this view places too great an emphasis on Lincoln's "political expediency," for he only intended to clarify his rumored "infidelity." Lincoln felt no obligation to share personal religious views that he believed bore little or no relevance to the campaign at hand. He therefore shows that his avoidance of sins of commission is the only relevant political consideration, not any sins of omission. The latter may have "eternal consequences" to be worked out "between him and his Maker," but this bears no import to political affairs. Lincoln chose to explain his understanding of religion and civil society to help his constituents know the legitimate expectations they should have regarding a candidate's public attitude toward religion.

This is why Lincoln does not state explicitly what he thinks about the Bible or any particular Christian doctrine. Like George Washington, James Madison, and other American Founders, Lincoln did not think the public profession of one's religious convictions contributed much for the community to consider when deciding on a candidate for office or when discussing the merits of a specific public policy. An undue emphasis on one's religious beliefs, moreover, could easily lead to factious politics, with no easy means of resolving disagreements. Here religion in the public square could give rise to factious majorities ruling according to their numerical might, as opposed to principled right, and therefore threaten the perpetuation of American self-government. In short, elections should not be turned into a forum for resolving religious quarrels.

In the handbill, Lincoln volunteers an account of his belief "in early life" in the doctrine of necessity, which seems to deny the free will of man. However, he emphasizes that five years had passed since he last made these arguments, they were never made in public, and they were understood by him to be shared by several Christian denominations. A case in point would be his own parents' church in Kentucky, Little Mount Separate Baptist Church. They were part of the "Separate" Baptist movement, otherwise known as primitive or "hard-shell" Baptists for their strict predestination doctrines.[29] In short, Lincoln's belief in the doctrine of necessity was a private matter not intended for the public ear and one that did not threaten Christian orthodoxy because none existed on the subject. He offers this personal information in the event that it might have been the source of the rumor of his religious infidelity. In the second paragraph, Lincoln shares his understanding of how the rumor might trouble the consciences of some of his constituents—hence, the reason for his no longer debating said belief even privately "with one, two or three."

Lincoln states that he doubts he could be moved to support a political candidate whom he knew to be "an open enemy of, and scoffer at, religion." Lincoln defends the community's "feelings" connected with religion; they should be immune from public "insult." While the private insult of a neighbor's religion is hardly intended by Lincoln, his emphasis on the feelings of "the community" leaves room for *discussing* the truth of a particular religion with one's neighbor without the malice and recklessness accompanying the intentional slight of a fellow citizen's convictions. Religion deals with a man's conscience and hence should be handled with care—especially if that man is a neighbor and fellow citizen.

During his first run for Congress in 1842, Lincoln showed respect for a community's religious sensibilities—despite personally experiencing "the strangest church influence" against him—in a letter written to a delegate to the Seventh Congressional District convention after the campaign was over:

> Baker is a Campbellite, and therefore as I supose, with few acceptions got all that church. My wife has some relatives in the Presbyterian and some in the Episcopal Churches, and therefore, whereever it would tell, I was set down as either the one or the other, whilst it was every where contended that no ch[r]istian ought to go for me, because I belonged to no church, was suspected of being a deist, and had talked about fighting a duel. With all these things Baker, of course had nothing to do. *Nor do I complain of them. As to his own church going for him, I think that was right enough*, and as to the influences I have spoken of in the other, though they were very strong, it would be grossly untrue and unjust to charge that they acted upon them in a body or even very nearly so. I only mean that those influences levied a tax of a considerable per cent. upon my strength throughout the religious comunity.[30]

In the eyes of churchgoers, his dueling episode with James Shields the previous year,[31] lack of church membership, and suspected deism crippled his campaign to be nominated as the Whig candidate of Sangamon County. Lincoln confesses that he found his campaign hampered by public doubts over his religious inclinations; yet, he does not begrudge his opponent (and close friend) for drawing the support of his own community church. Here, Lincoln grants not only the likelihood but the propriety of winning the support of those most acquainted with you. For example, in his first run for the Illinois State House, the twenty-three-year-old Lincoln received

277 out of 300 votes from his hometown precinct—the political equivalent of a congregation.[32] Even though it turned out to be a losing bid, Lincoln's first campaign for public office demonstrated the power of proximity or affection for what is near and dear, which he extends to one's church.

He also guards the "morals" fostered by the religious sentiments of the community from public "injury." To disregard the consequences of undermining a community's religious beliefs is to place too sanguine a confidence in the principles and practices of what one would substitute in their place. As George Washington expressed this in his Farewell Address:

> Of all the dispositions and habits which lead to political prosperity, Religion and morality are indispensable supports. In vain would that man claim the tribute of Patriotism, who should labour to subvert these great Pillars of human happiness, these firmest props of the duties of Men and citizens. The mere Politician, equally with the pious man ought to respect and cherish them.[33]

Lincoln leaves "the higher matter of eternal consequences" to the offending party "and his Maker," and preserves religious freedom, on the one hand, and promotes social responsibility, on the other. Again, George Washington set the example:

> The liberty enjoyed by the people of these states of worshipping Almighty God agreeably to their consciences, is not only among the choicest of their *blessings*, but also of their *rights*. While men perform their social duties faithfully, they do all that society or the state can with propriety demand or expect; and remain responsible only to their Maker for their religion, or modes of faith, which they may prefer or profess.[34]

As president, Lincoln explicitly acknowledged the nation's debt to the Almighty through proclamations of days of religious observance. Lincoln called for national days of thanksgiving, fasting, and prayer eleven times. In his last public address, following Lee's surrender at Appomattox, Lincoln states: "In the midst of this [celebration], however, He, from Whom all blessings flow, must not be forgotten. A call for a national thanksgiving is being prepared, and will be duly promulgated."[35] These proclamations, as well as other speeches involving religion in the public sphere, show the mutual benefit Lincoln believed religion and government could have on each other.

His speeches and writings reflect a penchant for drawing on religion for public purposes, as well as facilitating the natural and rightful expression of man's desire to worship the Creator. Lincoln, in other words, preserved the status of religion, independent of the needs of government, as worthy of the adherence of democratic citizens. Without going into many other ways Lincoln did this, let me note just a few examples of his political accommodation of religion: an 1862 Order for a Sabbath Observance "by the officers and men in the military and naval service";[36] an 1861 recommendation that Congress appoint and pay for hospital chaplains; his protection of the religious freedom of Southerners from Union generals who in some instances had undertaken to govern churches in the South; and most obviously by the ten executive proclamations of local and national days of fasting, thanksgiving, and prayer. Regardless of Lincoln's own religious beliefs, as a politician he spoke and acted so as to preserve the legitimate sphere of action for government and religion.

An early example of Lincoln's attempt to show the limits of religious expression in the public square is found in his 1842 Temperance Address, a speech ostensibly about moderation or temperance with regard to alcohol but at its core focused on tempering or moderating excess in political discussion. Ironically, this speech about speech judiciously employs religious imagery to subtly point out how excessive religious expression in public debate can subvert the political trust, humility, and compromise that grease the wheels of republican government.[37]

Lincoln's reference to the early temperance reformers as "old school" champions alludes to a then recent division among American Christians over the severity of original sin. In 1838 the Presbyterian Church suffered a schism, presaged by heresy trials earlier that decade, that produced an "Old School" and a "New School" bloc.[38] C. Bruce Staiger writes that as the Presbyterian Church sought to minister to the western settlements under its 1801 "Plan of Union," the incorporation of Congregationalists in their endeavor brought in "the liberalizing Pelagian and Arminian ideas of Unitarianism." The result was "a bitter theological quarrel between the strictly orthodox Calvinists of the Old School and the New School group which embraced the 'radical' New Divinity representative of the Congregational influence."[39] The debate centered around the doctrine of original sin, that men are born into the sin of Adam with only a few foreordained for salvation and the rest destined for damnation.[40] Opposed to the strict Calvinism of old guard Presbyterians, the New School held that man possessed free will. Charles Finney, the New School revivalist par excellence, described a man's conversion as an act of his will: "if the sinner ever has a new heart, he must . . . make it himself." Moreover, "All sin consists in selfishness; and all holiness or virtue, in disinterested benevolence."[41] Here lies the connection between the Second Great Awakening and the social reform movements that would sweep across America from the late 1820s through the 1830s.[42] A few examples of Lincoln's subtle employment of religious imagery should illustrate the threat he saw in religious movements becoming political causes.

In addition, Lincoln alludes to both the predestination and temperance controversies in his discussion of "persuasion," where he uses a more fitting and hopeful means of convincing a person of one's opinion: "On the contrary, assume to dictate to his judgment, or to command his action, or to mark him as one to be shunned and despised, and he will retreat within himself, close all the avenues to his head and his heart; and tho' your cause be naked truth itself, transformed to the heaviest lance, harder than steel, and sharper than steel can be made, and tho' you throw it with more than Herculean force and precision, you shall no more be able to pierce him, than to penetrate the hardshell of a tortoise with a rye straw." Not only does "hardshell" connote the old school understanding of original sin and predestination, held by so-called "hardshell" or "primitive Baptists" and the like,[43] but also "rye straw" alludes to the distilling cereal of rye whiskey, the frontiersman drink of choice. By alluding to the "hard doctrines" of old school, hardshell Calvinists along with frontier rye whiskey, he juxtaposes religious and drinking imagery as a not-so-subtle critique of old school rhetoric. To penetrate a "hardshell" with a "rye" straw was a roundabout way of saying that it would be as difficult to force a teetotaling (Old School) Calvinist to drink as it would be to persuade someone to give up drinking by condemning them. Given the Old School Presbyterian connotation to "old school" temperance reform, Lincoln's use of the phrase could not have been missed by his audience—seated as they were in the Second Presbyterian Church of Springfield. He could not have picked a more coincidental (and controversial) pairing of religious doctrine and social reform.

Lincoln reaches the peak of his purposeful, rhetorical excesses in this address in describing how political freedom shall find its consummation with the help of the temperance movement: "With such an aid, its march cannot fail to be on and on, till every son of earth shall drink in rich fruition, the sorrow quenching draughts of perfect liberty."[44] If one did not doubt Lincoln's sincerity in his appreciation of the temperance cause as a political movement, his statement that "every son of earth shall *drink* in rich fruition, the sorrow quenching *draughts* of perfect liberty" (emphasis added) should prove persuasive. To depict all men drinking, albeit from the cup of "perfect liberty," in a speech about temperance illustrates the deliberate ambiguity Lincoln presents about religiously motivated measures adopted to reform those who drank.[45]

Of course, *the* exemplar of Lincoln's counsel for political moderation, borne of political humility, comes in his second-most-famous speech—the Second Inaugural Address. Beginning his second term as president, Lincoln delivers a four-paragraph reflection on American theodicy—the problem of evil, specifically, slavery, in God's providence. Where the original draft of the Gettysburg Address contains no direct reference to God or providence,[46] the Second Inaugural Address places God's purposes in the American Civil War front and center. Lincoln interprets how the war had progressed under divine and human guidance, and where the Almighty may yet direct its consummation. Significantly, the address shows the extent to which Lincoln sees the reason and religion of men fall short in averting civil war. In a telling demonstration of republican statesmanship under the providence of God, Lincoln ironically uses both reason and religion to deliver the lesson.[47]

Foremost in his mind was uniting a divided nation. And only a common understanding of the war—its cause and meaning for the fractured country—could ensure a lasting peace. At the height of his rhetorical powers, Lincoln showed how both the war and emancipation came to the country despite the initial intentions of either side of the conflict. Another power must be at work, and Lincoln returned the country to that other, higher power in hopes that a common, national humility before the Almighty would help Americans both North and South to fix what they had broken. How else could Lincoln expect there to be "malice toward none" and "charity for all"? Only by the grace of God could all Americans experience and live out that "new birth of freedom" he called for at Gettysburg.[48]

After a brief opening paragraph that explains why there's no need for "an extended address," like that at his first inauguration,

Lincoln devotes the remaining three paragraphs to an explanation of the Civil War—how it began, and what must follow its consummation.[49]

In Paragraph 2, Lincoln states that at his first inauguration, no one North or South, Unionist or Secessionist, wanted a "civil war." Thus, neither North nor South was initially culpable for a war that would cost so much in blood and treasure. But something proved more important than avoiding war. For Lincoln as president, "*saving* the Union" initially without war (i.e., by the words of his First Inaugural Address) was the goal, but eventually he would "*accept* war rather than let it perish." For "insurgent agents," as Lincoln put it (and not "the South" or "Southern legislatures"), to "*destroy*" the Union without war through words of their own—"negotiation"—was their initial priority, but they soon would "*make* war rather than let the nation survive."

Implicit in shifting the focus from war—i.e., its avoidance—to the Union—i.e., its preservation—is an invitation to consider the significance of the Union. Why is it so important that it is worth defending by force, if words fail? What would be lost in its dissolution, or what would be gained by preserving it? Why is the United States so important? But despite separating the combatants into saviors and destroyers, Paragraph 2 closes with a statement of the war's arrival and not a judgment of its earthly cause by linking the starting of the war with the guilty party. This was not the time to foster sectional animosities. Lincoln's demonstration in Paragraph 2 of the failure of reason to avert the war will now be followed by a demonstration in Paragraph 3 of the failure of religion to do the same.

Paragraph 3, the most important paragraph of the speech, begins with his first reference to slaves—*the* issue that needs explaining as the Civil War nears its conclusion. He now says that slavery "somehow" was "the cause of the war," with insurgents seeking to bolster slavery's hold on the United States "even by war." The federal government only sought to "restrict" its extension. Somehow, the

Union and slavery (and freedom by implication) are connected in some moral sense. Emancipation was a surprise to both sides—one more "fundamental and astounding." In short, the war brought about a momentous change in the American regime, but one that was unintended by both sides. If unintended, then the Radical Republicans and Northerners, in general, could afford to tone down their pride at being "victorious in the strife."

So, neither side intended the war or the abolition of slavery, but both cataclysms took place anyway. What else needs to be explored? The ways of Providence in American history. Here Lincoln's "God talk" begins in earnest.

Lincoln points out that both sides shared the same holy writ and God, which would ordinarily lead one to expect a shared understanding of the ways of the Almighty and hence His view of the conflict. No war should have been started, since both sides should have viewed the cause of the conflict in the same way—God's way. No such luck!

In the lone interjection of the speech, Lincoln pauses to comment on the "seem[ing]" oddity (his euphemism for injustice) of the invocation of God to help one to enslave others: Lincoln asks the nation not to "judge" those who would do such a thing in order that judgment would not come to those judging. In the context of the verse he quotes (Matt. 7:1), the judgment feared is divine. Lincoln seeks to avoid a further reckoning on top of that which may already be working itself out as punishment for the offense of slavery. Lincoln concludes that the "Almighty has His own purposes" because the prayers of neither have been answered fully. This conclusion becomes the premise upon which Lincoln bases his theological supposition about the meaning of the war and slavery's passing from the American stage.

Lincoln begins his theological intertwining of the Civil War and slavery by citing Matthew 18:7. "Woe unto the world because of offences! for it must needs be that offences come; but woe to that man by whom the offence cometh!" This "woe" text encapsulates one of the fundamental paradoxes of Christianity: free will and the sovereignty of God, or, human, moral agency and hence responsibility coupled with original sin or man's fall from grace. Simply put, even though it appears that slavery was an offence that "in the providence of God, must needs come," the human beings responsible for its introduction and maintenance in the United States are still responsible for the enormity.

To begin his second term of office, Lincoln uses his inaugural address to give his understanding of his first term of office—a history of the United States from 1861 to 1865. And he cannot tell this story of the nation at war with itself without bringing God into the fray. The American people need a common understanding of the war—its ultimate and efficient causes—in order to move forward as a unified country. For the imminent termination of the war to produce the "lasting peace" he mentions in Paragraph 4, for the war between Americans really to be over, they must all have the same memory of it—the same history of it. And to Lincoln's mind, the ending of the war must be a "just" one to produce this peace that endures. Most important, a common view of the justice of the war requires a godly perspective. By his own earlier reasoning, Lincoln has his work cut out for him, for despite the nation's common Bible and God, the American people did not have a common, biblical view of slavery. Its justice or injustice was the source of disagreement among Americans that led to the Civil War.

Lincoln attempts to produce a common view of the war by withholding judgment upon the South alone for the evil of slavery. He supposes that slavery was an offense that came due to both Southern and Northern citizens, and one that God "now wills to remove" through "this terrible war."

Why should Americans, especially those on the Confederate side, believe this rendering of history? Why should Southern secessionists and former slaveholders believe now that slavery was wrong and the war a "scourge" of the Almighty? Because it brings coherence to the salient events and beliefs of the American people as they touch the war and slavery. How else to explain what Lincoln showed was inexplicable in Paragraph 2 and early in Paragraph 3? How else to account for a war no one wanted and an emancipation no one expected? If God visited a war upon the United States as punishment for the offense of slavery, and slavery disappears by virtue of that war, no American North or South can blame the other for the calamity and escape censure himself. Common guilt means common punishment—and if accepted as such, a common future is possible under God. Paragraph 3 offers a collective punishment for collective guilt in order to set up the collective healing process and peace of Paragraph 4.

Because of the common woe experienced by Americans as a result of the Civil War, Lincoln suggests in Paragraph 4 that they cannot afford any malice toward anyone, nor withhold charity toward all. What Americans broke, they must now fix—with God's help. In particular, in order to "finish the work" they are in (i.e., to conclude the war with a Union victory), to heal the wounds of citizen against citizen, to care for the soldier and his family, and to promote "and cherish" a peace that endures and is just, Americans must be firm "in the right, as God gives [them] . . . to see the right." Here Lincoln calls on the nation to do what the war could not do, which is to build a common life from the ruins of a divided country. Americans must now act in peace without malice toward their erstwhile enemies (i.e., commit no sins of commission) and with charity toward their enemies (i.e., commit no sins of omission). This would prove to be a tall order. Only as Americans rely upon God and His enlightenment, as He allows them "to see the right," does Lincoln believe the battle for Union on the field of war can be won off the field and in the hearts of every American. The temptation to malice will be great; the temptation to withhold charity, including forgiveness, will be great, as well.

But what allows Lincoln to encourage Americans to act with "firmness in the right"? Both sides had read the same Bible and prayed to the same God, but came to opposite conclusions that produced a devastating civil war. What has Lincoln done in his speech to bolster their confidence that they can not only "see the right," but also come to a common understanding of it despite their previous differences of opinion? If Americans have learned anything from the war and slavery's abolition, it's their inability to produce good on their own. Lincoln hopes to foster a republican humility and moderation, borne of a renewed reliance upon God, that can reconstruct a bitterly divided nation.

And so Lincoln starts them with what can be clearly understood from their common Bible and prayers to God: "With malice toward none, with charity for all."[50] On their own, Americans would be tempted to harbor malice in their hearts toward their perceived erring brethren, and find little incentive to act with goodwill and love toward the same. Only by the grace of God will they be able to experience "a new birth of freedom" as a self-governing people free of the taint of slavery. With one-eighth of the population now newly freed men, and still greatly concentrated in the South, the task of national reconstruction is made all the more difficult.

In addition, if the war is seen as a divine scourge and not an earthly one, then one's hatred of the enemy must dissipate or else be directed towards the heavens. But "the believers in a Living God" would not permit themselves this option, for they worship a God whose judgments they believe to be "true and righteous altogether." This includes the malice Northerners would wish to express against Southerners (and vice versa), as well as that by former slaves toward their former masters. Charity, not malice, must mark their actions toward each other—North versus South, former slave versus former master, white versus black. Alas, the scapegoating of blacks that followed the failure of Reconstruction facilitated the eventual rapprochement of Northern and Southern whites.

Given the aim of the speech, which is essentially the aim of his second term as president—namely, uniting a divided country—Lincoln had to hide or diminish the culpability of the South for the Civil War. But he could not ignore it, for he also sought to unite the country as a slave-free one. In other words, as he declared at Gettysburg, he intended the American people, North and South, to experience "a new birth of freedom." This meant that Southern secessionists would not be held solely responsible for causing the war; but it also required that they change their mind about the meaning of America. The Union was now to be in practice what Lincoln always understood it to be in principle—a union devoted to protecting the equal rights of all of her citizens. It was a bargain of sorts, which Lincoln explained with a political-theological rhetoric far exceeding any of his public career.

Following his second inauguration as president, Lincoln received a congratulatory letter from New York's Republican Party boss, Thurlow Weed, to which Lincoln replied:

> I expect the latter [meaning 'the recent Inaugural Address'] to wear as well as—perhaps better than—any thing I have produced; but I believe it is not immediately popular. *Men are not flattered by being shown that there has been a difference of purpose between the Almighty and them.* To deny it, however, in this case, is to deny that there is a God governing the world. It is a truth which I thought needed to be told; and as whatever of humiliation there is in it, falls most directly on myself, I thought others might afford for me to tell it.[51]

Through reason and religion, Lincoln shows how reason and religion failed to avert the American Civil War in order to induce the humility that will be needed for the work ahead. What failed to prevent war among Americans must now succeed in order to unite them.

For me, to study Abraham Lincoln as "Communicator in Chief" is to learn about American self-government, to learn about the abiding tension between our commitment to the equal rights of humanity and our obligation to secure those rights by the consent of the governed. Understanding the relevance of religion and, especially, Christianity, to Lincoln's politics helps us better understand his political project: namely, the defense of the American constitutional union as an expression of his faith in God's purposes for himself and his country. As Lincoln put it before the New Jersey Senate en route to his first inauguration:

> I am exceedingly anxious that this Union, the Constitution, and the liberties of the people shall be perpetuated in accordance with the original idea for which that struggle was made, and I shall be most happy indeed if I shall be an humble instrument in the hands of the Almighty, and of this, his almost chosen people, for perpetuating the object of that great struggle.[52]

CHAPTER 3

Lincoln, Douglas, and Popular Sovereignty: The Mormon Dimension

John Y. Simon

THE FAMED 1858 DEBATES BETWEEN ABRAHAM LINCOLN AND Stephen A. Douglas centered on Douglas's strident defense of popular sovereignty. Douglas defended the right of citizens of Kansas Territory to vote slavery "up or down" while Lincoln insisted that the Missouri Compromise of 1820 had already settled the issue. To Lincoln, popular sovereignty jeopardized the intent of the founders to place slavery "in the course of ultimate extinction." Throughout the debates, Lincoln refrained from mentioning Utah Territory, where settlers employed popular sovereignty to maintain a theocracy despised by others. Yet, on the Mormon issue, Douglas was especially vulnerable. In the previous year, President James Buchanan had sent an expedition of 2,500 men to enforce federal authority in Utah. This army established a permanent base some thirty miles from Salt Lake City.

Founded in upstate New York in 1830, The Church of Jesus Christ of Latter Day Saints, popularly called the Mormons by themselves and others, had established a center at Kirtland, Ohio, and later moved to locations in western Missouri. Founded by Joseph

Smith through revelation, the Mormons followed his leadership in all matters religious and secular. An alien presence everywhere, the Mormons clashed with their neighbors. Governor Lilburn Boggs of Missouri finally declared that the Mormons "must be treated as enemies and must be exterminated or driven from the state, . . ."[1] In 1839, the Mormons began to settle in Hancock County, Illinois, where they started to erect a capital city at Nauvoo.

Illinois Whigs and Democrats courted Mormon votes. Douglas, a young, ambitious Democrat, proved most successful. He had come to Illinois at the age of twenty and, after a brief stint as schoolmaster, had embraced law and politics. Elected to the state legislature in 1836, he joined young Lincoln, then in his second term, and ran for Congress in 1837, losing by only a few votes to Lincoln's law partner John T. Stuart. Elected in 1840 as Illinois secretary of state, he left that office almost immediately to accept an appointment to the Illinois Supreme Court. His circuit included Hancock County.[2]

Douglas had already courted the political favor of the Mormons, despite their distaste for Democrats. They resented President Martin Van Buren, who had ignored their plight, and Governor Boggs, their persecutor. As a member of the legislature and as a state official, Douglas had been influential in securing a special charter for Nauvoo that provided broad powers of self-government, in establishing the Nauvoo Legion (that gave extensive military force to local government), and in fostering the appointment of Mormon leaders to positions in local government. Left behind from the Missouri years were various indictments, and Justice Douglas twice blocked the extradition of Joseph Smith, acts that Smith remembered gratefully.[3] When Mormons voted the Whig presidential ticket in 1840, 200 Mormons struck Lincoln's name as elector, a development charged to Douglas's influence.[4] Nonetheless, Lincoln voted for legislative acts authorizing Mormon autonomy and pointedly congratulated John C. Bennett, their leading lobbyist.

Within two years, Douglas had achieved an alliance with the Mormons. Smith declared Douglas "a *Master Spirit*, and *his friends are our friends*—we are willing to cast our banners on the air, and fight by his side in the cause of humanity, and equal rights—the cause of liberty and the law."[5] Yet Smith still had reservations, warning Douglas that "if ever you turn your hand against me or the Latter-Day Saints you will feel the hand of the Almighty upon you." As for threats, Smith intoned "I prophesy in the name of the Lord God of Israel, unless the United States redress the wrongs committed upon the Saints . . . in a few years the government will be utterly overthrown and wasted, . . ."[6] In 1842, Democrat Thomas Ford won election as governor with enthusiastic support from Mormon voters. By this time Nauvoo had an estimated population of 12,000, while Chicago had fewer than 4,500, Springfield 2,500, and no other Illinois city more. Since Mormon voters invariably voted as Joseph Smith wished, their political impact exceeded these numbers. In 1843, at a public meeting in Nauvoo, Hyrum Smith raised his arms and proclaimed, "Thus saith the Lord, those that vote this ticket . . . this Democratic ticket, shall be blessed; those who do not shall be accursed." Later, Joseph Smith said, "I have not enquired of God about the election; I suppose he would have told me if I had enquired. Bro. Hyrum says he has. He is as good a man as God ever made, and I never knew him to tell a lie. God told him the church must vote the Democratic ticket."[7]

One year later, the Mormons had entered a time of troubles. Porter Rockwell, a member of Smith's bodyguard (a group of thugs sometimes tastefully dressed in white robes and named the Danites), had fired three bullets into the head of Governor Boggs, and Missouri officials were pursuing Smith (who had since declared himself a candidate for president of the United States). Smith had disclosed to his closest associates a revelation that God had commanded them to practice polygamy, a ritual which Smith himself had pioneered. When one of these associates denounced polygamy in the pages of the *Nauvoo Expositor*, Smith suppressed the newspaper and began to exercise his broad civil and military powers in alarming fashion. He commanded a private army of an estimated 2,000 men. As conflict between Mormons and non-Mormons reached fever pitch, Smith and his brother Hyrum entered Carthage jail with promises of state protection. Nonetheless, they were murdered by an angry mob.

In the following year, Douglas negotiated what passed for peace in Hancock County as the Mormons prepared to move.[8] Brigham Young assumed leadership, but reactions to Smith's death and especially the furor over polygamy fractured the community. Consequently, when Young led his celebrated expedition to Salt Lake City, the church was virtually purged of members who resisted polygamy. As Young left Illinois, denouncing his country as corrupt, Douglas remained a true friend.

Although planning to leave the United States, the Mormons found themselves Americans once again when victory in the Mexican War brought Utah Territory within the national boundaries. Young called upon Douglas for help with fort and mail contracts and for assistance in forming Deseret, the Mormon state designed to stretch from Salt Lake across Nevada through modern New Mexico into southern California, with seaports at San Diego and Los Angeles. In the Compromise of 1850, a more modest Utah Territory included Nevada and the matter of slavery was left to popular sovereignty.

When Douglas attempted to employ the same language in organizing Kansas Territory in 1854, "with or without slavery, as their constitution may prescribe at the time of their admission," Northern indignation over violation of the Missouri Compromise led to the organization of a new political party. Lincoln had joined the Republican Party before 1856 when its platform denounced the "twin evils of slavery and polygamy." Governor Young attempted to join church and state in Utah, using his broad powers to eliminate federal control. As he announced, "I am and will be Governor, and no power can hinder it until the Lord Almighty says, 'Brigham, you need not be Governor any longer,' . . ."[9] One federal judge had his courtroom sacked, his law books burned, and his records stolen away. As President James Buchanan began to organize an expedition to tame Utah, Douglas executed an abrupt reversal.

In June 1857, Douglas denounced Brigham Young as a dictator who intimidated his people through "horrid oaths and terrible penalties" to recognize Young's government "as paramount to that of the United States, in civil as well as religious affairs." Young's power rested upon the support of aliens, nine-tenths of the people, who refused naturalization and citizenship. Young had encouraged Indian hostility to other settlers and maintained bands of "Danites or Destroying Angels" to murder anyone who would "denounce the infamous and disgusting practices and institutions of the mormon government." In light of this, Washington was entirely correct in sending an expedition against "out-laws and alien enemies." Better still, Congress should abolish territorial status to increase its power to deal forcefully with wrongdoers, to "apply the knife and cut out this loathsome, disgusting ulcer."[10]

Douglas used his denunciation of the Mormons as a prelude to his defense of the Dred Scott decision, which somehow squared with the concept of Popular Sovereignty since slavery required "police regulations and local legislation." Critics would charge that his proposal for revocation of the territorial government of Utah might well have been applied to Kansas. "The Utah troubles had sadly deranged the finespun Democratic theory of popular sovereignty. The practical view which the Mormons take of that doctrine, seemed to bode the party no good."[11]

Two weeks later, Lincoln replied:

> If it prove to be true, as is probable, that the people of Utah are in open rebellion to the United States, . . . they

ought to be somehow coerced to obedience; and I am not
now prepared to admit or deny that the Judge's mode of
coercing them is not as good as any. . . . To be sure, it
would be a considerable backing down by Judge Douglas
from his much vaunted doctrine of self-government for the
territories; but this is only additional proof of what was
very plain from the beginning, that that doctrine was a
mere deceitful pretense for the benefit of slavery. . . . But
in all this, it is very plain the Judge evades the only question the Republicans have ever pressed upon the Democracy in regard to Utah. That question the Judge well knows
to be this: "If the people of Utah shall peacefully form a
State Constitution tolerating polygamy, will the Democracy admit them into the Union?"[12]

In Lincoln's 1857 reply to Douglas, the Utah theme occupied a
small corner of a larger effort designed to air the issues of the Kansas controversy and the Dred Scott decision. Even as Lincoln spoke,
however, Buchanan was assembling an expedition bound for Utah
to install a governor to replace Brigham Young, accompanied by
new judges and other territorial officials, escorted by 2,500 troops,
eventually commanded by Albert Sidney Johnston. As for Young, he
had at least 2,000 men under arms to say nothing of other militant
Mormons. At a public meeting Heber C. Kimball announced "God
Almighty helping me, I will fight until there is not a drop of blood
in my veins. Good God! I have wives enough to whip out the United
States; . . ."[13] Buchanan claimed that the "despotism of Brigham
Young" challenged "the supremacy of the Constitution and laws."
Nevertheless, the federal government had no right to interfere with
the religious practices of the Mormons however "revolting to the
moral and religious sentiments of all Christendom." Young, however, had encouraged Indian tribes to hostility against Americans,
and troops were necessary to subdue the "frenzied fanaticism" of

"these deluded people."[14] Before the year ended, Mormons had resisted federal troops and had participated with local Indians in the massacre of some 120 members of a wagon train at Mountain Meadows in southern Utah.

The eventual resolution of the "Mormon War" that left troops stationed in Utah had little effect on life in that territory. Despite the replacement of Brigham Young as governor and the addition of federal officials, Mormons continued to follow the leadership of Young, practice polygamy, and resent federal authority. As both Lincoln and Douglas had acknowledged in 1857, polygamy was no violation of federal law. In 1860, Republican Representative Justin S. Morrill of Vermont introduced a bill to punish the practice of polygamy, a bill that roused Southern fears that congressional legislation to exercise police powers within any territory carried with it an implied power to prohibit slavery as well. Such concerns, however, did not trouble Representative Roger A. Pryor of Virginia, as he was

> shocked and humiliated by the bestial abominations of that outcast community[.] They are a reproach in the eyes of the nations—a reproach upon civil liberty, as exhibiting to what extravagance of licentious development republican institutions may conduce; and a reproach upon religious freedom, as betraying the excesses of depravity which may flourish under shelter of indiscriminate toleration.

As such, Pryor supported the bill

> to avert the scorn of Christendom, and protect our country from the blight of the most consuming curse that can fall upon a nation, let us not hesitate, because of any scruple of legal technicality, to employ the most efficacious expedient

for the suppression of polygamy within the limits of the Republic.[15]

Instead of supporting Morrill's bill, Douglasites proposed to divide current Utah Territory in two with the line drawn through Great Salt Lake. The eastern portion would be joined to the territory of Jeffersonia, with its capital at Denver, while the western half would be joined to Nevada, with a capital at Genoa.[16] Douglas argued that miners flooding the Carson Valley of Nevada and the Pike's Peak region would soon outnumber Mormons in each region and take appropriate action to outlaw polygamy under territorial law. His ally, Representative John A. McClernand of Illinois, expressed, at length, Douglas's position that the excesses of this faith

eventuated in the exodus of the Mormons from the State, because they were unwilling to submit to the laws; because, in an attempt to trample the authority of the State under foot, they were overcome. Their maxim then was, and still is, rule or ruin. Leaving Illinois, they went forth and established themselves in their present seat in Salt Lake valley . . . in the midst of the Rocky Mountains, and in the heart of the continent, remote from any Power capable of molesting them. . . . It is upon the great line of emigration from east to west—from the Atlantic to the Pacific. It is a commanding military position, giving them the control of the lives and property of the teeming thousands passing through their jurisdiction. . . . Emigrants from the Atlantic States to California and Oregon would become a prey to the Mormon banditti that would infest their track. . . . These Mormons should never be admitted as a distinct political community among the States. . . . The government of these Mormons is a hierarchy concentrated in one man, who exerts an absolute temporal and spiritual power over his followers. He thinks for them; and they obey him from a dread of his temporal and spiritual power. The power of the Pope of Rome . . . is much less absolute than that of Brigham Young, the prophet, priest, and *de facto* Governor of the Mormons. . . . Brigham Young exercises not only the power to join man and woman in wedlock, but to divorce them at pleasure. . . . There is not now so absolute a hierarch living or reigning in any other quarter of the globe. The civil authorities kept up there by this Government are powerless—a mere mockery; and must continue to be so until a new and controlling social element is infused into Mormon society. As to polygamy, . . . It is a scarlet whore. It is a reproach to the Christian civilization; and deserves to be blotted out, if it be practicable to do so. But how shall it be done? . . . First, it makes polygamy an indictable offense, and upon conviction of the offender against the law, subjects him to fine and imprisonment. This is the whole extent of a remedy proposed by the committee's bill—a bill which assumes and relies upon the Mormons—polygamists themselves, to execute its provisions.[17]

Despite such arguments, the anti-polygamy bill passed on April 5 by a vote of 149 to sixty. While some Southern Democrats had voted for the bill, Illinois Democrats opposed it because they preferred Douglas's plan of dividing Utah Territory. The matter died ultimately when the Senate declined to take up the bill.

Lincoln had already discussed this legislation. To him, the idea of dissolving the territory reminded him of a similar inconsistency. "If I cannot rightfully murder a man, I may tie him to the tail of a kicking horse, and let him kick the man to death!" More seriously, Lincoln asked,

But why divide up the territory at all? . . . Something must be wrong there, or it would not be necessary to act at all.

And if one mode of interference is wrong, why not the
other? Why is not an act dividing the territory as much
against popular sovereignty as one for prohibiting polygamy? If you can put down polygamy in that way, why may
you not thus put down slavery? Mr. Lincoln said he *supposed* that the friends of popular sovereignty would say—if
they dared speak out—that *polygamy* was wrong and slavery right; and therefore one might thus be put down and
the other not; . . .[18]

Nothing came of either plan, and Utah Mormons watched the
unfolding of the secession crisis with a mixture of alarm and satisfaction. The news of Douglas's death in June 1861 reawakened resentment of a former ally who had later deserted the righteous. As
for Lincoln, he "had never raised his voice in our favor when he was
aware that we were being persecuted."[19] As the nation went to war,
the federal garrison was withdrawn from Utah for service elsewhere
and the Mormons prepared to relish their role as spectators of Civil
War. Brigham Young regarded that war as a just punishment.
"Those who are against the Kingdom of God must suffer."[20] Lincoln's call for temporary protection of the telegraph and mail routes
between Fort Bridger and Fort Laramie went directly to Brigham
Young, who must have felt ill-requited when Lincoln signed a new
Morrill Act punishing polygamy and sent volunteers from California
to take over the policing of Utah. By 1863, Lincoln had entered into
a truce, allegedly telling a Mormon emissary to "tell Brigham Young
that if he will let me alone, I will let him alone."[21]

An authentic Lincoln quotation? Perhaps. Nonetheless, this line
expresses something of Lincoln's attitude for the entire period during which he was aware of this new religion. Unlike Douglas, who
so enthusiastically courted Mormon favor and so emphatically denounced this unpopular sect when past support threatened future

political prospects, Lincoln took a cooler approach to the many issues presented in both Illinois and Utah Territory.

Through the debates with Douglas, Lincoln might well have
pointed to Utah as well as to Kansas as an abject failure of popular
sovereignty. Bleeding Kansas had become a battleground of proslavery and antislavery forces, including "border ruffians" from Missouri who invaded Kansas to promote the interest of slavery, parties
of determined migrants from both Northern and Southern states
settling in Kansas determined to prevail in the battle between freedom and slavery, and the lawless, including John Brown, who recognized no legal barriers in this battle. Nonetheless, deaths in the
struggle for Mormon supremacy in Utah could match or exceed
casualties in Kansas. In the debates, Douglas repeatedly attempted
to discredit Lincoln by associating him with the interests of black
people, even beyond their status as slave property. Through the
campaign of 1858 and afterward Douglas played on issues of race
prejudice. Speaking to an audience in which only white men could
vote, Lincoln sought to defuse the issue, to clarify his definitions of
what rights the Declaration of Independence gave to men regardless of skin color. In his celebrated Freeport question, he challenged Douglas to explain if settlers in any territory could free
themselves of the institution of slavery. Douglas's answer—that this
could be accomplished through unfriendly local legislation—helped
Douglas in Illinois though damaging his reputation among Southerners who believed that slavery could never be lawfully excluded.

Douglas' answer would not fit Utah, where polygamy had the
enthusiastic support of both church and state. Could a practice so
repugnant to the voters of Illinois ever be lawfully challenged, much
less abolished? This was a question Lincoln failed to ask Douglas,
whose earlier alliance with the Mormons was well known to voters.
In 1858, one correspondent urged Lincoln to respond to charges of
abolitionism by charging Douglas with Mormonism.[22] Unfair as
both charges would have been, Utah was a problem that Douglas

had helped to create. Lincoln ignored this strategic suggestion, perhaps on the same grounds that he had earlier denounced Know-Nothing efforts to mobilize anti-Catholic bigotry for electoral advantage. The solution offered in 1860 of dividing Utah in half and assigning each portion to a broader territory offered only hope that polygamy would be overwhelmed in each area when miners outnumbered Mormons. Perhaps Utah deserved as much attention as Kansas in Illinois politics.

Lincoln, however, did not see it in that light. Instead, he kept a sharp eye on the wrong of slavery, leaving other wrongs to other voices. Repeated efforts to have Utah admitted as a state during the Civil War proved fruitless; the admission of Nevada, despite its smaller population, clearly indicated that Utah presented a special problem.

In Lincoln's day and later, polygamy represented a Mormon religious tenet that could not be abandoned for the sake of statehood. In 1879, the Supreme Court decided a test case brought by a Mormon invoking the First Amendment as sanctioning polygamy based upon religious belief. In ruling against polygamy, the court separated belief from practice. Not until 1890 did the church reluctantly abandon support of polygamy to clear the way for statehood, not granted until 1896.

By failing to exploit Douglas's vulnerability on the Mormon issue, Lincoln pursued an honorable course. Knowing that he could not conscientiously denounce polygamy in stronger terms than those already used by Douglas, he chose silence over demagoguery. Further, he declined to change the focus of the debates from one evil to another.

CHAPTER 4

The Campaign of 1860: Cooper Union, Mathew Brady, and the Campaign of Words and Images

Harold Holzer

ON WASHINGTON'S BIRTHDAY 1860—AS THE ANNUAL PATRI-
otic parade was forming in the center of Springfield, Illinois, with
brass bands marching, children of Revolutionary War veterans cele-
brating, and banners waving to honor the nation's first president—
the man who would become the nation's sixteenth president quietly
boarded a train to begin a long trip to New York City.[1] It was a
journey, as he well knew, that would make or break his White
House dreams—which, legends of modesty notwithstanding, were
surely very much in his mind on that wintry February 22, 1860.

That same morning, Springfield's Democratic newspaper, the
Illinois State Register, both acknowledged and mocked Abraham
Lincoln's ambitions by publishing this notice:

> SIGNIFICANT—The Honorable Abraham Lincoln departs
> today for Brooklyn under an engagement to deliver a lecture
> before the Young Men's Association of that city, in Beecher's
> Church. Subject, not known. Consideration, $200 and ex-
> penses. Object, presidential capital. Effect, disappointment.[2]

Of course, we know that is not exactly what happened. The trip would increase Lincoln's presidential capital immeasurably, but for none of the reasons the *Illinois State Register* enumerated. Lincoln was not scheduled to speak before a "Young Men's Association," but rather, for New York's Young Men's Central Republican Union. This was a group created four years earlier to boost John C. Frémont's campaign for president. Now it was dedicated to stopping their once-favorite son, and overwhelming favorite for the 1860 nomination, Senator William H. Seward.

Most audiences find it difficult to imagine why. But as my fellow New Yorkers understand, upstate-downstate competition—then as well as now—can sometimes ignite the fierceness of blood feuds. Seward hailed from upstate New York. To his fellow Republicans in New York City, that was enough to disqualify him. Besides, they insisted, with far more political logic, only a western-based Republican nominee could hope to attract enough votes in the West to elect the next president. An easterner, their argument went, would be unable to do so.

The *Register* made another error as well—an understandable one, since Lincoln himself didn't know the truth of it. He would not be speaking, after all, at Beecher's Church in Brooklyn, but at Cooper Union in Manhattan. For years, historians have mistakenly claimed that the oration was moved across the East River because Lincoln was so popular that organizers needed a larger hall to accommodate his admirers. Not so. For one thing, Cooper Union actually held fewer people than the Plymouth Church. The simple fact is, Lincoln delayed his trip for so long that the Beecher Church lecture series, to which he was originally invited, simply ended—and a new hall had to be found.

The change proved significant for symbolic reasons as well, also seldom mentioned. Beecher's Church was a national shrine to abolitionism. Its pastor, Henry Ward Beecher, was one of the most famous antislavery orators in the country. His sermons attracted tourists and press coverage every Sunday. He and his congregation once bought a slave from its pulpit, brought her to Brooklyn, and amidst tremendous publicity, set her free.

For Lincoln to have appeared there would have sent a strong signal, North and South, that he identified himself with those who demanded the immediate destruction of slavery everywhere. And, as we know, Lincoln was then campaigning for the idea of killing slavery slowly—by limiting its spread into the new national territories. The change of venue to Cooper Union was unexpected and, to Lincoln, unknown, but it served him well. The free college for self-made men was a far more appropriate venue for his cautionary message than Beecher's church.

It's hard to recreate an era in which one major speech—delivered outside the glare of television, bloggers, and the twenty-four-news coverage we take for granted today—could attract the kind of attention that Lincoln's Cooper Union address did. One must imagine again a bygone age in which the public was passionately interested in politics, when people thronged to rallies, debates, and orations, eagerly read newspaper and pamphlet reprints of political speeches, and voted in mass numbers—80 percent of eligible white males in 1860, nearly double the level we get today, tragically.

That is why Lincoln immediately appreciated that his very first speech in the media center of the nation presented him with a great opportunity to convince Easterners that he was more than a frontier debater, and a further chance to produce a document that the New York publishers might reprint and circulate nationwide. He devoted as much time and energy to its preparation as he did to any address of his career, before or after. His intense labor makes another persistent Cooper Union legend particularly ludicrous.

The legend appears to date to March 1860, when Lincoln traveled from Springfield up to Chicago to appear in court in what turned out to be his last big trial as a lawyer: the famous "sand bar" case, a complex civil dispute over valuable new shorefront land accumulating because of the slow but steady accretions of Lake Michigan. In his final turn as a railroad attorney, Lincoln represented the interests of his most important client, the Illinois Central. But the trip was not all devoted to legal work.

While in the city, Lincoln also agreed to sit for a wet-plaster life mask at the studio of local sculptor Leonard Wells Volk, a relative by marriage of Lincoln's longtime political foe, Stephen A. Douglas. Volk proposed to use the cast of Lincoln's face as the model for a bust.

Twenty years later, long after Lincoln achieved immortality, and Volk, artistic fame with a series of reproductions of the mask and bust alike, the sculptor wrote a magazine article about his experiences with his most famous sitter. As his subject waited for the "anything but agreeable" process to begin, Volk remembered, their conversation turned to Lincoln's recent triumph in New York, and, as Volk remembered it, Lincoln revealed to him "that he had arranged and composed this speech in his mind while going on the cars from Camden to Jersey City."[3]

By the time Volk published this supposed revelation, another President, James A. Garfield, had fallen victim to an assassin, and people who had known the nation's first martyred chief executive, like Volk, found themselves back in demand, spinning supposedly reliable first-hand stories for eager audiences. By then, Lincoln's myth-worthy creative abilities and almost saintly modesty had emerged as crucial elements of his image.

Volk's recollection, clouded though it was by the passage of time, seemed well in keeping with the Lincoln legend. A president who had supposedly been able to create his greatest masterpiece on the back of an envelope while riding on a train to Gettysburg surely could have written his Cooper Union address on a train to New York—even in the few hours it took to ride only through New Jersey.

Of course, the Cooper Union myth is as false as the Gettysburg myth. The truth is, Lincoln never in his life labored more rigorously over a speech than he did to prepare his 7,700-word Cooper Union masterpiece. It required weeks of painstaking research, writing, and rewriting, all without the help of secretaries or speechwriters. Needless to say, it would not do for a candidate to be seen breathing heavily on his way to the nomination—so much of the story of Lincoln's labors was buried to emphasize his creative genius and self-effacement. To Volk was left the crucial job of extolling Lincoln's modesty, and meanwhile creating and circulating the first Lincoln image from life, which he did in many variations in the months and years after Cooper Union.

There is yet another Cooper Union legend that deserves to be punctured. Years after the event, *Tribune* editor Joseph H. Medill testified that when Lincoln arrived in Chicago en route to New York, he gave advance copies of his newly written speech "to quite a number of us, requesting that we study it carefully and make such corrections and suggestions as we saw fit." Lincoln planned to stay overnight in the city, and return to the newspaper offices the next day to collect their comments.

According to Medill, when Lincoln showed up the following morning, "we handed him our numerous notes with the reference places carefully marked on the margins of the pages where each emendation was to be inserted. We turned over the address to him with a self-satisfied feeling that we had considerably bettered the document and enabled it to pass the critical ordeal more triumphantly than otherwise it would. Lincoln thanked us cordially for our trouble, glanced at our notes, told us a funny story or two . . . and took his leave."

Yet "when the speech was finally delivered" in New York, Medill was shocked to discover, "it was exactly word for word with the original copy which Lincoln gave us. Not a change suggested had been adopted. I never knew whether Lincoln intended to play a joke on us, or whether he really believed that the alterations were not effective. I never mentioned the matter to him, and he said nothing more to me."[4]

It is a good story. It has a Lincolnian ring of authenticity to it. One can easily imagine Lincoln arriving in town and heading straight for the local Republican newspaper office, to swap stories and seek advice on his upcoming speech in the East. After all, he liked to audition his major addresses in front of friends and allies. He had done so previous to delivering his House Divided speech in 1858. Medill and his fellow *Tribune* journalists were especially loyal, longtime supporters, and they had just endorsed him for president. Lincoln trusted no newspapermen more.

But in this case, their story was untrue. Lincoln did not leave his manuscript with Joseph H. Medill in Chicago for the simple reason that he didn't travel to Chicago to begin with. He traveled east via Indiana.

To be charitable, maybe Medill did not intentionally fabricate the story. Maybe he simply confused the details. Perhaps Lincoln sent copies of the *finished* speech for review when he was polishing the talk for publication months later. Only then would Lincoln have had "copies" to share with the *Tribune* men. En route to New York, he had just one hand-written manuscript, and it is almost certain that he kept it close at all times.

In any case, Medill published the entire speech in the paper two days after Lincoln delivered it, adding this lavish editorial praise from Horace Greeley: "No man ever before made such an impression on his first appeal to a New York audience." The paper now quickened its pace of stories from all over the country reporting growing Lincoln-for-president fever. "The more politicians look over the field in search of an available man," it declared, "the more often they are convinced that Old Abe is the man to run the race with."[5]

Clearly, political oratory was more serious in the nineteenth century. Speeches were essays, not cartoons; marathons, not sound bites. But it must be admitted that style was just beginning to become almost as important as substance, and sculptor Volk was onto something new and influential when he captured Lincoln's likeness and started a cottage industry in affordable reproduction sculptures.

Let us remember, too, that when Lincoln stopped in New York he not only visited Cooper Union, but also the studio of master photographer Mathew Brady. No one kept a precise record of who thought up this excursion—Lincoln or his hosts. Throughout his years of prominence, Lincoln always seemed to be "ushered"—that is the word one sees in other reminiscences—to the photographers, rather than initiating the idea himself. It always struck me as a remarkable coincidence that his "ushers" always managed to get these ideas just when Lincoln was ready to deliver a major speech. The results provided wonderful illustrations to unforgettable words.[6]

But they were made in the days before photographs could be widely reproduced, and before Lincoln was famous enough to inspire engravers and lithographers to copy them for the public. In 1860, however, the man, the moment, and the technology all collided in perfect unison. And it happened at Brady's New York.

The result (fig. 1) did nothing less than change the Lincoln image. It looks nothing like the primitive images of his younger days, partly because of the magic of the retoucher's tools, softening the harsh lines in the face. But the pose deserves to be called a masterpiece for other reasons, and it took a genius like Brady to arrange it. It is not just a headshot. Note the props: there is a pillar of state to signify strength and leadership (an iconographic symbol of strength ever since artists began depicting Christ bound to a pillar for the flagellation, or Samson hauling down the pillars of the Philistines to punish them for godlessness). Nearby was a pile of books to represent knowledge and wisdom. The distance of the camera is also perfect—close enough to give a good impression of Lincoln's strong features, yet distant enough to hide its imperfections and highlight the subject's great height and powerful frame.

Brady made sure, too, that Lincoln's so-called "wild Republican hair" was patted down smoothly—and this must have required some cosmetic assistance in the studio after Lincoln's long walk uptown to the galleries. He had occasionally forgotten to fix his hair before sitting for the camera—and one result, made in Chicago three years earlier, would prove particularly disagreeable to his wife, Mary. She objected specifically and strenuously to "the disordered condition of the hair."[7]

Brady made sure his subject's hair was in perfect order. And then, in an inspiration, he remembered: "I asked him if I might not arrange his collar, and with that he began to pull it up."

"Ah," said Lincoln, "I see you want to shorten my neck."

"That's just it," Brady recalled, "and we both laughed."[8]

That long, dark, withered neck—visible like a totem in earlier pictures—made Lincoln look like an uncouth laborer. Brady's pose transformed him into a gentleman. The picture captured Lincoln in all his western vigor, refracted by a new and convincing dignity. It was a work of art. It is no wonder that Lincoln later said: "Brady and the Cooper Institute made me President."[9]

As an artist of the day agreed, "My friend Brady insisted that his photograph of Mr. Lincoln—taken on the day he made his speech in New York—much the best portrait, by the way, in circulation of him during the campaign—was the means of his election. That it helped largely to this end I do not doubt. The effect of such influences, though silent, is powerful."[10]

And there, in a nutshell, is the yin and yang, if you will, of Lincoln's entire 1860 campaign. After he returned from his Cooper Union tour, the candidate himself remained home, and silent. He wrote no new speeches, no new public letters. His "campaign," such as it evolved, was conducted at rallies, parades, and meetings by surrogates and supporters—with the nominee represented by re-prints of his speeches and broadly circulated images.

To be accurate, mass photography—the little *cartes-de-visite* im-ages that Americans collected in leather albums—did not become universally popular until a few months *after* the 1860 campaign. But Brady's Cooper Union image did emerge as a campaign icon—in adaptations churned out for campaign pins, patriotic envelopes, car-toons, book covers, broadsides, and print portraits for home display. Before the days of the thirty-second TV campaign commercial and the perennially airborne candidate making stops in several media markets daily, these were how presidential candidates reached the voters.

But modern viewers need to keep several things in mind to un-derstand both the political culture and publishing technologies in 1860. It was an era of mass participation in politics, and endless parades and rallies in small towns and big cities alike. It was an era in which great speeches would be reprinted in the newspapers in full, and then reproduced by the thousands in cheap pamphlets—as was Cooper Union.

Pictures were widely reproduced, too—but only if public de-mand warranted it. Today's political commercials and other ephem-era—buttons and bumper stickers, to mention the last survivors of a vanishing genre of modern-day campaign material—are manufac-tured by, and for, the campaigns themselves. In Lincoln's day, by contrast, artists and printmakers created the pictures and posters—responding to what they perceived to be a public demand. The im-ages were thus produced from the bottom up, not the top down. They truly reflected popular interest in the political process and in the heroes they depicted.

But even though Lincoln triumphed at Cooper Union, there was no immediate call for his now-iconic picture. In fact, when asked about it six weeks later, Lincoln told a supporter: "I have not a single one now at my control; but I think you can easily get one at

New-York. While I was there I was taken to one of the places where they get up such things, and I suppose they got my shadow, and can multiply copies indefinitely."[11] He was right, of course, if rather too folksy about it: they could indeed multiply copies indefinitely, but for a while, there was no commercial demand impelling them to do so.

Not until Lincoln won the nomination in May did *Frank Leslie's Illustrated Newspaper* really launch the Cooper Union photo phenomenon (fig. 2) by publishing this first, full-page, engraved adaptation. Then, a few days after Lincoln's election six months later, *Frank Leslie's* great rival, *Harper's Weekly*, issued its own woodcut version, reversing it into a mirror image, and adding a herd of buffalo incongruously outside what was in reality a New York window, perhaps to remind readers that the new president-elect had gone all the way from the prairie to the White House. In between the appearance of these two full-page illustrations came more engravings, lithographs, tintypes, and other adaptations than one lecture, or one chapter, can possibly accommodate. *Harper's* had published a small engraving of the print during the campaign, and it quickly inspired New York engravers Ensign, Bridgman, & Fanning to issue a hand-colored copy for home display (fig. 3). But even a representative sampling proves the point—Lincoln's and Brady's point as well—that the picture did indeed help make him president.

The avalanche of Cooper Union iconography included illustrated political envelopes (fig. 4), illustrated patriotic writing paper (fig. 5), illustrations for illustrated campaign biographies, and a handsome engraving specially issued for the campaign by J. C. Buttre (fig. 6), advertised price—10 cents.[12]

The New York lithography firm of Currier & Ives, known for its lively output of campaign portraiture, issued several adaptations of the Cooper Union pose (figs. 7, 8) and, motivated by commercial, not political, profit, were not afraid to attach the face to a grotesquely imagined body in the campaign cartoons that made the

Republican presidential nominee look as ridiculous as the Brady original had made him look dignified (fig. 9). The little-known but vigorously original weekly newspaper *Momus* produced a cartoon of Lincoln as a rail-splitter—wielding an axe that cleaves the divided Democratic Party asunder—just two weeks after Lincoln's nomination (fig. 10).

In the meantime, reprints of the speech had already appeared in special editions published in newspapers around the country (figs. 11, 12). The combination of words and pictures proved unbeatable.

Given the evidence, it would be difficult to minimize the national impact of Lincoln's Cooper Union address. But it would be more difficult still to assign it automatically a greater importance than those of the images produced to accompany it. One rather crude adaptation of the Brady photograph for an engraved campaign poster (fig. 13) inspired a little girl in upstate New York to urge Lincoln to grow a beard to improve his appearance. In Europe, the pose continued to serve as a model for Lincoln textiles (fig. 14) and prints (fig. 15), long after those emblematic whiskers had been added to the original—even after the president's assassination.

And in an America whose public was as eager to preserve the image as were the image-makers to save money by adapting it rather than creating new pictures (fig. 16), the Cooper Union Lincoln remained a vivid part of the American scene (fig. 17) long after the words of Lincoln's later, elegiac speeches had eclipsed those he uttered in New York on February 27, 1860.

Figure 1. The "Cooper Union photograph" of Abraham Lincoln, made by Mathew Brady, New York, February 27, 1860. (Library of Congress)

ABRAHAM LINCOLN, OF ILLINOIS, THE PRESIDENTIAL CANDIDATE FOR THE REPUBLICAN PARTY.—PHOTOGRAPHED BY BRADY.—SEE PAGE 345.

Figure 2. Engraver unknown, after Mathew Brady, *Abraham Lincoln, of Illinois, the Presidential Candidate for the Republican Party.* Published in *Frank Leslie's Illustrated Newspaper*, New York, June 20, 1860. (The Lincoln Museum, Fort Wayne, Indiana, neg. no. 3706)

ENSIGN, BRIDGMAN & FANNING,   100 WILLIAM STREET, NEW YORK,

ABRAHAM LINCOLN,
SIXTEENTH PRESIDENT OF THE UNITED STATES.
No. 20.

Figure 3. Ensign, Bridgman, and Fanning, after Mathew Brady, *Abraham Lincoln, Sixteenth President of the United States*. Hand-colored woodcut engraving, New York, 1860. (The Lincoln Museum, Fort Wayne, Indiana, neg. no. 2054)

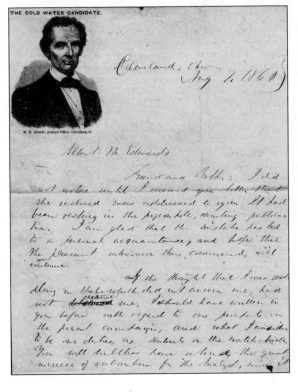

Figure 4. Above: M. H. Allardt, after Mathew Brady, *The Cold Water Candidate.* Engraved illustration for a campaign envelope, Cleveland, 1860. (Harold Holzer).

Figure 5. Left: M. H. Allardt, after Mathew Brady, *The Cold Water Candidate.* Engraved illustration for campaign notepaper, Cleveland, 1860. (Harold Holzer)

Figure 6. J[ohn]. C[hester]. Buttre, after Mathew Brady, [*Abraham Lincoln*].
Steel engraving, New York, 1860. (Harold Holzer)

Figure 7. Currier & Ives, after Mathew Brady, *Abraham Lincoln, / Republican candidate for / Sixteenth President of the United States*. Lithograph, New York, 1860. (The Lincoln Museum, Fort Wayne, Indiana, neg. no. 1987)

Figure 8. Currier & Ives, after Mathew Brady, *Abraham Lincoln, / Sixteenth President of the United States*. Lithograph, New York, 1860. (The Lincoln Museum, Fort Wayne, Indiana, neg. no. 2056)

Figure 9. Above: Currier & Ives, after Mathew Brady, *The Rail Candidate*. Lithograph, New York, 1860. (Library of Congress).

Figure 10. Right: R. Hooper, after Mathew Brady, *The Last Rail Split by "Honest Old Abe."* Woodcut engraving, published in *Momus*, New York, June 2, 1860. (Library of Congress)

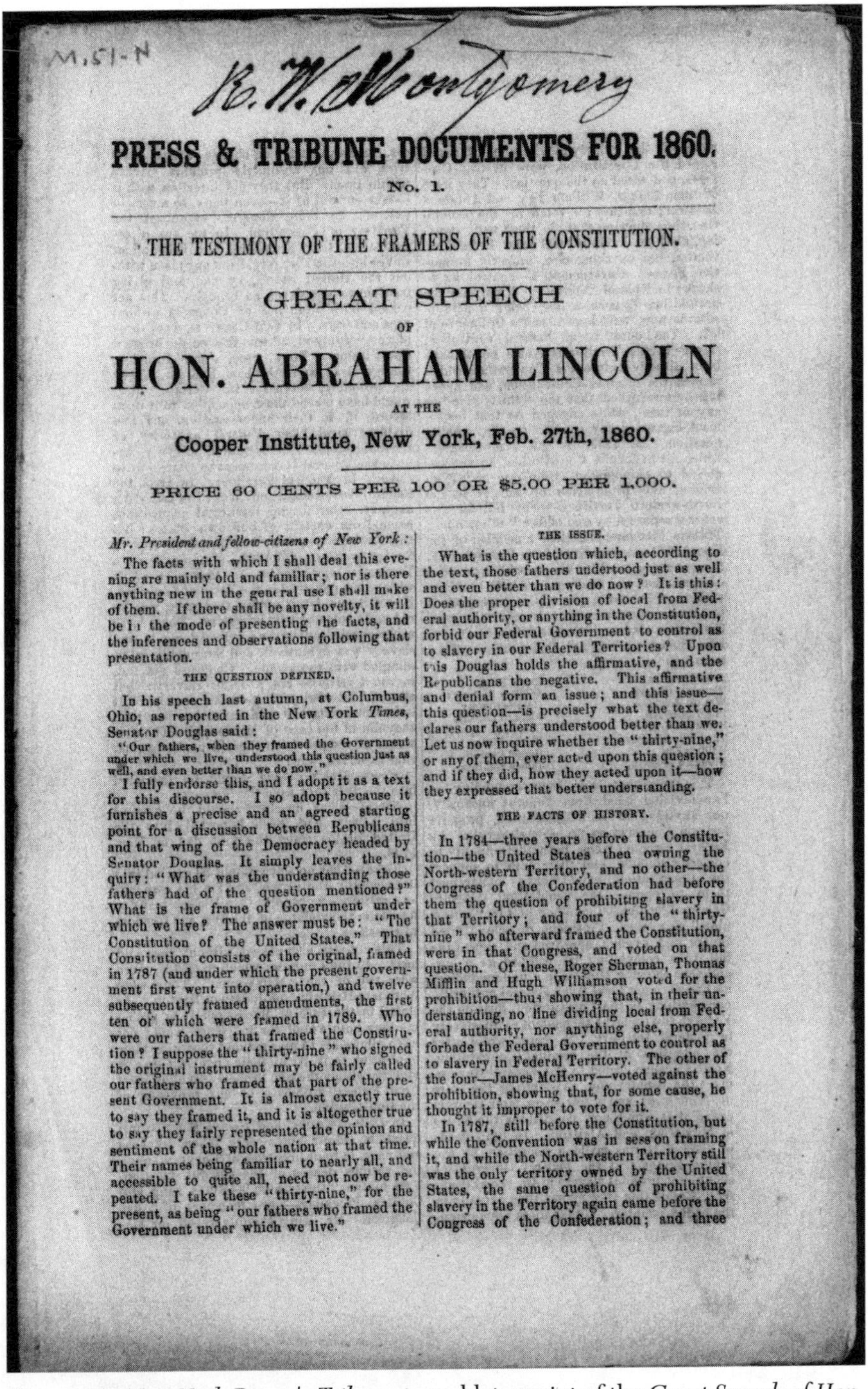

PRESS & TRIBUNE DOCUMENTS FOR 1860.

No. 1.

THE TESTIMONY OF THE FRAMERS OF THE CONSTITUTION.

GREAT SPEECH

OF

HON. ABRAHAM LINCOLN

AT THE

Cooper Institute, New York, Feb. 27th, 1860.

PRICE 60 CENTS PER 100 OR $5.00 PER 1,000.

Mr. President and fellow-citizens of New York:

The facts with which I shall deal this evening are mainly old and familiar; nor is there anything new in the general use I shall make of them. If there shall be any novelty, it will be in the mode of presenting the facts, and the inferences and observations following that presentation.

THE QUESTION DEFINED.

In his speech last autumn, at Columbus, Ohio, as reported in the New York *Times*, Senator Douglas said:

"Our fathers, when they framed the Government under which we live, understood this question just as well, and even better than we do now."

I fully endorse this, and I adopt it as a text for this discourse. I so adopt because it furnishes a precise and an agreed starting point for a discussion between Republicans and that wing of the Democracy headed by Senator Douglas. It simply leaves the inquiry: "What was the understanding those fathers had of the question mentioned?" What is the frame of Government under which we live? The answer must be: "The Constitution of the United States." That Constitution consists of the original, framed in 1787 (and under which the present government first went into operation,) and twelve subsequently framed amendments, the first ten of which were framed in 1789. Who were our fathers that framed the Constitution? I suppose the "thirty-nine" who signed the original instrument may be fairly called our fathers who framed that part of the present Government. It is almost exactly true to say they framed it, and it is altogether true to say they fairly represented the opinion and sentiment of the whole nation at that time. Their names being familiar to nearly all, and accessible to quite all, need not now be repeated. I take these "thirty-nine," for the present, as being "our fathers who framed the Government under which we live."

THE ISSUE.

What is the question which, according to the text, those fathers understood just as well and even better than we do now? It is this: Does the proper division of local from Federal authority, or anything in the Constitution, forbid our Federal Government to control as to slavery in our Federal Territories? Upon this Douglas holds the affirmative, and the Republicans the negative. This affirmative and denial form an issue; and this issue—this question—is precisely what the text declares our fathers understood better than we. Let us now inquire whether the "thirty-nine," or any of them, ever acted upon this question; and if they did, how they acted upon it—how they expressed that better understanding.

THE FACTS OF HISTORY.

In 1784—three years before the Constitution—the United States then owning the North-western Territory, and no other—the Congress of the Confederation had before them the question of prohibiting slavery in that Territory; and four of the "thirty-nine" who afterward framed the Constitution, were in that Congress, and voted on that question. Of these, Roger Sherman, Thomas Mifflin and Hugh Williamson voted for the prohibition—thus showing that, in their understanding, no line dividing local from Federal authority, nor anything else, properly forbade the Federal Government to control as to slavery in Federal Territory. The other of the four—James McHenry—voted against the prohibition, showing that, for some cause, he thought it improper to vote for it.

In 1787, still before the Constitution, but while the Convention was in session framing it, and while the North-western Territory still was the only territory owned by the United States, the same question of prohibiting slavery in the Territory again came before the Congress of the Confederation; and three

Figure 11. New York Press & Tribune pamphlet reprint of the Great Speech of Hon. Abraham Lincoln at the Cooper Institute, New York, Feb. 27th, 1860. Price 60 cents per 100 or $5.00 per 1,000. (Cooper Union Collection; photograph by Don Pollard)

M.57.

Detroit Tribune Tract.—No. 5.

SPEECH OF ABRAHAM LINCOLN,

OF ILLINOIS.

Delivered in the Cooper Institute, February 27, 1860.

MR. PRESIDENT AND FELLOW-CITIZENS OF NEW YORK: The facts with which I shall deal this evening are mainly old and familiar; nor is there anything new in the general use I shall make of them. If there shall be any novelty, it will be in the mode of presenting the facts, and the inferences and observations following that presentation.

In his speech last autumn, at Columbus, Ohio, as reported in the New York *Times*, Senator Douglas said:

"Our fathers, when they framed the Government under which we live, understood this question just as well, and even better than we do now."

I fully endorse this, and I adopt it as a text for this discourse. I so adopt it because it furnishes a precise and agreed starting-point for a discussion between Republicans and that wing of Democracy headed by Senator Douglas. It simply leaves the inquiry: "What was the understanding those fathers had of the question mentioned?"

"What is the frame of Government under which we live?"

The answer must be: "The Constitution of the United States." That Constitution consists of the original, framed in 1787 (and under which the present Government first went into operation), and twelve subsequently framed amendments, the first ten of which were framed in 1789.

Who were our fathers that framed the Constitution? I suppose the "thirty-nine" who signed the original instrument may be fairly called our fathers who framed that part of the present Government. It is almost exactly true to say they framed it, and it is altogether true to say they fairly represented the opinion and sentiment of the whole nation at that time.— Their names being familiar to nearly all, and accessible to quite all, need not now be repeated.

I take these "thirty-nine," for the present, as being "our fathers who framed the Government under which we live."

What is the question which, according to the text, those fathers understood just as well and even better than we do now?

It is this: Does the proper division of local from federal authority, or anything in the Constitution, forbid our Federal Government to control as to Slavery in our Federal Territories?

Upon this Douglas holds the affirmative, and Republicans the negative. The affirmative and denial form an issue; and this issue—this question—is precisely what the text declares our fathers understood better than we.

Let us now inquire whether the "thirty-nine," or any of them, ever acted upon this question; and if they did, how they acted upon it—how they expressed that better understanding.

In 1784—three years before the Constitution—the United States then owning the Northwestern Territory—and no other—the Congress of the Confederation had before them the question of prohibiting slavery in that Territory; and four of the "thirty-nine" who framed the Constitution were in that Congress, and voted on that question. Of these, Roger Sherman, Thomas Mifflin, and Hugh Williamson voted for the prohibition—thus showing that, in their understanding, no line dividing local from federal authority, nor anything else, properly forbade the Federal Government to control as to slavery in federal territory. The other of the four—James McHenry—voted against the prohibition, showing that, for some cause, he thought it improper to vote for it.

In 1787, still before the Constitution, but while the Convention was in session framing it, and while the Northwestern Territory still was the only Territory owned by the United States—the same question of prohibiting slavery in the territory came again before the Congress of the Confederation; and three more of the "thirty-nine" who afterwards signed the Constitution, were in that Congress, and voted on the question. They were William Blount, William Few and Abraham Baldwin; and they all voted for the prohibition—thus showing that, in their understanding, no line dividing local from federal authority, nor anything else, properly forbids the Federal Government to control as to slavery in federal territory. This time the prohibition became a law, being part of what is now well known as the Ordinance of '87.

The question of federal control of slavery in the territories, seems not to have been directly before the Convention which framed the original Constitution; and hence it is not recorded that the "thirty-nine," or any of them, while engaged on that instrument, expressed any opinion on that precise question.

In 1789, by the first Congress which sat under the Constitution, an act was passed to enforce the Ordinance of '87, including the prohibition of slavery in the Northwestern Territory. The bill for this act was reported by one of the "thirty-nine," Thomas Fitz-

☞ Printed, and for Sale, at the DETROIT TRIBUNE Office: 50 cts. per 100: $5 per 1000.

Figure 12. Detroit Tribune Tract reprint of the Speech of Abraham Lincoln, of Illinois. Delivered in the Cooper Institute, February 27, 1860. (Cooper Union Collection; photograph by Don Pollard)

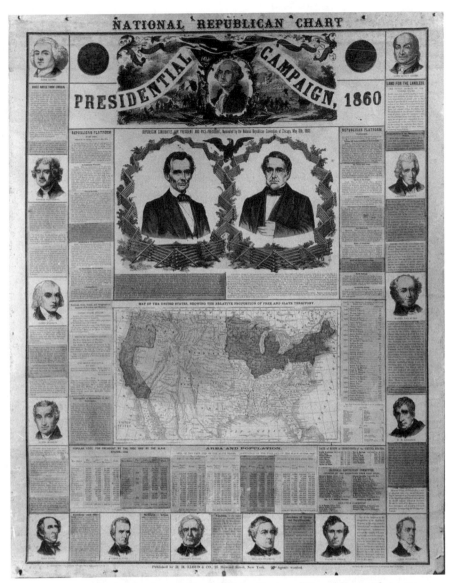

Figure 13. H. H. Lloyd, after Mathew Brady, *National Republican Chart / Presidential Campaign 1860*. Woodcut engraving, New York, 1860. (The Lincoln Museum, Fort Wayne, Indiana, neg. no. 394)

Figure 14. S. Chevre, after Mathew Brady, *Union For Ever /
A. Lincoln. / President.* Woven silk portrait published by
Isaac Dreyfus, Basel, ca. 1865. (Harold Holzer)

Figure 15. J. W. Whatley, after Mathew Brady, *Abraham Lincoln. / 16th President of America. / Assassinated by J. Wilkes Booth, April 14th, 1865.* Lithograph, London, 1865. (The Lincoln Museum, Fort Wayne, Indiana, neg. no. 2318)

Figure 16. Currier & Ives, *Abraham Lincoln. / Sixteenth President of the United States / Assassinated April 14th 1865.* Lithograph, New York, 1865. (Library of Congress)

If God had not loved the common people he would not have made so many of them.

Abraham Lincoln.

Figure 17. The Rotograph Company, Souvenir program for a Lincoln dinner, including a picture-within-the-picture of an engraving after Brady, New York, ca. 1909. (Harold Holzer)

CHAPTER 5

"I See the President":
Abraham Lincoln and
the Soldiers' Home
Matthew Pinsker

"I SEE THE PRESIDENT ALMOST EVERY DAY," NOTED POET
Walt Whitman in an entry from his wartime journal, dated Wednes-
day, August 12, 1863. "I saw him this morning about 8½ coming in
to business." Whitman, who visited the wounded at Union hospitals
and lived on L Street in Washington during part of the conflict,
observed that Abraham Lincoln, "somewhat rusty and dusty," along
with an "unornamental *cortège*" of twenty-five or thirty cavalry
troops, made absolutely "no sensation" on the city's streets. The
Long Island native was less immune to the routines of the nation's
capital and maintained a careful vigil over the president's daily commute while he lived in the city. He reported that in their brief encounters, Lincoln's "dark brown face" with its "deep-cut lines" was
often plainly visible to him, adding wistfully that there was a "deep
latent sadness" evident in his eyes. The close scrutiny apparently
did not go unnoticed. "We have got so that we exchange bows,"
Whitman claimed, "and very cordial ones."[1]

This striking portrait of President Lincoln heading to work raises
a provocative question. Where was he spending his nights if not at

the White House? Most Americans, and even some scholars, have been unaware that Lincoln maintained a wartime retreat from 1862–1864, spending over a quarter of his presidency in residence there, usually each year from early summer to late autumn. He was actually one of a handful of nineteenth-century presidents to use this place called the Soldiers' Home as his sanctuary and private White House.[2]

Telling the story of Lincoln's three seasons at the Soldiers' Home is the first object of this essay, but not its only purpose. Whitman's fascinating journal entry suggests a larger meaning. As any photographer knows, a slight shift in focus or subtle change of lens can sometimes create dramatic new images from otherwise familiar scenes. Few scenes in American history are more familiar than Lincoln's presidency, but no study of that period has ever attempted to see the president from the perspective of his daily journeys between the Soldiers' Home and White House. The book that I have written takes the fleeting glimpse of a poet and tries to make it the starting point for a new look at Lincoln's presidential leadership. In the following pages, I would like to share some of those insights. The result is as much metaphor as narrative, offering a window into the elusive boundary that separates a president's public and private experiences.

Originally known as the Military Asylum, the Soldiers' Home was an institution created in the early 1850s for disabled army veterans who could not support themselves. The federal government had purchased land for the proposed community near the District's northwestern boundary, about three miles from the White House, along the road toward Silver Spring, Maryland. By nineteenth-century standards, this venture was unprecedented, a significant expansion of government services and an untested experiment in accommodating people with disabilities. Not surprisingly, the operation struggled at first. Political support flagged and there was talk of abandoning the effort. Anxious to cultivate more allies in Washington, the military commissioners in charge of the Home soon began the practice of inviting presidents and secretaries of war to spend summers at private cottages on their grounds.

The cottages at the Soldiers' Home offered an attractive alternative to the White House, especially in hot weather, because they were well situated on cool, shaded hills. They also offered the advantage of being outside the city while not too far from the presidential office. It took an ordinary carriage driver about half an hour to navigate the three-mile journey across the District. In the Civil War era, the grounds covered nearly three hundred acres, offering a panoramic view of the capital and surrounding countryside. At the outset of the Lincoln administration, a local newspaper praised the area as "one of the most charming rural retreats in the vicinity of Washington."[3]

There were five principal buildings clustered together at one corner of the grounds: an imposing main hall for approximately 150 residents, or inmates as they were then called; and four rustic but still elegant domiciles scattered nearby. Local banker George W. Riggs, Jr., the previous owner of the property, had built the largest of these cottages in the early 1840s to serve as his family's "country" residence. With two prominent gables, a stucco-covered brick exterior and an extended porch or veranda, the country home was designed in the English Gothic Revival style that had been popularized by prominent nineteenth-century designer Andrew Jackson Downing. The government had built two of the other cottages, called Quarters 1 and 2, in the mid-1850s, at the same time that they constructed the Scott Hall, the main edifice named after General in Chief Winfield Scott, who had been the founding spirit behind the Soldiers' Home. The other building, known as the Corlisle Cottage, was situated slightly apart from the others in a more secluded grove. All of these residences typically served as housing units for officers or personnel associated with the institution.

James Buchanan, the first president to reside at the Soldiers' Home, stayed at Quarters 1. The bachelor president was satisfied with his decision and reported to his niece Harriet Lane in 1858 that he "slept much better at the Asylum than at the White House." It was probably Buchanan who first recommended the Soldiers' Home to Lincoln during their brief encounters in 1861. Within a few days after the Inaugural, the *New York Times* reported that both the new First Lady and her husband had separately ridden out to look over the grounds. By April, a local newspaper announced that President Lincoln and his family intended to follow Buchanan's example and occupy the same "charming spot" that the previous incumbent had enjoyed so much.[4]

The report about Lincoln's summer plans appeared on Sunday, April 14, 1861—the same day that Federal troops surrendered Fort Sumter. In the gathering storm of Southern rebellion, the prospect of a presidential vacation suddenly appeared far less charming. Mary Lincoln continued to hold out some hope for a temporary escape, but it was to no avail. In mid-July, she wrote to a friend that the family expected to go out to the Soldiers' Home, "a very beautiful place," within about three weeks. "We will ride into the city every day, & can be as secluded, as we please," she predicted hopefully.[5] Just ten days after this note, Union forces suffered a devastating setback at Bull Run in the war's first major engagement. With her husband now more preoccupied by work, Mary Lincoln remained at the White House, continuing with her plans to renovate the presidential mansion and dutifully visiting wounded soldiers. In August, however, she struck out on her own, heading to the fashionable resort at Long Branch, New Jersey, and then for an extended social and shopping excursion across New York.

It was not until the beginning of the next summer that the Lincolns made good on their plans to occupy a cottage at the Soldiers' Home. By then, the need for a family retreat had become both more pressing and more personal. In February 1862, twelve-year-old Willie Lincoln had died after a bout with what the newspapers had labeled pneumonia but what was probably typhoid fever. This blow was especially hard for his doting mother, who had already lost one child, Eddie, to illness years before. In the aftermath of Willie's death, Mary Lincoln found life at the White House too distracting for proper mourning. Subsequently, the president agreed, despite his ever-increasing workload, to move the family out to the Soldiers' Home in June 1862.

In retrospect, it is startling to consider how disorganized and informal the process of relocating the First Family was in that era. Senator Orville Browning, a close friend from Illinois, showed up at the White House one evening only to discover that the Lincolns had already vacated the official residence for the season. There were no special security measures taken on their behalf—no guards or escorts at their disposal. The president left for the Soldiers' Home with his wife, their youngest son Tad and probably only a handful of servants: a cook, a housekeeper and perhaps a valet. There are no official records of their new residency—no documentation for which cottage they inhabited, no inventory of the White House belongings they carried along with them, and no register of the many guests who soon began visiting their "*country* retirement," as Mary Lincoln proudly called it.[6] Everything about their experience at the Soldiers' Home must be pieced together from fragments principally found in diaries, letters, recollections, and newspaper accounts.

Following their arrival, the Lincolns apparently decided that unlike President Buchanan, they would displace the acting governor of the Home, who was then occupying the former Riggs country residence. Situated directly next to the asylum, the Riggs home was comfortable but offered constant reminders about the painful stakes of military conflict. Crippled veterans regularly filled its small courtyard. One side of the elegant cottage now also faced a national military cemetery, hastily dedicated after the defeat at Bull Run and, by the summer of 1862, full of fresh graves. Thus, even while attempting to escape from their private grief and the national crisis, the Lincolns still found themselves surrounded by the somber echoes of war.

Yet nothing about the sorrowful nature of their surroundings appeared to diminish the joy that the Lincolns found in their temporary seclusion. "How dearly I loved the 'Soldiers' Home,'" the First Lady later recalled.[7] The president's feelings have not been similarly recorded, but he returned each summer and stayed as long as weather permitted, even when his wife and his sons were out of town. In 1862, the Lincolns remained in residence from mid-June until early November, a total of nearly five months. The next year, the president returned for another period of about four and a half months. His stay in 1864 was slightly more compressed, extending from early July until sometime after mid-October. Altogether, President Lincoln lived at the Soldiers' Home for about thirteen out of his forty-nine months in office. For most of that period, his wife and youngest son Tad were with him, though Mary Lincoln traveled outside of Washington frequently, shopping in New York or vacationing in Vermont, leaving her husband alone at the cottage for weeks at a time. Eldest son Robert was usually away at college or traveling with friends. He spent no more than a few weeks with his father each summer.

Like many modern-day commuters, Lincoln scrambled in the mornings to avoid traffic and get a head start on his daily work. "He rose early," recalled John Hay, one of his top aides. "When he lived in the country at Soldiers Home, he would be up and dressed, eat his breakfast . . . and ride into Washington, all before 8 o'clock."[8] Others involved in the daily presidential routine shared similar recollections. An Army captain responsible for accompanying the president during a period of rising military tension recalled that he used to enter the cottage each day at about 6:30 a.m., often discovering that Lincoln was already awake, "reading the Bible or some work on the art of war."[9] Not surprisingly, some contemporary observations, like Whitman's journal entry, hint at a less punctual president, but the phenomenon of rising early and heading off to work was a deeply ingrained part of Lincoln's wartime life.

During his first summer at the Soldiers' Home, Lincoln often rode without any escort, but after some nervous consultations among friends, political advisors, Union military commanders and his anxious wife, the president was compelled to accept at least some minimal show of protection. The army ordered a Pennsylvania infantry company to guard the cottage and by the autumn of 1862, members of a New York cavalry unit that Whitman so memorably dismissed as an "unornamental *cortège*" began accompanying Lincoln on almost all of his daily trips. From December 1863 until the war's end, a unit specially recruited from Ohio replaced them and provided the president with his primary escort.

The president and his cavalry escort had a choice of routes into the city, either via the Seventh Street Turnpike or North Capitol Street or Fourteenth Street. The turnpike was then the principal route in and out of the city, complete with a tollgate that the president was generously allowed to ignore. The road had strategic as well as political value. A key element of the city's elaborate defense network, Fort Massachusetts (later renamed Fort Stevens) sat perched just inside the District line along this pike. It was one of sixty-eight major forts that ultimately ringed the city, a martial beltway that stretched across suburbs in Maryland and through Union-occupied northern Virginia. The Soldiers' Home was not officially part of this network, but the tower at the main hall provided a communications outpost that ultimately proved vital for the defense of the city when it fell under attack in 1864.

As Lincoln and his escort crossed Boundary Street, the turnpike became Seventh Street Road, and they officially entered a city that was then expanding rapidly within the District. However, for several blocks the dusty road remained sparsely inhabited and hardly resembled a major avenue in a national capital. As many noted both at the time and since, the city was as incomplete as the nation torn apart by sectional conflict. The Washington Monument stood half-finished, looking more like a Roman ruin than a great national symbol. Until 1863, the Capitol Dome was also still under construction. There was a handful of spectacular buildings—the White House, Treasury Department, Post Office, Patent Office and Smithsonian "castle"—but there was also an inescapable sense of under-achievement about Washington. Depending on the season, the city's wide avenues were either dusty or muddy, with adjoining land often barren of buildings and whole sections of the town simply cut apart and isolated by open and filthy waterways. "The whole place looks run up in a night," wrote London journalist Edward Dicey, ". . . and it is impossible to remove the impression that, when Congress is over, the whole place is taken down, and packed up again till wanted."[10]

For Lincoln, though, the city must have seemed large enough with its 61,000 people at the start of the war and 230 miles of streets. Prior to becoming president, he had spent the previous twelve years living in a modest wood frame house in Springfield, Illinois, a town with only a few thousand inhabitants. He had lived in Washington once before, during the late 1840s as a homesick congressman holed up in a boardinghouse near Capitol Hill, but the town was even less developed then. Moreover, by the end of the war, the city's population had tripled, approaching 200,000 people and was considered, by most Americans at least, to be a bustling, engaging place.

Once in the city, Lincoln and his entourage probably turned off Seventh onto Rhode Island and there connected to Vermont Avenue. It was on this stretch of the route that the president would have passed by Whitman's home near the corner of Vermont and L Street in the mornings on his way toward Lafayette Square and days full of crisis at the wartime White House.

While her husband tended to the nation's business, Mary Lincoln strained in her own way to contribute to his cause. Frustrated by her private grief and poor health, nineteenth-century gender conventions, and her husband's near-constant state of exhaustion, the First Lady found it difficult to connect to him and to support him in his enormous endeavors. Mary Lincoln subsequently invested herself in projects that she imagined might help her husband. Some of these experiments proved to be spectacular and costly political failures, such as her extravagant spending on White House renovations or her occasional attempts to punish the spouses and daughters of the president's more prominent rivals. Other efforts were more helpful, such as her admirable habit of visiting Union hospitals, several of which were located near the cottage. The First Lady often made the rounds of hospital wards without seeking any press coverage, making them straightforward exercises in charity. Moreover, these were not encounters for the faint-hearted. A Union soldier stationed at nearby Fort Stevens described the hospitals most frequently visited by Mary Lincoln in a letter to his father:

> I went toward Washington yesterday to visit the hospitals on the edge of the city. I went to three—Mount Pleasant, Carver, and Columbia College. They all seem neat and well kept . . . [but] wounds are everywhere. Some are most shockingly mangled. I did not go about much, for I do not like such scenes.[11]

If such scenes so disturbed a combat soldier, it is difficult to imagine how they affected Mary Lincoln, who normally recoiled from bloodshed.

President Lincoln visited the wounded as well, but most of his day was invariably spent locked inside the White House. His office was a magnet for visitors, both serious and laughable, though there was little effort to distinguish between them. In a wickedly biting recollection, one English visitor described the casual collection of guests who congregated at the White House prior to the president's arrival on typical summer mornings: "If you had only been with us that morning upon the steps of the White House," George Borrett wrote with tongue planted firmly in cheek, "where we waited, with one or two more loungers like ourselves, to see the President come in from his country house." He ridiculed the entire proceedings, from the "bow-legged, cow-quartered, dead-alive quadrupeds" that served as the cavalry escort's horses to the presidential carriage that "might have been centuries since it was washed or painted." "The Constitution has some queer provisions," he noted dryly, "I wonder whether it compels the President's coachman to brush his hat the wrong way."[12]

Lincoln's office was on the second floor of the White House, along the southern side of the building. Here even greater crowds spilled out into the hallways and down the stairs. The wartime president had only a handful of aides to help him manage his affairs. The result was inevitably chaotic, a situation only exacerbated by Lincoln's peculiar style of conducting business. "Sometimes there would be a crowd of senators and members of Congress waiting their turn," remembered Illinois Congressman Isaac Arnold. "While thus waiting, the loud ringing laugh of Mr. Lincoln—in which he would be joined by those *inside*, but which was rather provoking to those *outside*—would be heard by the waiting and impatient crowd."[13] Nothing seemed to alleviate the delays. "The House remained full of people nearly all day," reported Hay, noting that at lunchtime the president "had literally to run the gantlet through the crowds who filled the corridors."[14]

During the wartime period, Lincoln was only in his mid-fifties, but the pressures and tragedies of the conflict aged him dramatically. Old friends such as Arnold "were sometimes shocked with the change in his appearance" and could barely recognize a man they had once considered blessed with "a frame of iron and nerves of steel."[15] Many wartime observers echoed Whitman in commenting on the president's "deep latent sadness." Journalist Noah Brooks, who had met Lincoln in the 1850s, described the nation's Commander in Chief as having been "grievously altered" since his days as a "happy-faced Springfield lawyer."[16] Artist Francis B. Carpenter, who worked on a canvas at the White House for a period of about six months, simply called Lincoln's countenance "the saddest face I ever painted."[17]

The tension so evident in the president's appearance underscores the importance of his attempts to find sanctuary at the Soldiers' Home. In the evenings when the Lincolns were together at their cottage, they tried earnestly to relax. As with many families from that era, they found their greatest release in social activities, usually in the parlor and often by reading aloud. Although known for his storytelling, recollections by guests at the cottage suggest that the president was more likely to turn to his favorite poets or dramatists when he was outside of the office and not trying to make a political point or neutralize an unwanted request. There were evenings full of the famous anecdotes and even some sentimental ballads, but they appeared to be less common. The Lincoln parlor generally embodied a dignified nineteenth-century ideal.

"Where only one or two [friends] were present [Lincoln] was fond of reading aloud," Hay insisted. "He passed many of the summer evenings in this way when occupying his cottage at the Soldiers' Home." According to the loyal aide, who once drifted to sleep while listening to lines from *Richard III*, the president would read from Shakespeare "for hours with a single secretary for [an] audience." Lincoln appeared to Hay to be especially fond of the famous soliloquy in *Richard II* where the King contemplated the meaning of death, a passage that the young assistant claimed he had heard Lincoln recite "at Springfield, at the White House, and at the Soldiers' Home":

> For God's sake, let us sit upon the ground,
> And tell sad stories of the death of kings:—

How some have been depos'd, some slain in war,
Some haunted by the ghosts they have deposed;
Some poisoned by their wives, some sleeping kill'd;
All murthered. . . .[18]

Naturally, many of the Shakespearean plays and passages that Lincoln seemed to admire most dwelt upon themes of rebellion, usurpation, and ambition run amok. The historical dramas that he quoted from so freely, such as the plays about the Henrys or the Richards, depicted an England divided by civil war as two rival clans, the House of York and the House of Lancaster, vied for control of the realm. The tragedies he preferred, like *Macbeth* or *Hamlet*, concerned the nature of evil and civil disorder created by disruptions in the succession of kings. These are themes that he appreciated long before the war, but ones that developed special resonance for him as the conflict erupted in the aftermath of his own election. "Some of Shakespeare's plays I have never read," he explained, "while others I have gone over perhaps as frequently as any unprofessional reader."[19]

Not all of Lincoln's readings invoked such dark and brooding topics. He was also fond of comic verse from popular poets such as Thomas Hood or Fitz-Greene Halleck. He favored a group of nineteenth-century American prose humorists, men such as Petroleum V. Nasby (a pen name for David R. Locke) who posed as a crude Southern sympathizer in a series of wonderful wartime satires. The president often read from Artemus Ward (Charles F. Browne), probably the best known nineteenth-century American humorist before the emergence of Mark Twain. Lincoln also appreciated the character Orpheus C. Kerr (Robert H. Newell), whose biting commentary on the ways of the nation's capital struck a special chord with the politician. A number of cottage guests testified to Lincoln's talent for mimicry, which he employed with delightful effect when reading from comic pieces by one of these authors.

Recreating the physical scene where these readings and intimate social gatherings took place is a difficult task. Most of the guests recorded only fleeting observations about the interior design of the cottage, the layout of the parlor or the style of the furniture. Still, some interesting details have emerged. The main parlor at the former Riggs cottage appears to have been opposite the front entryway. It had gib windows that opened onto a porch facing the northern edge of the grounds and the nearby cemetery. A fireplace occupied one wall, useful during late autumn evenings when the air around the cottage grew chillier. The residence was also equipped with gaslights. By the standards of the Victorian era, the parlor was only lightly furnished with a handful of sofas and chairs and appears to have been separated from a dining area and the stairwell merely by a folding screen. Mary Lincoln tried to refurbish the interior of the cottage in the spring of 1864 by hiring a local upholsterer to add gilt-edged wallpaper to several of the rooms and to lay down what was then considered fashionable grass matting on the upstairs hallways.[20]

President Lincoln invariably removed his boots when entering the cottage and walked around in his slippers. When it was particularly hot, he also carried a large palm-leaf fan to help circulate the air. The image he presented to visitors was casual—a rumpled, often tired country gentleman preparing for bed. Englishman George Borrett recalled during his 1864 visit that he and other guests were "ushered into a moderate-sized, neatly furnished drawing-room." After waiting a few minutes, they were informed by a grumpy valet that Mrs. Lincoln had already retired for the evening and did not feel well. They prepared to leave, but then suddenly, "there entered through the folding doors the long, lanky, lath-like figure" of President Lincoln. Borrett described the president "with hair ruffled, and eyes very sleepy," noting with amusement that his large feet were "enveloped in carpet slippers." Lincoln then proceeded to hold forth with his visitors on various political and legal topics before ending the audience with a recitation from Alexander Pope's famous poem, "Essay on Man."[21]

It is impossible to specify an exact number of visitors who spent such evenings at the Soldiers' Home cottage. There were probably hundreds who passed through the parlor during the First Family's three seasons in residence, with a core group of about a dozen regulars and an unknown number of overnight guests. My book contains stories or insights from about seventy-five of these visitors. No easy label captures them. They were Union generals and lower-ranking officers, Cabinet members and mid-level political appointees, journalists, and old Illinois friends, congressmen, and their wives, Washington socialites and foreign dignitaries. Most were friends but some were strangers. It was an eclectic assortment of human diversions for a family in sore need of distraction.

The cottage visitors were certainly a fortunate group, and not just because of their proximity to greatness. Some were simply lucky to find the place. Although the Soldiers' Home was a public destination, favored by local residents for Sunday drives and afternoon strolls, it was not always easy to locate in the evenings. Several guests reported that their hacks or taxi drivers got lost on the path to the cottage. "Our driver missed the way," recalled one of the president's old acquaintances visiting from Illinois, "passing by the Home into the forest below." The man claimed that he and his other friends did not make it out of the "labyrinth" until nearly 2 o'clock in the morning and missed a chance to see the president.[22] Traveling on the Seventh Street turnpike at such hours could be dangerous as well. There was a racetrack nearby and several taverns and houses of prostitution in the vicinity. "Rode home in the dark amid a party of drunken gamblers & harlots," reported Hay in his diary, after returning from an evening with the president.[23]

But for the Lincolns, practically nothing could disturb their image of an idyllic country retreat. "We are truly delighted, with this retreat," Mary Lincoln happily concluded early in their first season, "the drives & walks around here are delightful, & each day, brings its visitors."[24] The family not only came out each season after 1862—and would have done so again in 1865—but also husband and wife made the Home a frequent destination for their regular afternoon carriage rides. They began riding out in March 1861 and continued the habit throughout the next four years. Whitman reported seeing them together in the summer of 1863 "toward the latter part of the afternoon, out in a barouche, on a pleasure ride through the city." He noted that over a year after Willie Lincoln's death, Mary Lincoln was still "dress'd in complete black, with a long crape veil." According to the poet, these rides were taken without military escort. "The equipage is of the plainest kind," he wrote in his journal, "only two horses, and they nothing extra."[25]

The day before President Lincoln was fatally shot in April 1865, he took an afternoon ride on horseback without his wife, though accompanied by a small cavalry escort trailing behind him. Maunsell B. Field, who was then a senior political aide in the Treasury Department, recalled that he was himself heading out toward the Soldiers' Home when the president and his entourage came up behind him. Field claimed they "conversed together upon indifferent subjects" for a brief period. He noticed that the president was in a melancholy mood and seemed tired. Then Lincoln spurred his horse and headed off, presumably for his own customary ride around the grounds before returning to work at the White House. If Field's memory was accurate, this was the last time anyone would see the president traveling between his public and private worlds.[26]

The story of the Soldiers' Home frames Lincoln's entire presidential experience. He first rode out to the retreat a few days after his Inaugural. He last returned on the day before he was killed. Between those moments, he lived there for a total of thirteen months. Even more critically, he lived at this retreat during some of the key periods of the conflict, such as when he developed his emancipation policy in 1862 or maneuvered successfully toward re-election in 1864. Lincoln's challenge as a national leader was unprecedented. In that era of grave crisis, he naturally sought support within his private life to help sustain his public duty. The Soldiers' Home offered a sanctuary where he could work out this vital struggle.

It was not easy. During his first season at the Soldiers' Home, Lincoln faced critical decisions over emancipation, conscription, and the controversial fate of his leading general, George B. McClellan. All of these grave decisions were related to one frustrating and tragic reality—the war was not ending. In the first year of the conflict Lincoln had done his part, holding together an improbable Union coalition that included both Democrats and Republicans and ultimately four out of the fifteen slave states. But the slow pace of mobilization and the failure of Union military commanders to win decisive victories created pressure on President Lincoln to raise the stakes of the war.

He wrestled with each of the decisions that escalated both the war's level of violence and its larger meaning. As the president veered back and forth between his difficult choices in the summer and autumn of 1862, he sometimes stumbled and lost his poise. He persevered, however, and ultimately found a workable balance by year's end. This achievement was driven at least in part by the sustenance Lincoln discovered both inside his new sanctuary and through the rhythm and unanticipated interactions of his daily commute.

One of the finest examples of how the commute sometimes offered the president unexpected intelligence comes from a brief but revealing glimpse recorded in the *New York Tribune* on July 8, 1862 under the heading, "THE PRESIDENT AND THE WOUNDED":

> The President on the Fourth, while on his way to his Summer Residence at Soldiers Home, meeting a train of

ambulances conveying wounded men from the late battles to the hospitals, just beyond the city limits, rode beside them for a considerable distance, conversing freely with the men, and seeming anxious to secure all the information possible with regard to the real condition of affairs on the Peninsula and the feeling among the troops from those who had borne the brunt of the fight.[27]

Earlier on Independence Day, the president had told a delegation of veterans, "I am indeed surrounded, as is the whole country, by very trying circumstances."[28] Now here was the nation's wartime president trailing forlornly along the ambulance trains heading out to the several temporary hospitals that were located near his summer residence, "seeming anxious" to uncover the "real condition of affairs" in the field. On the eighty-sixth anniversary of the nation's birth, the head of the government appeared almost lost.

And yet behind the pathos of this scene lay one secret to Lincoln's enduring popularity. However bewildered the president might have appeared to the *Tribune*'s Washington correspondent, he was nonetheless at ease with the nation's ordinary people, someone capable of "conversing freely with the men" and willing to listen to "those who had borne the brunt of the fight." Lincoln's genuine accessibility often helped win over skeptics who felt empowered by his apparent interest in them. Many leaders in similar circumstances would have locked themselves away in the White House, attempting to escape from the constant criticism. In this fashion, the president's decision to relocate to the Soldiers' Home takes on a broader meaning, serving not just as his family's private retreat but also as a striking example of his outreach efforts. The daily commute promised regular, unstructured interaction with the people, which sometimes had value beyond calculation, as the clipping from the *Tribune* attests.

Sometimes, however, the random interactions on the rough roads outside the Soldiers' Home threatened danger. In the summer of 1863, the First Lady endured a harrowing accident while traveling from the cottage to a nearby military hospital. As the president waited anxiously for news from both the battlefields at Gettysburg and Vicksburg, his wife was thrown from a carriage. Mary Lincoln's wounds were initially considered minor, but they soon became infected and she nearly died. Robert Lincoln, rebuked by his father for not returning to Washington quickly enough, later claimed the episode permanently damaged his mother's already fragile emotional state. Not long after the accident, she left Washington for nearly eight weeks, seeking greater seclusion and rest in Vermont. Some contemporaries wondered if the accident was not really a botched assassination attempt. Later in the war, there would be more claims about kidnappers and assassins lurking along the dark roads out to the Soldiers' Home.

Yet the president enjoyed the distance his wartime retreat offered and continued to weigh these presumably hypothetical security risks against real political benefits. Often Lincoln used the casual setting of the Soldiers' Home to discover critical information about the war and his political situation. It was at the Soldiers' Home in August 1864, for example, that he vigorously defended his policies to politicians such as Carl Schurz, Alexander W. Randall, and Joseph T. Mills. These meetings illustrate, in the words of one participant, Lincoln's remarkable "elasticity of spirits," and document with surprising clarity his determined strategy during a summer of discontent. Nothing better demonstrates Lincoln's willingness to play hardball, however, than a secret meeting he conducted at the Soldiers' Home in September 1864 with Copperhead political leader Fernando Wood. This is an encounter that has generally escaped previous Lincoln scholars, but offers provocative insight into the lengths that the president was willing to consider taking in order to secure his reelection.

Lincoln's final season at the Soldiers' Home literally began and ended under siege. The family ventured out to the cottage in early July 1864 only to be ordered back to the White House in the middle of the night by Secretary of War Edwin Stanton when Confederate troops threatened the city's defenses on July 10. President Lincoln then risked his own life on two separate occasions as he tried to view the Rebel assaults against Fort Stevens. The family soon returned to the cottage, but as the summer wore on, there were an increasing number of reports from soldiers, servants, and neighbors around the Soldiers' Home indicating threats against the president's life, specifically those targeting him as he made his daily commute. By the time he returned to the White House in late autumn, the War Department had ratcheted up his personal security by several degrees. In addition to an infantry company and a cavalry escort—both now on full alert—the president also received for the first time a personal bodyguard made up of former Washington police detectives. They would remain on a high state of alert until the following spring when the Confederacy collapsed and the war finally appeared to be ending.

The evolution of the presidential security arrangements constitutes a critical element of the Soldiers' Home story. President-elect Lincoln had arrived in Washington in 1861 amidst fears of an assassination plot against him. Under pressure from concerned advisors, he had been persuaded to enter the city secretly and in partial disguise. This was new terrain since no American president had ever been murdered in office. Given that history, and the heated political spirit of the times, President-elect Lincoln received some fierce criticism and ridicule for his "cowardly" entry into office.[29] As a result, he generally declined further security precautions on his behalf during the war's first year. But once his family was living outside the city at the Soldiers' Home in the fall of 1862, he faced no choice. The Confederate movement across the Potomac in September demanded extra security around the cottage. Only at this time

did Lincoln finally accept the assignment of both a cavalry and infantry company to help protect the First Family.

This turned out to be a decision that changed the nature of the
war for President Lincoln in an unexpected way. Obviously the military guards did not succeed in saving the president's life. They did,
however, improve it. Despite his initial objections, Lincoln grew to
appreciate the presence of soldiers in his midst. They helped dis-
tract him from his concerns and helped him recreate some of the
spirit of fraternity that he had once enjoyed as a younger politician
and circuit-riding attorney in Illinois.

During the many weeks when his family was away, Lincoln
seemed to crave such company, in particular reaching out not only
to the soldiers, but also to a shifting handful of aides and colleagues
who became close friends and helped alleviate some of his loneli-
ness. Many of these friendships were temporary or superficial, but
one, in particular, had lasting consequences for the Union cause.
Lincoln's second secretary of war, Edwin Stanton, also maintained
a cottage at the Soldiers' Home. Here, he and his children inter-
acted with the president and his family and helped cement a part-
nership that contributed mightily to the Federal victory. All of these
bonds ultimately proved to be a great irony of Lincoln's life at the
Soldiers' Home. What began as an attempt to find seclusion for his
family became a rare opportunity for an overburdened president to
experience moments of intimate camaraderie.

This insight raises a final but essential point. To see Lincoln
through a new lens inevitably means to hear new voices. Like all
books on the Lincoln presidency, this one rounds up many of the
usual suspects among Civil War diarists and memoir writers. White
House staffers Hay and John Nicolay are frequent contributors. The
journals of Cabinet members such as Salmon P. Chase and Gideon
Welles provide important material. Recollections from various secondary figures, like painter Francis Carpenter or journalist Noah
Brooks, have been mined extensively for references to the Soldiers'

Home. But the heart of the Soldiers' Home narrative comes from testimony not generally reported in Lincoln biographies.

Readers will discover figures such as David V. Derickson and Willard Cutter. Captain Derickson led the infantry unit assigned to the Soldiers' Home, a company that included his eighteen-year-old son Charles. A politically minded businessman from Meadville, Pennsylvania, he quickly established himself as a regular presence in President Lincoln's life. He forged a remarkable friendship with the president that quickly became the object of jealous gossip. His recollections, and those of his son, offer important new details about the First Family.

Cutter was a private in Derickson's company, and also from Meadville. Like the president, he escaped personal tragedy himself in 1862 by coming to the Soldiers' Home. Cutter had left behind in Pennsylvania a recently widowed mother who naturally feared for the life of her young son. The result was a blessing for historians even though it was an occasional annoyance to the soldier. "You seem to be awful tender-hearted," he wrote to his mother in 1864, "I hope you don't think you are the only woman that has a son in the army."[30] Nonetheless, the dutiful young man wrote to his family about once each week, detailing his adventures in Company K, the infantry unit assigned to guard the Lincoln family from September 1862 until the end of the war. Though not a good speller, or an especially imaginative observer, Cutter was nonetheless a faithful chronicler. What makes his particular bundle of approximately 150 letters so extraordinary, however, is its provenance. For years, the Cutter letters have been passed along from one generation of his family to the next—kept in private possession until the 1980s. They have been used by local Civil War reenactors, but never before by scholars.

There are many more secondary figures like Derickson and Cutter whose names almost never appear in Lincoln biographies, but whose stories enhance the historical narrative. "Aunt" Mary Dines, a runaway slave who served as the family's cook at the Soldiers' Home cottage, shares recollections of Lincoln visiting her "contraband" or runaway camp in Washington. There are rare documents from other soldiers, such as the court-martial transcript of Captain George A. Bennett, who led the Ohio cavalry escort assigned to the president near the war's end. The unpopular officer endured a revolt from within his company by troops who accused him of embezzling government rations. Although no letters or diaries have emerged from the residents of the Soldiers' Home itself, the institution's quarterly rolls nevertheless reveal dramatic details about the troubled lives of the crippled veterans who lived right next to the president.

How is it possible that so much testimony and such an important presidential setting could have thus far escaped the serious attention of Lincoln scholars? The answer I believe has important consequences for academics such as me and for groups such as The Lincoln Forum. On college campuses, historians routinely encourage an interdisciplinary approach to the study of the past. The idea is to strive towards a more comprehensive and sophisticated view of history by borrowing insights and practices from other disciplines, such as the social sciences or the study of literature. But when it comes to learning from other approaches within the field of history itself—such as those undertaken by preservationists, genealogists, or reenactors—there is much less enthusiasm. It is not easy, for example, to find a college professor who both teaches the Civil War era and takes Civil War enthusiasts seriously. The reverse is also true. Too often history buffs ignore the efforts by academics to provide context to specific episodes in the past. This mutual disdain has been an obstacle in the progress of the historical profession. Historians of different varieties with their separate audiences and contrasting styles need to learn to rely on each other more. We need a greater sense of *intra*-disciplinary history.

The story of the Soldiers' Home proves this point eloquently. The Lincoln Forum and other Washington-area Civil War groups pressed for years for greater recognition of the site. Finally, they secured attention from the National Trust for Historic Preservation during the 1990s. Under the leadership of Richard Moe, the National Trust worked with then First Lady Hillary Rodham Clinton to designate the Lincoln family cottage as a historic monument and to begin the long process of renovation and public education. My work began as an outgrowth of these efforts. In other words, here was intra-disciplinary history at its best. Enthusiasts, preservationists, and academics worked together to protect a place of national significance while simultaneously exploring and enriching an understanding of the past. These achievements are important because observers can no longer "see the President" as Whitman did so memorably in 1863. Yet we must always strive to recreate that vivid spirit in our work on the written page and in the preservation of historic places.

CHAPTER 6

Varieties of Religious Experience: Abraham and Mary Lincoln

Jean Baker

IN 1902 WILLIAM JAMES, YOUNGER BROTHER OF HENRY AND Alice James, veteran of the Civil War and student of religion and medicine, delivered a series of lectures at the University of Edinburgh entitled "Varieties of Religious Experience." His audience, made up of conservative members of the Church of Scotland, sat stunned by his audacious approach to religion. James had taken as his subject what he called subjective religion—that is dreams, witchcraft, and pantheism as well as the Eastern religions of Hinduism that were suspect to most orthodox Christians. To James, religion included the feelings, acts, and experiences of individual men and women "in their solitude, so far as they apprehend themselves to stand in relation to whatever they may consider the divine."

In this doctrinally loose and institutionally expansive view, personal religion had its center everywhere: in mystical states of consciousness, in early religious training from parents, and, as was the case with both Lincolns, in life experiences. James believed that individuals often adopted different faiths and religious understandings over the course of their lives. What he described as "unions with the higher universe" varied during a person's life, according to what occurred during that life.[1]

I would like to use James's understanding of religion as a point of departure for a discussion of both Abraham and Mary Lincoln's religion. My hypothesis is that both Lincolns demonstrated the validity of James's claims—Lincoln to the extent that he intensified his belief in God's omnipotence even as he remained "unchurched" in his commitment to the sacraments. Meanwhile Mary, who at the beginning of her life was more conventional about spiritual matters, changed her understanding of a transcendent reference point from orthodox Presbyterianism to briefly Episcopalianism and then to spiritualism. She more than Lincoln adopted James's most liberal view of what religion was, becoming committed to the recall of the world beyond and visions of the dead that were unacceptable to orthodox churchgoers. She made spiritualism part of her conventional Christianity, whereas her husband moved from skepticism about church rituals and practices to the view of an omnipotent, ultimately unknowable God. Both Lincolns introduce us to the broad range of American religious beliefs in the nineteenth century.

As a child, Lincoln had no orthodox religion—his stepmother once said that he had no religion at all, although we know he read the Bible and memorized passages from it.[2] He lived too far away from any organized church for attendance, although his father was a member of the Little Pigeon Creek Baptist Church in Indiana. Now these Baptists were fundamentalists with an attachment to rituals. Often they met informally out of doors. The period of Lincoln's youth featured great revivals, accompanied by congregations in full ecstasy: jerking, barking, and of course in the central sacrament of the Baptists, immersing. I believe Lincoln, who studied the law and admired Euclid, was repelled by behaviors he considered irrational. But Lincoln underwent his own "immersion" in a Baptist family in a Baptist community whose central doctrine was a belief in the sovereignty of God.

For most of his life Lincoln lived on the margins of orthodox religion, always suspicious of the rituals and the necessary suspension of reality that any faith in resurrection requires, but always convinced that the churches made the best effort of all institutions to ask and answer the essential existential questions of human life. After his marriage and the birth of his children he attended Presbyterian Churches in both Springfield and in Washington, because those were the churches his wife chose and because he liked their ministers: James Smith and Phineas Gurley.

But this nonmembership in a Christian community does not make Lincoln an atheist, or even an agnostic, although perhaps it renders him a deist. He refers to God in his letters. (Students of his religion—a subtopic in Lincoln studies—scour his writings for every use of the words *Lord*, *God*, and *Christ*, the latter appearing only once.) For example, in the 1840s, Lincoln wrote his friend Joshua Speed that he was the instrument of God in bringing Speed together with his wife Fanny. In his 1846 congressional campaign against the Methodist minister Peter Cartwright (who had disparaged Lincoln's Christianity), Lincoln denied in a handbill that he had ever disavowed the scriptures or had spoken "with intentional disrespect of religion in general." Lincoln averred that he was a believer in the doctrine of necessity—that the "human mind is impelled to action, or held in rest by some power, over which the mind itself has no control."[3] He also said that he would never support an open enemy of religion or what he called a "scoffer." What Lincoln did not accept were the essential sacraments and New Testament doctrines of Christianity: the virgin birth, the Holy Ghost, the Eucharist, and the resurrection.

Meanwhile his future wife Mary Todd lived an entirely different religious life, growing up in a family of Presbyterians in Lexington, Kentucky. The Todds and her maternal line, the Parkers, had emigrated from Scotland in the mid-eighteenth century and, along with their trunks and linens, they had carried the Presbyterian faith of

Scotland and a fierce need to be autonomous in religion as well as government. In fact, the family left for religious reasons. The branch of the family that settled in the new state of Kentucky around the time of the Revolution came with other family members, their Scots-Irish Presbyterianism thus reinforced by the similarity of beliefs among their neighbors who were also kin.

Like many American denominations, they did not believe that human nature was irrevocably depraved, and thus they softened one of the central faiths of all Calvinists and indeed of Old School Presbyterians—that is, that God predestined the salvation of some of his flock. Predestination led to resignation and fatalism as well as hard work because no one knew who was chosen. Perhaps God might be influenced by a worthy life on earth. Such views clashed with the American beliefs in God's gift of free will to man. The familiar couplet "In Adam's fall / We sinned all" might be at the center of the liturgy of many Christians in the early part of the nineteenth century, but the view never infused the behavior of a group of pioneers who intended to shape their destiny.

When six-year-old Mary Todd's mother died of puerperal fever in 1825 following the birth of her seventh child in thirteen years, her family was supposed to find comfort in the doctrine of Christian resurrection. Heaven, according to the preachers in the McCord Presbyterian church in Lexington where young Mary went every Sunday and listened to three- to four-hour sermons, was a better place than earth. According to one parishioner, "the uncertainties of life are so great and eternity so important that to have our dear ones safe is a consolation so great that the more we dwell on their removal, the better we are able to afford the loss." And in a similar expression, "nothing less than affliction can sufficiently teach us the futility of every dependence but that which is upon God."[4]

But Christian acquiescence to a searing human loss was something that Mary Todd found difficult as a child and as an adult. Like her husband she was unorthodox in her Christianity and never found much comfort in the doctrine that Christ died for the sins of humans. And perhaps that was true of all the Todds. For at her mother's funeral, the family walked from their home to the church three blocks away singing the lugubrious and fiercely unaccepting words of Isaac Watts's hymn: "And must this body die, / This mortal frame decay, / And must this active frame of mine, / Lie mouldering in the clay."[5]

After the death of her mother, Mary was still surrounded by Presbyterianism: She went to school with Presbyterians (though her first school was run by an Episcopalian) and, though she loathed her with an anti-Christian zeal, her new stepmother was also a Presbyterian, as were Mary's friends. But she was also exposed to another tradition—the religion of black slaves, nine of whom served in the Robert Todd household. From slaves like Chaney and Mammy Sally, she learned that death was not permanent and that life on earth might not be so different from hell. In her own tragic existence, she more than once lamented her life was indeed a hell. For slaves the separation between the living and the dead was not so sharp as it was for whites. Instead a comforting interchange took place between the physical and the spiritual world. In Lexington, Kentucky, as elsewhere in the South, blacks kept alive their African spiritualism, mixing it with the required Christianity of the white master. In black folk religion the dead returned, sometimes to see their babies, sometimes (and this was especially the case with wandering souls) wearing their burial clothes and sometimes under the direction of a conjurer. A mourner had only to walk backward or rub dead moles' feet at daybreak to help a dead mother return, at least for a visit.[6]

When she was eighteen, Mary Todd followed her sisters to Springfield, Illinois, where, as all the world knows, she met and in 1842 married Abraham Lincoln. By this time she was as well educated as any woman in America, having gone to school for twelve years. In her pursuit of education she enacted a tenet of her church, for the Presbyterians had long insisted on a well-educated clergy and fellowship (as the early Baptists did not) in an institution that was governed by elected elders from the congregation. But in her early years in Springfield, Mary Lincoln attended the Episcopal Church with her older sister Elizabeth. And when the day came for her marriage, out of respect for her sister and brother-in-law, she and Lincoln were joined together under the face of God by an Episcopal minister.

From Mary Lincoln's letters during this period when she lived in Springfield both before and after her marriage we get some sense of her religiosity—that is her commitment to the church and her own spiritual state. Her letters to friends and family, from 1842 to 1861, reveal a perceptive young woman who is well aware of the tension between the secular world of frivolous pleasure and God's world of good works and submission. She seems imbued with guilt, at a unique level of consciousness. To her friend Merce Levering, who has urged on the party-loving Mary the importance of a life of "good morals and religion," Mary replies: "Would it were in my power to follow your kind advice . . . and turn my thoughts from earthly vanities, to one higher than us all, every day proves the fallacy of our enjoyments, & that we are living for pleasures that do not recompense us for the pursuit." Among those pleasures for Mary Lincoln would always be her love of parties and her interest in party politics, both of which in the view of some Old Light ministers were considered vain and frivolous and certainly inappropriate for women.[7]

In 1850, four-year-old Eddie Lincoln, the second of Mary and Abraham's sons, died of tuberculosis after a long siege of fever and coughing. James Smith, the new rector at the First Presbyterian Church and a native of Scotland, organized the funeral and although we do not know what he said in a homily delivered at the Lincoln's home, most likely he emphasized standard Christian views of death—the acceptance of God's will, the resurrection of the dead, and the gift of heaven, the latter Christ's sacrifice on the cross, to the living. Mary Lincoln found, in this and the other family deaths, that acceptance of God's will and resignation to the reality of death were difficult. They remained so throughout her life.

Grieving Christian parents in the nineteenth century, who on average lost one of their four children to some bacterial infection, were encouraged to find comfort in the abstract Christian notion of resurrection, and the kingdom of heaven served as a solid defense for those who watched their children die. Mothers like Mary Lincoln were supposed to be mollified by the expectation that heaven was a better place than earth for their children and a place where they could expect to rejoin their dead children. Accordingly the Lincolns were not the only parents to engrave on a tombstone as they did on Eddie's: "Of Such Is the Kingdom of Heaven." Nor were they the first to find some solace in poetry. Together the grieving parents may have written a poem to their darling Eddie that appeared in the *Springfield Journal*. It concluded with the lines "Affection's wail cannot reach thee now / Deep though it be, and true. Bright is the home to him now given / For such is the Kingdom of Heaven."

After Eddie's death Mary Lincoln left the Episcopal Church to join the Presbyterians, the religion of her youth, occupying as she later described the same pew in Springfield's Presbyterian Church for ten years—that is from 1850 when Eddie died to 1861 when the family went to Washington. Mostly she attended with her children, the concept of Sunday School being fairly rare, although not unknown, in western states before the Civil War. But even with the help of Reverend Smith, Mary Lincoln never achieved the recommended compliance with God's will, even as her husband was coming to accept the doctrine of an omnipotent God. In a different vein, Mary Lincoln accepted the Calvinist doctrine of predestination and personalized it, believing that God's will was set against her.[8]

We have very little evidence about Lincoln's specific religious views during this period, although he did go to church more often after he was elected president and moved to Washington. His wife later suggested that, after Willie Lincoln's death in 1862, her husband gave religion more thought. Certainly in his public messages there are more references to the "assistance of the Divine Being"; he spoke of the "providence of God, Maker of the Universe." He found comfort in the Bible, telling Speed that it was a good book and would make Speed live and die happier.[9] He referred to God in his First Inaugural, saying that he still had confidence that the Almighty, the Maker of the Universe would, "through the instrumentality of this great and intelligent people, bring us through this as He has through all the other difficulties of our country."[10] In 1863 he acknowledged that he often wished he was more devout than he was.

Meanwhile after Willie's death Mary Lincoln prayed as good Christians do, but according to her half-sister Emilie, she never accomplished the recommended

> passive acceptance of fate if she could divert predestination into more pleasant channels. She said to me one day, "What is to be is to be and nothing we can say, or do, or be can divert an inexorable fate, but in spite of knowing this, one feels better even after losing, if one has had a brave, wholehearted fight to get the better of destiny."

But Mary Lincoln, though she put up a number of brave, wholehearted fights, never got the best of destiny: In her painful human journey through a life marked by the early death of her mother, the later death of three of her sons, the assassination of her husband before her eyes, and the disloyal behavior of her one remaining son who consigned her to a mental institution, she constantly raged against her destiny. And although a Presbyterian, she never could be consoled by the idea of accepting fate in secular terms or in the conviction of Presbyterians, God's will. Instead she believed that she was being punished in her cost-benefit acknowledgement of her sins. Nor could she adopt the solace of resurrection. Throughout her life she was Job, not Mary or Martha.[11] She expressed this sense of abandonment by God in a letter to a friend: "our second boy, a promising bright creature of four years we were called upon to part with several years ago and I grieve to say that even at this day I do not feel sufficiently submissive to our loss."[12]

Instead Mary Lincoln took another route, and found her consolation in spiritualism, which had become a popular therapy for not only the mothers of young children who died, but increasingly during the Civil War, for the parents of soldiers who died on the battlefield or in the lethal military camps.

Mary Lincoln's indoctrination into spiritualism had probably taken place first in Lexington from the household slaves whom she became so close to after her mother's death. And even in Springfield during the 1840s and 1850s there were clairvoyants and mediums who could put the living in touch with the dead. In Washington some of Mary Lincoln's friends were spiritualists who found consolation from séances and the physical reappearance of those who had passed through, as this generation liked to say, "the pearly gates." In fact three blocks from the White House lived one of the most celebrated mediums in the city.[13]

Mary Lincoln, adopting James's view of religion as including visions of the hereafter, tried to lift the veil separating the dead and the living. In a letter to Charles Sumner she described the "very slight veil separat[ing] us, from the 'loved & lost' and to me, there is comfort, in the thought, that though unseen by us, they are very near." Through spiritualism, Mary Lincoln lifted that veil. Able to hear and see her sons, she announced to her astonished half-sister Emilie Helm a year after Willie's death that "he lives, . . . He comes to me every night, and stands at the foot of my bed with the same sweet, adorable smile he has always had; he does not always come alone; little Eddie is sometimes with him."[14]

And later after her husband's assassination and her third son Tad's death in 1872, she traveled to Moravia, New York, in the heart of the dark parlor country where she had already seen twenty-two spirit faces, including Tad's. In fact, during the early 1870s, her life became a pilgrim's journey to spiritualist centers. Then in New York she posed in the studio of William Mumler, a spirit photographer, and to her delight the camera caught a shadowy but unmistakable—and of course fraudulent—image of her husband behind her.

Meanwhile, before his death Lincoln's faith was crystallizing into a conviction that many historians find best expressed in his powerful Second Inaugural delivered in March of 1865, shortly before his assassination. In one of the shortest inaugural addresses ever delivered, in 703 words, Lincoln connects his religious beliefs to the war and identifies what historians call a political religion. What Lincoln says is that the war was part of God's plans. He does not say that the war is a punishment for slavery. Nor does he take a providential view and argue that God is on the North's side. There is none of the sentiment that God has a special covenant with America and that as Herman Melville proposed, the United States is "the peculiar, chosen people—the Israel of our time; . . . the ark of liberties."[15]

For Lincoln, man can not know what God's purposes are, but all men understand that there is evil in the world. Quoting from the New Testament Book of Matthew, Lincoln said: "Woe unto the world because of offences." If slavery is an offence—and with all his acknowledged human fallibility Lincoln believed it was—and God now wills it to be removed—then "he gives to both North and South, this terrible war." Of course, says Lincoln, we hope that the war will end (indeed it was ending), but

> if God wills that it continue, until all the wealth piled by the bondsman's two hundred years and fifty years of unrequited

toil shall be sunk, and until every drop of blood drawn with the lash, shall be paid by another drawn with the sword, as was said three thousand years ago, so still it must be said "the judgments of the Lord, are true and righteous altogether."

This is certainly one of the harshest rebukes ever delivered by an American president to the American people. It is Old Testament monotheistic testimony and the important thing for understanding Lincoln's religion is his utter submissiveness to the will of God. "The Almighty has His own purposes"—emphasis on His. But in the majestic ending he offers—as "God gives us to see the right"— Lincoln offers a counsel of charity and love.[16] Hearing the Second Inaugural, Frederick Douglass concluded that "the address sounded more like a sermon than a state paper."[17]

In a letter to Eliza Gurney in September 1864, Lincoln expresses what he implies in the Second Inaugural: "The purposes of the Almighty are perfect, and must prevail, though we erring mortals may fail to accurately perceive them in advance. . . . we must work earnestly in the best light He gives us, trusting that so working still conduces to the great ends He ordains."[18] Thus Lincoln, the early skeptic, who as a young man parodied sermons, has reached a position of utter submissiveness to the will of the Lord, not as mediated through Jesus Christ as conventional Christians believed but through a flawed human being's acceptance of the will of Jehovah.

There is a certain irony that Mary and Abraham Lincoln changed sides in their explanations of religion and God's relationship to man. She began as an orthodox Christian anxious to submit to the will of the Lord and ended outside of mainstream expression with spiritualism. On the other hand, by submitting to God's will and coming to believe it unfathomable, Lincoln, whose life ended on Good Friday, removed from humans a certain degree of agency, even as he became a secular icon of tremendous importance to his nation. Ultimately both Lincolns fulfilled William James's perspective that human beings have "varieties of religious experience." While Mary Lincoln exposed her husband to texts and ministers, he gave to her an understanding of unorthodoxy and various ways to challenge the givens of established faith. For neither was religion a static affair.

CHAPTER 7

The Poet and the President: Abraham Lincoln and Walt Whitman

Daniel Mark Epstein

PRESIDENT ABRAHAM LINCOLN HAD AN OLD FRIEND FROM IL-
linois who was good-hearted but not very bright. So this fellow who
was not very bright got elected to Congress. And soon after arriving
in Washington he paid Lincoln a surprise visit in his office at the
White House.

There was always a mob of people waiting to see Lincoln, but
the president spied his old acquaintance in the crowd outside, and
called out to him warmly.

"Come on in here Bob, and tell me everything you know. It
won't take long."

It won't take me long to recount what Lincoln knew about Walt
Whitman, although the little he knew was significant. What Whitman knew about Lincoln, on the other hand, is an inexhaustible
subject, and the inspiration of a great poem.

A week before the Battle of Gettysburg, President Lincoln took
up residence in the Soldiers' Home, on a hill three miles north of
the White House. Anybody with the slightest interest in seeing

Lincoln might spy him traveling along an unvarying route to and from the White House every morning and evening.

Whitman became a president-watcher, loitering near the corner of Vermont Avenue and L Streets. His hopes and efforts often met with success. And you couldn't be a president-watcher in those days without being watched in turn by the president and his guard. Who's that jolly-looking old duffer with the baggy pants stuffed into his boots, the shaggy one with the haversack and the bulging pockets? There he is again, right about where we left him yesterday. Walt Whitman the poet, studying the president. So the word passed through the ranks.

Whitman's personal magnetism is well documented. It won him such friends as John Burroughs, the naturalist. Burroughs had seen nothing like Whitman in all of nature. He described him at this time thus: "his large benevolent look . . . of infinite good nature and contentment . . . the rich mellow voice indicative of deep human sympathies and affinities . . ." It was the benevolent look that had so much healing power in the hospitals where Whitman worked as a volunteer nurse.

Now as the lonely president passed, worrying over Lee's army and whether or not it was moving into Pennsylvania; worrying over when, exactly, he would remove General Hooker from command and replace him with General Meade; as the sad president passed with the weight of the nation on his soldiers, the fate of several hundred thousand men and their fearful wives and mothers, Whitman fixed him with "that benevolent look . . . of infinite good nature," that gaze that merged "deep human sympathy" with an "impersonal and elemental force."

At some point, that week or the next, the president looked back at Whitman, met his gaze and acknowledged it, with a nod of his head or a slight wave of his hand. That eye-to-eye contact began to form a bond, as order formed out of chaos. The poet had become a welcome and comforting fixture on the road to Lincoln's summer retreat. Whitman wrote in his journal, "I see the President almost every day."

Whitman recalled how he would "pass a word with" Lincoln sometimes, as he rode by. The Commander in Chief probably needed the love and comfort the poet delivered in his slow gaze. He needed this as much as any feverish soldier in Armory Square Hospital. And the sight of Lincoln's transparent goodness inspired Whitman.

Lincoln's gloom lifted during the last days before Gettysburg. His leadership grew bold as he replaced Hooker with Meade, and he remained confident of victory even though the newspapers were spreading panic. Is it too much to imagine that Whitman was in some small part responsible for the change in Lincoln's mood? Maybe so. I don't want to make too much of it. Yet it is such subtle influences that create the finer fabric of history.

Virginia Woolf wrote a wonderful essay on biography called "Granite and Rainbow." She makes the case that in order to write biography the writer requires both the granite of hard facts and rainbow of imagination. To write legitimate history the historian must be clear where the granite ends and the rainbow begins.

My book, *Lincoln and Whitman: Parallel Lives in Civil War Washington*,[1] is very much a book of atmosphere, an effort to recreate the mood of the nineteenth-century world in which Lincoln and Whitman lived and moved; often the success of this effort is dependent upon a single detail or artifact that other scholars have found unremarkable.

My major goal in writing this book was to profile two great Americans, Lincoln and Whitman, and show each of them in a new light. My second goal was to show that each of these men had a profound influence on the other.

To say that Lincoln influenced Whitman is to say what everybody knows. Whitman's greatest poem, "When Lilacs Last in the

Dooryard Bloom'd," is an elegy to Lincoln; and Whitman's journalism and essays are full of his memories of the president.

But to say that Whitman influenced Lincoln is to join in a heated argument that has been going on for about seventy-five years. I didn't dwell on that argument in the main text of my book. But I'm going to take some time to expand on it here, where it will be of greater interest than it might be to the general reader.

In 1916, Henry Rankin, a former student in Lincoln & William Herndon's law office, published a detailed memoir describing Lincoln's reading aloud from Herndon's copy of *Leaves of Grass*. According to Rankin "discussions hot and extreme sprung up between office students and Herndon concerning its poetic merit." A few verses:

> I mind how we lay in June, such a transparent summer
>   morning,
> You settled your head athwart my hips and gently turned
>   over upon me,
> And parted the shirt from my bosom-bone, and plunged
>   your tongue to my bare-stript heart . . .
> I turn the bridegroom out of bed and stay with the bride
>   myself,
> I tighten her all night to my thighs and lips.

Poetry indeed! These long, racy unrhymed verses did not look like any poetry the provincial law students had ever seen. The talk of Whitman that animated the law office during the spring of 1857 relieved the anguished discussion of the Supreme Court's recent decision about Dred Scott, which aroused Lincoln from a spell of political torpor. Yet even Scott's fate led them back to *Leaves of Grass*:

I am the hounded slave. I wince at the bite of the dogs,
Hell and despair are upon me, crack and again crack the
    marksmen,
I clutch the rails of the fence, my gore dribs, thinned with
    the ooze of my skin.

Lincoln worked quietly at his desk, raking his coarse hair with his long fingers. Or he came and went, apparently oblivious to the disturbance the new book was causing in the workplace. He'd lost a year to politics, stumping for John C. Frémont during the presidential campaign of 1856. And he was having a spell of depression, what he called the "hypo." So he turned his back on the students, and Herndon, as they challenged each other's taste in poetry and questioned one another's morals, reading passages of *Leaves of Grass* and attacking or defending Whitman as the spirit or the letter moved them.

One day after the debaters had left, a few clerks, including Rankin, remained, copying documents. Lincoln rose from his desk. This was always a sight because sitting down Lincoln appeared to be of average height. But his limbs were so long that when he unfolded and stretched them it was as if a giant had sprung up out of a common man.

In his memoir, published in 1916, Rankin recalled:

> Quite a surprise occurred when we found that the Whitman
> poetry and our discussions had been engaging Lincoln's si-
> lent attention. . . . Lincoln took up *Leaves of Grass* for his
> first reading of it. After half an hour or more devoted to it
> he turned back to the first pages, and to our general sur-
> prise, began to read aloud.
>   I celebrate myself
>   And what I assume you shall assume,

> For every atom belonging to me as good belongs to you.
> I loafe and invite my soul,
> I lean and loaf at my ease, observing a spear of summer
> grass.
>
> Other office work was discontinued by us all while he
> read with sympathetic emphasis verse after verse. His ren-
> dering revealed a charm of new life in Whitman's versifica-
> tion. Save for a few comments on some broad allusions that
> Lincoln suggested could have been veiled, or left out, he
> commended the poet's new verses for their virility, fresh-
> ness, unconventional sentiments, and unique forms of
> expression. . . .
>
> At his request, the book was left by Herndon on the of-
> fice table. Time and again when Lincoln came in, or was
> leaving, he would pick it up as if to glance at it only for a
> moment, but instead he would often settle down in a chair
> and never stop reading aloud such verses or pages as he
> fancied.

Rankin also recalls Lincoln taking the book home with him. "He
brought it back the next morning, laying it on Bateman's table and
remarking in a grim way that he 'had barely saved it from being
purified in fire by the women.'" By the "women" he meant, of
course, his wife, Mary Todd. The anecdote goes a long way in explaining why Lincoln is not on record as mentioning Whitman as
one of his literary idols.

Rankin's testimony, published in his 1916 book, *Personal Recollections of Abraham Lincoln*, is very convincing evidence that Lincoln read Whitman. When people ask me what inspired me to write
my book, this is one of the first things I mention. Unfortunately,
Rankin's story lacks independent corroboration.

Modern historiography lives by strict rules. A piece of data is not
considered a fact unless it can be corroborated by an independent

source. Historians, the great and the near-great, live and die by this rule, or by breaking the rule, or demonstrating that someone else has broken the rule. I want to take a few moments to discuss this, following the lead of the distinguished historian Douglas L. Wilson.

Professor Wilson, in his book *Lincoln Before Washington*, revisits the story of Ann Rutledge. Wilson, who was the coeditor of *Herndon's Informants*, observes that there is an overwhelming body of testimony that Lincoln was in love with the beautiful maiden from New Salem, and intended to marry her. Yet Paul Angle, who did not have access to the documents, spoke of the Rutledge hoax, as a spiteful fabrication of Herndon, who hated Mary Lincoln. The great scholar James G. Randall was given access to the Herndon-Weik documents in 1941. Randall had a number of objections to the evidence offered by Herndon's informants, and effectively dismissed the case.

Wilson asks this question: "If the testimony on the basic elements of the Ann Rutledge story is so overwhelming as it assuredly is, why has the opposite view so roundly prevailed?"

And his answer is this: "the key to understanding the banishment of the Ann Rutledge story from the Lincoln biography is not simply the historical evidence itself but the standards by which the leading critic, J. G. Randall, insisted that the evidence be judged."

Randall was concerned with the proper use of historical evidence. Let me quote Randall on the subject:

> Historians must use reminiscence, but they must do so critically. Even close-up evidence is fallible. When it comes through the mists of many years, some of it may be true, but a careful writer will check it with known facts. . . . Unsupported memories are in themselves insufficient as proof.

So, memories of witnesses to historical events, being fallible, are not sufficient proof. Contemporary evidence or "known facts" must exist to check them against. People who have read *Herndon's*

Informants know, that as overwhelming as the Ann Rutledge evidence is, it cannot pass Randall's test, which Randall likens to evidentiary rules in a court of law. Randall treats the Rutledge story like an accusation against Lincoln that must be proved beyond a reasonable doubt.

Here's the problem: If all historians stuck to Randall's strict laws of evidence, some very important works of history would never have been written. Wilson argues persuasively that the Rutledge story ought to be on the record.

Now let's return to Lincoln and Whitman. In 1916, Rankin published his detailed memoir describing Lincoln's reading aloud of *Leaves of Grass*. It's the most compelling piece of evidence that Lincoln had read Whitman. It's internally consistent.

In 1928, the Lincoln biographer William E. Barton published a full-length book entitled *Abraham Lincoln and Walt Whitman*. It's an odd book. The Reverend Barton appears to have had no inspiration in writing this book except to highlight Lincoln's virtues at the expense of Whitman's character flaws, and to disassociate the poet and the president wherever he can. Whitman scholars took note of this. As early as 1932, the scholar Charles Glicksburg declared that Barton's book was "marked throughout by a hostile spirit toward Whitman." Glicksburg attacked Barton's argument that Lincoln was unaware of Whitman's existence. Gay Wilson Allen, the first great modern biographer of Whitman, said that Barton's book was "exceedingly biased" against Whitman. Let us put aside, for the time being, any speculation about Reverend Barton's animus against Whitman.

Reverend Barton devotes a chapter of his book to the testimony of Rankin. He raises the sorts of questions that Randall would have raised, and several more. He is concerned that Rankin waited so long to tell the story, until all those who might have corroborated it were dead. He wonders why Herndon never reported on Lincoln's reading of Whitman. He questions not only Rankin's memory of the incident, he questions whether Rankin was ever in Lincoln's law office. He says he has searched every file in every county in which Lincoln practiced and examined every scrap of paper looking for evidence of Rankin's handwriting, and found none.

What Barton fails to do is explain why Rankin, whose book is otherwise modest and credible, would devote four pages to a richly detailed lie about a poet who wasn't popular even in 1916. Rankin said "the scene was so vividly recalled then as to become more firmly fixed in my memory than any other of the incidents at the Lincoln and Herndon office."

Nevertheless, Reverend Barton had blown the whistle, and since 1928, the evidence of Lincoln's reading *Leaves of Grass* has not formally been admitted to the record. Herndon never mentioned it and Lincoln never mentioned it. Barton did mention in passing that Herndon owned a copy of *Leaves of Grass* which he procured in 1857, a fact that figures importantly in my case, which I'll get to presently. Barton knew about Herndon's copy of Whitman because he had purchased Herndon's book collection.

Many people have asked me why Lincoln never acknowledged his admiration of Whitman or *Leaves of Grass*. I have two answers, somewhat related. The first is that while it is well documented that Lincoln read Ralph Waldo Emerson, and actually met with Emerson in person, Emerson's name never appears in any of Lincoln's writings or in his recorded conversation. So why should he have mentioned Whitman? Second, during most of the nineteenth century, the general public considered Whitman as a pornographer. Lincoln was a consummate politician. Suppose that Dwight D. Eisenhower had read *Tropic of Cancer* in the 1950s. Suppose that Eisenhower had been deeply impressed by Henry Miller's prose style. Do you believe Ike would have told everybody about it? I don't think it would have been politically savvy.

So Lincoln didn't talk about *Leaves of Grass*. And the Rankin story, so credible in itself, has been left dangling without support.

This is really where my book begins. The first forty pages of my *Lincoln and Whitman* are devoted to a close textual analysis of Whitman's poems and Lincoln's speeches, with a view to demonstrating the influence of Whitman's poetry on Lincoln's oratory.

Now I don't want to leave you with the impression that my book is a work of literary criticism. In fact, only two chapters deal directly with literary particulars; the rest of my book is the story of Lincoln's and Whitman's lives during the Civil War, Whitman's work in the military hospitals, and Lincoln's trials in the White House. It shows how these men's paths crossed, and how they made subtle but meaningful contact.

But let's briefly consider literary style. As a poet, I think I bring something to the table that has hitherto been lacking in the discussion of Lincoln and Whitman. Most Whitman scholars have not read all of Lincoln's speeches; and most Lincoln scholars have not read all of Whitman's poems. To my knowledge, no one before now has ever undertaken to compare these writers.

I've been writing and publishing poetry for forty years. And I grew up in the era of the New Criticism. The hallmark of the New Criticism, of course, is close textual analysis. It was this discipline that I brought to Lincoln and Whitman.

The first challenge I faced was determining which edition of *Leaves of Grass* was in Herndon's collection. There are great differences between the first edition of 1855 and the second edition of 1856. In this matter, the Reverend Barton became an unwitting accomplice. Somehow I don't think he would be pleased with this. Barton, who owned Herndon's library in 1928, clearly states that Herndon purchased this book in 1857, just before Lincoln's debates with Douglas. If Herndon had purchased the book in 1855, or even in 1856, it would be more likely that his *Leaves of Grass* was the 1855 edition. The fact that Herndon purchased the book in 1857, and the likelihood that the book was purchased at Blanchard's bookshop in Chicago, where Herndon often traveled on business, points to the 1856 edition. The 1856 edition had a nationwide distribution while the 1855 edition was more regional in its sales, mostly the New York area.

Finally, Emerson had endorsed the 1856 edition, and Herndon was an Emerson fanatic. So I decided to use this edition for my analysis. The 1856 edition incorporates all the poems of 1855, while adding about twenty new poems.

My second task was easier. Between June of 1857 and June of 1858, Lincoln only made three public speeches. First, there's the speech at Springfield, Illinois, responding to Douglas's recent speech on Kansas and Dred Scott; second comes the baffling "Lecture on Discoveries and Inventions"; and last comes the magisterial "House Divided" speech given at the close of the Republican State Convention in the spring of 1858.

These were the speeches I thought most likely to show Whitman's influence. Of course, in order to register any change in Lincoln's style, I had to be familiar with his speeches back to 1838.

In reading Whitman and then Lincoln, what I found was stunning, and very exciting. In my book I analyze the Lincoln speeches one by one, chronologically, showing the influence of specific Whitman poems. In the brief time we have here, I must limit myself to a few choice examples.

Of all of Lincoln's speeches, perhaps the most peculiar is one that he made as a sort of popular entertainment, a bid for the nonpolitical lecture circuit. It's called "Lecture on Discoveries and Inventions." This is really a prose poem, a historical ode to human ingenuity since Adam invented the fig-leaf apron:

> All creation is a mine, and every man, a miner.
> The whole earth, and all *within* it, *upon* it, and *round about* it,
> Including *himself*, in his physical, moral, and intellectual nature, and his susceptabilities, are the infinitely various

"leads" from which man, from the first, was to dig out his destiny.

In the beginning, the mine was unopened, and the miner stood *naked*, and *knowledgeless*, upon it.

In 1858, only one other writer in America was spinning out lines like these: Whitman. The very title of Lincoln's lecture echoes the Poem of Whitman, American. "Trippers and askers surround me, ask the latest news, discoveries, inventions . . ." Lincoln's prose poem is a catalogue of discoveries and inventions beginning with spinning and weaving, the discovery of iron and tool-making. In a voice like Whitman, Lincoln celebrates the powers of locomotion, "wheel-carriages, and water-crafts—wagons and boats . . . he sings the motive power of sailing vessels, windmills, pumps and water-wheels, the steam engine . . ."

It's exactly like Whitman's "Song of the Occupations," a poem where Whitman sings of "the anvil, tongs, hammer, the axe, and wedge, the square miter, joiner . . . the steam-engine, lever, crank axle . . . Coal mines, all that is down there, the lamps in the darkness."

More than half of Whitman's fifteen-page poem is taken up with a catalogue of the same discoveries and inventions that Lincoln celebrates. Including elaborate mining imagery.

All of these parallels are striking. But it is when Lincoln gets to talking about speech and writing that it is most difficult to tell his voice from Whitman's. This time let me begin with Whitman's "Poem of the Many in One":

Language-using controls the rest;
Wonderful is language!
Wondrous the English language, language of live men,
Language of ensemble, powerful language of resistance,

> Language of a proud and melancholy stock, and of all who
>   aspire . . .
> Great are the myths, I too delight in them,
> Great are Adam and Eve, I too look back and accept them,
> Great the risen and fallen nations, and their poets, women,
>   sages, inventors . . .
> Great is language—it is the mightiest of the sciences.

What, to Lincoln, is the ultimate divine discovery and invention? Speech, and writing, "the art of communicating thoughts to the mind, through the eye—is the great invention of the world. Great in the astonishing range of analysis and combination, . . . great in enabling us to converse with the dead, the absent, and the unborn, at all distances of time and of space. . . ."

Leaves of Grass introduced several ideas to Western civilization, ideas so boldly expressed that readers in England, France, and America were shocked by them. These include the equality of all things and beings, the sacredness and supremacy of personality, and the belief that the poet is commensurate with his people, incarnating the sexual and working life of America as well as its geography.

But perhaps no idea of his is more surprising and eerie than his insistence that his words and personal presence transcend time and space.

> It avails not, neither time or place—distance avails not,
> I am with you, you men and women of a generation, or ever
>   so many generations hence,
> I project myself, also I return—I am with you, and know
>   how it is.

So it is a notable and significant fact that Lincoln paraphrases Whitman's singular concept in this line from a speech given in 1858:

Great is writing "in enabling us to converse with the dead, the absent, the unborn, at all distances of time and space. . . ." This congruity with Whitman, along with the similarity in tone, is not mere coincidence. The two men were not drawing upon a common source. Lincoln was neither a major poet nor a philosopher. And Whitman's ideas and style were remarkable, if for no other reason—in that they were not to be found elsewhere.

What is evident here is a distinct literary influence.

Now I don't mean to suggest that Lincoln wrote any speech with *Leaves of Grass* at his elbow. But Whitman's thoughts are infectious. They infuse his whole book, as he repeats them tirelessly in artful variations. Lincoln's memory was famously retentive. The bold sexuality that we find in Lincoln's speech against Douglas in June of 1857, where the orator denounces the slave-owner's abuse of slave women, would not have been possible before Whitman. And the architectural metaphors of the House Divided speech are clearly foreshadowed in Whitman's "Broad-Axe Poem."

A study of these texts proves beyond any reasonable doubt that Lincoln had read Whitman in 1857. Whitman's fingerprints are all over the three speeches I have mentioned. Before reading Whitman, Lincoln's oratory was analytic and clear, the medium of a lawyer. It was spiced with tall tales, Bible stories, Aesop, and barnyard metaphors. After reading Whitman, Lincoln became a far more dynamic speaker. He learned to raise his oratory to the level of dramatic poetry as the occasion demanded it.

As I mentioned earlier, my book is not a book of literary criticism. Once I have made my point, supporting Rankin's testimony of 1916 that Lincoln read Whitman, I move on to the discussion of the men's parallel lives in Washington. I do not analyze the Gettysburg Address, or the Second Inaugural for traces of Whitman. By 1863, Lincoln has assimilated all influences, and developed a voice so distinctive that he sounds like no one but himself.

Yet it is my opinion that without Whitman, the House Divided speech would not have such great poetic power. And it is possible without that power, newly gained from reading *Leaves of Grass*, Lincoln might not have become the Republican candidate for president in 1860.

Whitman was unaware of this. Although the two men had many friends and acquaintances in common, including Hay, Lincoln's private secretary, Horace Greeley, the publisher, and Senator Charles Sumner, Lincoln and Whitman never sat down together to dine or converse. But during the war, Whitman was so fascinated by Lincoln that he became a president-watcher. He studied Lincoln from near and from afar. As the president passed to and from the Soldiers' Home during the summer months, Whitman would stand on the corner of Vermont and L Streets. They developed an acquaintance. This was observed by the president's guard, as each day the men would wave to each other, and sometimes exchange a few words.

Whitman wrote: "We have got so that we always exchange bows, and very cordial ones." Whitman also wrote in his diary, after seeing Lincoln in his office: "I love the President personally." While we know what these close encounters meant to Whitman, we will never know exactly how comforting the poet's presence in Washington was to the embattled president.

My book is about how these great men, our greatest poet and greatest president, influenced each other. It's about how they worked to change America, to preserve the union.

Lincoln once was asked by a spiritualist for a blurb for one of his books. Lincoln didn't want to offend the author, but on the other hand, he didn't want to put the presidential seal of approval on such hocus-pocus.

So he wrote: "For the type of people who like this book, it is the type of book those people will like."

CHAPTER 8

1862—A Year of Decision for President Lincoln and General Halleck

John F. Marszalek

ABRAHAM LINCOLN WAS PRESIDENT OF THE UNITED STATES, and Henry W. Halleck was commanding general of the nation's army during the gravest domestic crisis in American history. On their shoulders rested the decisions that would be instrumental in determining whether the nation would remain whole or be splintered in two. From July 1862 to March 1864, these two men, along with Secretary of War Edwin M. Stanton, held more power than anyone else on the American continent had ever possessed up to that time.[1]

Halleck and Lincoln came to their dominating positions from different places and differing backgrounds. Lincoln was born into the poverty of the frontier, while Halleck came from the merger of two old-line families in his native New York State. Both Lincoln and Halleck had poor relationships with their fathers, Halleck even leaving home to live with relatives and, for a time, signing his name Henry Wager instead of Henry Wager Halleck. Lincoln was primarily self-taught, while Halleck attended the best schools that his state and the nation could offer: Hudson Academy, Fairfield Academy,

Union College, and the United States Military Academy. Lincoln was a successful lawyer and politician in his home state of Illinois; Halleck became famous in the army, doing engineering work in the East, traveling to Europe and writing a book on military theory, participating in the Mexican War in California, becoming a founding father of the Golden State, and resigning from the military to become a lawyer and the nation's leading theoretical and practical expert on land law. And while Lincoln almost became vice presidential candidate for the fledgling Republican party in 1856, Halleck became the equivalent of a millionaire in San Francisco during that same period. Then again, Lincoln's election to the presidency in 1860 precipitated the Civil War. And the coming of that conflict brought Halleck back into the army, with the venerable Winfield Scott even unsuccessfully urging his choice as commanding general.

By December 1861, Lincoln was president of the United States and Halleck headed the army in Missouri, a key area in the war. The two men did not know each other personally, but the president could not help but be impressed with the general's efficiency. The California lawyer turned military leader found chaos in Missouri when he replaced John C. Frémont there in the fall of 1861, and methodically, he placed the military on an organized basis. He let it be known that Missouri would remain in the Union. Secessionists, in fact, would pay a special monetary levy he placed on them for any depredations against the state's Unionists. Halleck established himself as a no-nonsense leader in an important area of the Civil War.

During this same time, Lincoln seemed to be having difficulty finding his military footing. In the spring, Lincoln had been forced to sneak into Washington for his inauguration and, for a time, the nation's capital was cut off from the rest of the nation. His Secretary of War, Pennsylvania political boss Simon Cameron, was proving himself to be ineffective and was dragging Lincoln down with him. The Battle of Bull Run (Manassas) was an embarrassment, and the coming of George B. McClellan to head the Army of the Potomac resulted in delay rather than action.

As the divided nation entered 1862, therefore, Halleck seemed to be doing great things, while Lincoln looked weak. If a Gallup Poll had been taken on January 1, 1862, asking the American populace about their confidence in their leaders, Halleck would very well have received a high approval rating, while Lincoln would have scored correspondingly low.

The year 1862 proved to be one of important decisions for these two men. During that year, in fact, their approach to decision-making made their legacies. "Decision" is a common word, of course, and most people know what it means. Yet a dictionary definition provides help for evaluating Lincoln and Halleck during this crucial year. The primary dictionary definition of the word "decision" is: "The passing of judgment on an issue under consideration." The next definitions are: "The act of reaching a conclusion or making up one's mind" and "firmness of character or action; determination." The word "decision," therefore, includes within it the ideas of judgment, conclusion, making up one's mind, firmness, character, and determination.[2]

Entering 1862 with the nation unhappy with him and the military situation, Lincoln realized that he had to act. In early January 1862, he decided to send his inefficient secretary of war, Cameron, to Russia as minister, replacing him with a former cabinet member from the Buchanan administration, Stanton. The Ohioan had long been an antislaveryite, as late as 1861 working with Cameron on a position paper calling for the enlistment of black troops. Yet he had also supported Southern Democrat John C. Breckinridge in the 1860 presidential election as the only hope for preserving the Union. Stanton clearly straddled a lot of fences. Lincoln probably chose him because of this ability and because such disparate figures as Secretary of State William Henry Seward and Secretary of the Treasury Salmon P. Chase both supported him.

In Stanton, Lincoln found someone who proved to be decisive with a vengeance. With Stanton's support, Lincoln issued, on January 27, 1862, the "President's General War Order No. 1" calling on all United States military forces to begin moving forward no later than February 22. Lincoln was particularly concerned about the inactivity of McClellan's Army of the Potomac; in fact, he issued another order four days later specifically calling on that army to move.

McClellan did not advance, but in the western theater, there was a spurt of activity. Even before the promulgation of Lincoln's order, Union General George H. Thomas routed the Confederates on January 19, 1862, at Mill Springs, Kentucky. Then, even more dramatically, on February 6, Ulysses S. Grant's army and Andrew Foote's navy captured Fort Henry on the Tennessee River. Grant then took Fort Donelson on the Cumberland ten days later. Chase, the usually critical secretary of the treasury, was ecstatic. "I have just heard the glorious news from Fort Donelson," he wrote a friend. "The underpinning of the rebellion seems to be knocked out from under it—thanks to Divine Providence in the first place & next to the urgency of the President seconded by the genius of Halleck & the skill and courage of the generals & soldiers in the field."[3] Notice that Chase praised only one individual by name: Halleck. Lincoln, Grant, and even God had to settle for less specific references.

We know, of course, that it was the daring of Grant, overcoming the hesitation of Halleck, that launched the successful assaults on Henry and Donelson. Yet, these successes did come under Halleck's overall leadership. McClellan was giving Lincoln excuses in the East, while Halleck was producing results in the West.

Yet, all was not perfect on the Mississippi River and its environs. Lincoln rightly worried about the lack of coordination between Halleck's forces and Don Carlos Buell's Army of the Ohio; he prodded both men to come to an understanding. Halleck responded by recommending Buell's promotion from brigadier to major general, asked Buell to come to the Cumberland River and merge with Grant, and there take command of the western offensive. Grant or Buell, it would still be an offensive under Halleck's supervision.

Becoming absolutely specific, Halleck next demanded of McClellan that the commanding general make him overall commander in the West. "Give it to me, and I will split secession in twain in one month," Halleck promised. The next day, he made the same point even more forcefully. "I must have command of the armies in the West," he insisted. "Hesitation and delay are losing us the golden opportunity. Lay this before the President and Secretary of War. May I assume the command? Answer quickly."[4]

McClellan did not respond favorably to Halleck's demand for command, but Stanton did. Because Lincoln was grieving the death of his son Willie, however, Stanton could not get the president's permission to elevate Halleck. But clearly Stanton was impressed with the general. "The brilliant results of the energetic action in the West fills the Nation with joy," he said.[5]

Soon after, Lincoln did make Halleck commander of a new Division of the Mississippi, while, at the same time, stripping from McClellan his commanding generalship over the entire Union army. With a stroke of a pen, Lincoln made Halleck McClellan's equal and took to himself and Stanton coordination of the army efforts in the East and the West.

McClellan finally moved, but soon became mired on the Peninsula. In Halleck's Division of the Mississippi and in areas adjacent to his command, success followed upon success. On February 25, Buell entered Nashville. Then the March 8 victorious battle of Pea Ridge in Arkansas guaranteed Union control of Missouri. Shiloh on April 6 was a near-disaster, but Grant made it into a Union victory on April 7. John Pope took Island No. 10 that same April 7th day, while New Orleans fell on April 27. Two days later, Halleck, having merged Grant's, Buell's, and Pope's armies, personally began to lead the Union march on Corinth and its railroads. It took him a month to travel the twenty-two mile distance from Shiloh, Tennessee, to Corinth, Mississippi, and then the Confederate army under P. G. T. Beauregard escaped. Yet, Corinth was a Union victory, and it was accomplished with little loss of lives. Within another week, the Confederates also evacuated Memphis. At the end of June, Admiral David G. Farragut steamed by Vicksburg, for a time uniting the upper and lower Mississippi River into Union hands.[6] Whether he deserved it or not, Halleck's name was associated with energetic movement, while, in the East, McClellan remained bogged down on the Peninsula.

Once again Lincoln acted. He ordered Pope, an old friend from Illinois and one of Halleck's subordinates, to come to Washington to act as advisor and then to become commander of a new Eastern army. Soon after, Lincoln wrote directly to Halleck asking him to pay "a flying visit for consultation." Halleck responded that "being somewhat broken in health and wearied out by long months of labor and care, a trip to Washington would be exceedingly desirable." Yet he was needed with his army, he said, so he would not come.[7]

Actually, Halleck did not want to go to Washington because he was worried about Lincoln's constant calls for troop reinforcements from the West for McClellan in the East. He complained to his wife that, because of such demands, he "felt utterly broken-hearted. My first impulse was to resign and go home to California. But this my duty to the country forbade."[8]

In fact, Lincoln was not calling Halleck to Washington to convince him to send some of his troops to the East, or, as Halleck also feared, "to involve me in the quarrel between Stanton and McClellan" and among cabinet members. After visiting McClellan in Virginia and Scott at West Point, Lincoln decided to make Halleck the army's new general in chief to provide the military with the leadership he knew it needed. Surely, Pope's and Stanton's advice played a role in Lincoln's decision to choose Halleck, but, in fact, Lincoln made the decision himself.

Whatever the case, Halleck seemed to be the appropriate choice. He was the nation's leading authority on military theory; he had brought organization to the West and coordinated a series of successes there. Perhaps he could bring organization and success to the East. And he would take a great deal of work off Lincoln's shoulders. The president made his decision to hire Halleck for numerous good reasons. Now he expected Halleck to make some decisions, too. "I am very anxious—almost impatient—to have you here," Lincoln wrote. "Having due regard to what you leave behind, when can you reach here?" he implored.[9]

Learning of Halleck's appointment, Chase recognized its significance, and he immediately tied it to Lincoln's proposed antislavery activity which he had just learned about. "These [antislave] measures," he said, "& the substitution of an able general for McClellan, & the genius & indefatigable labor of Halleck presiding over all, will I hope soon end this rebellion."[10] Soon after Lincoln made his decision to hire Halleck, he, in fact, did decide to issue a proclamation freeing slaves in areas rebelling against the United States. Halleck and emancipation: Lincoln hoped they would speed the war's successful conclusion. As for McClellan, Lincoln left that decision to Halleck.

Before Lincoln could promulgate his decision on slavery, therefore, Halleck had to make a major decision on the war effort. Should McClellan's Army of the Potomac continue its campaign against Richmond from the Peninsula, or should it leave the Peninsula and mass with Pope's Army of Virginia for a direct movement on Richmond? When Lincoln and Halleck met in Washington, Lincoln gave his new general authority over the entire army and that included McClellan. In fact, he told Halleck to decide whether or not to keep McClellan in command or to fire him.[11] In short, Lincoln gave Halleck permission to make a major military decision to open the way for his own decision on slavery.

Halleck immediately went to McClellan's headquarters, arriving there on July 25. He diplomatically told his former commander that he was there "to ascertain from him his views and wishes in regard to future operations." McClellan responded that he planned to attack Petersburg and cut off Confederate communications; then, he would go after Richmond. Halleck said he thought it made more sense for McClellan to mass with Pope and attack Richmond with the combined armies. If he believed he could take Richmond himself, however, he should make the attack. McClellan immediately said he could take Richmond—but only if he had 30,000 more troops. Halleck countered that 20,000 was all he could promise. After sleeping on it for a night, McClellan agreed to attack Richmond with the additional 20,000 men. Soon, however, he was demanding more.[12]

Halleck was not happy with what he had seen or heard. He found McClellan a general who did not "understand strategy," "surrounded by very weak advisers." He also worried whether McClellan would be cooperative. Halleck reminded the general of his own previous loyalty to McClellan when their positions had been reversed, and he asked for the same support now. They were friends, after all, Halleck pleaded, and they had to work together for the good of the nation.[13]

McClellan answered with soothing prose. Nevertheless, he had not changed his mind about the way the war should be fought. He agreed, McClellan said, with Halleck's "ideas as to the concentration of forces," but he also said "It is unnecessary for me to repeat my objections to the idea of withdrawing this army from its present position." As for slavery and the unremitting radical pressure Lincoln faced to end it, McClellan said, "we should avoid any proclamations of general emancipation, and should protect inoffensive citizens in the possession of that as well as of other kinds of property." As Lincoln began seriously considering how to promulgate his Emancipation Proclamation, therefore, one of his leading generals was calling for the preservation of slavery, while his commanding general made no protest because he agreed.[14]

On August 3, Halleck made his military decision. He ordered McClellan to remove his troops from the Peninsula and mass with Pope at Acquia Creek. McClellan responded that this order caused him "the greatest pain I ever experienced." If he could not change Halleck's mind, which he tried to do, he said he would "with a sad heart obey your orders." Significantly, he did not indicate how long this would take, and then dragged his feet.[15]

Halleck was not happy with McClellan's uncooperative attitude, but amazingly he was also displeased with the full cooperation he was receiving from Lincoln and his cabinet. Such support "only increases my responsibility," he told his wife, "for if any disaster happens they can say 'We did for you all you asked.'" "I can't get Gen. McClellan to do what I wish," he continued. "The President and Cabinet have lost all confidence in him, and urge me to remove him from command. (This is strictly *entre nous*.) In other words, they want me to do what they are afraid to attempt [themselves]. I hope I may never be obliged to follow their advice in this matter." In short, having made the important military decision to order Mc-Clellan to evacuate his army from the Peninsula, Halleck, rather than thinking of ways to enforce that order, was worrying about having to make another decision, this time to fire the general. His response to McClellan's slowness in massing with Pope was, there-fore, ineffective.[16]

After Lee defeated Pope at Second Bull Run (Manassas) in late August, Washington seemed in danger. Yet, Halleck still did not confront McClellan about his foot dragging on the Peninsula which prevented his massing with Pope. Instead, he implored McClellan: "I beg of you to assist me in this crisis with your ability and experi-ence. I am utterly tired out." McClellan wrote back condescend-ingly: "To speak frankly—and the occasion requires it—there appears to be a total absence of brains, and I fear the total destruc-tion of the army." Despite hearing this obviously insulting language, Old Brains Halleck, the next day, could only telegraph McClellan's headquarters to inquire: "Is the general coming up to Washington; and, if so, at what hour will he be here? I am very anxious to see him." At no time did Halleck ever think of taking field command himself as Pope, for example, urged him to do. Significantly, Lincoln never made such a suggestion. McClellan took command again by default.[17]

While Halleck refused to take responsibility—acting like a "moral coward" as Secretary of the Navy Gideon Welles cruelly put it—Lincoln was making what proved to be the most important decision of the war. Throughout the conflict, Lincoln was regularly castigated as being soft on slavery. Concerned about border-state reaction, he had indeed maintained a delicate balancing act on the issue. By 1862, however, he knew he had to make a major decision about it. What form would that decision take? Slowly, while he, along with Stanton, grappled with running the military, and then chose Halleck to do it for him, he began composing the Emancipation Proclamation. The radical wing of his own party pushed through Congress the Second Confiscation Act on July 17, 1862, which freed the slaves from all individuals guilty of treason and rebellion against the United States. On July 13, four days before this law's passage, and just two days after he had appointed Halleck, Lincoln had already told Chase and a few others of his intention to use his war powers to abolish slavery. When he told his entire cabinet of his decision, they convinced him to wait for a military victory.[18]

Lincoln, therefore, had to continue looking to Halleck. Now he needed a battlefield victory before he could issue the Emancipation Proclamation. Ironically it was McClellan, the man Halleck could not bring himself to fire, who provided the occasion for Lincoln's important announcement. McClellan forced Robert E. Lee to withdraw from the Antietam/Sharpsburg battlefield on September 17, 1862. Lincoln then issued his proclamation five days later, freeing the slaves in those areas of the Confederacy still in rebellion on January 1, 1863. Lincoln soon grew irritated again at McClellan's continued inactivity and this time he stopped waiting for Halleck to act. He fired McClellan himself on November 7.

Lincoln took a terrible beating for issuing his carefully worded preliminary statement of freedom. White Southerners, who understood better than others just how significant this pronouncement was, were outraged. Northerners, whose own commitment to racial equality was hardly total, demonstrated their opposition to the pronouncement by giving Lincoln's rivals, the Democrats, a gain of thirty-four seats in the House of Representatives. In numerous state and local elections, the Republicans suffered similar losses. In the field, more than a few Union soldiers expressed open contempt for the statement. Lincoln issued the Emancipation Proclamation as an attempt to win the war through an attack on slavery, but its initial result was to hurt Lincoln's party and hinder the war effort.

What was worse, this September 22 pronouncement would not even go into effect until January 1. Perhaps it never would go into effect; perhaps Lincoln would decide that the war effort would not be benefited by following this controversial September 1862 decision with another, final, statement in January, 1863. After all, he had told Horace Greeley just a month before his September promulgation that his main aim in the war was to preserve the Union, and he would do it either by ending or by keeping slavery, whichever worked best. And the lambasting the Republicans took in the fall elections certainly shook Lincoln. What would he do?[19]

Lincoln faced an important decision, and he did not waver. He signed the final Emancipation Proclamation on January 1, 1863.

That same day, Halleck refused to make a decision which was hardly as difficult. As Ambrose Burnside, McClellan's replacement, prepared to launch another frontal attack against Fredericksburg following his earlier disastrous assaults, Lincoln turned to Halleck once again. He told him, during a meeting early on January 1, 1863, to go to Burnside's army, evaluate the situation, and tell that general what should be done.

Halleck refused, but Lincoln gave him another chance. Writing on that same day, the day he issued his momentous antislavery statement, Lincoln had Stanton hand this letter to Halleck during the secretary of war's New Year's Day reception. Lincoln pulled no punches with his general: "Gather all the elements for forming a judgment of your own," he said, "and then tell General Burnside that you do approve or that you do not approve his plan. Your military skill is useless to me if you will not do this." "If in such a difficulty as this you do not help, you fail me precisely in the point for which I sought your assistance."[20]

Halleck bristled at these words. "I am led to believe," he wrote through clenched teeth, "that there is a very important difference of opinion in regard to my relations toward generals commanding armies in the field, and that I cannot perform the duties of my present office satisfactorily at the same time to the President and to myself." With that, he resigned. Lincoln refused the resignation, writing across his letter to Halleck: "Withdrawn, because considered harsh by General Halleck." Unlike his decision to fire McClellan and replace him with Burnside, Lincoln could not see any available replacement for Halleck, even though he found "Old Brains" exasperating. In fact he still saw some good in the man. He believed Halleck was "wholly for the service. He does not care who succeeds or who fails, so the service is benefited." Although Halleck refused to make a decision, Lincoln made the decision to keep Halleck.[21]

As 1862 faded into historical memory and the new year of 1863 arrived, Lincoln was still suffering in public opinion. He was the president losing the war: not doing enough according to some, being too radical according to others. Unlike January 1862, however, Halleck was now also down in public opinion. The successful leader in the western theater was now the indecisive general in Washington.

Yet, history's conclusion on the two men is not identical to the contemporary perceptions, and 1862 determined that fact. Halleck has a low historical reputation because of his inability to make decisions, a view formed in 1862. Because of his ability to act in 1862, Lincoln is counted as the nation's greatest chief executive and among the leading figures in all of human history.

The reason history remembers these two men as it does can best be understood by going back to the definition of the word "decision" cited earlier. In issuing the preliminary and final Emancipation Proclamations, Lincoln demonstrated judgment, character, firmness, determination, the ability to make up his mind, and the ability to bring the matter to a conclusion. Halleck, in his dealings with McClellan and Burnside, refused to render judgment or make up his mind, he lacked firmness, character, and determination, and he was unable to bring matters to a conclusion. Welles saw this difference at the time. He praised Lincoln for the Emancipation Proclamation, and in the same December 29 diary entry he condemned Halleck for having "neither military capacity nor decision."[22]

In sum, General Halleck's and President Lincoln's year of decision established their historical legacies: Lincoln as the Great Emancipator and Halleck as the unwilling indecisive general. Nothing either man did after 1862 changed history's mind about them.

CHAPTER 9

"I Felt It to Be My Duty to Refuse": The President and the Slave Trader

William Lee Miller

THE NEW PRESIDENT IN MARCH OF 1861 WOULD FIND IN THE same paragraph of the Constitution that that made him Commander in Chief this rather surprisingly unqualified, unchecked, quite explicit grant: "He shall have the Power to grant Reprieves and Pardons for Offenses against the United States." This new president would make the most extensive, and the most generous, use of that power of any president. His generosity in the use of the power to grant pardons, commutations, and reprieves would come to be much praised. It would eventually be part of his legend, and even in his lifetime, it was celebrated.

But it was not praised by everyone. There would be critics who would insist that his tender mercy was often inappropriate and over-done, not what a statesman and commander in chief ought to do, and not what justice and the national interest nor the discipline of armies required.

One charge was that he was too easily swayed by the entreaties of large numbers of citizens, of eminent figures, of friends of the accused, and friends of his own. General William T. Sherman, who would be one of the persistent critics of Abraham Lincoln's "charity," complained that Lincoln found it hard to hang spies (that is, to allow spies to be hanged when with a stroke of his pen he could save their lives) "when a troop of friends follow the sentences . . . with earnest appeals."

Another charge was that he was a politician too responsive to appeals by politicians. It is true that when you read through the cases of Union soldiers found guilty by court-martial, that when a congressman asked for a pardon for some "boy," he almost invariably got it.

But the most common complaint by Lincoln's critics was that he was too easily moved by a personal, emotional appeal, particularly from women. His own attorney general, Edward Bates, was one of those who made this criticism. Bates, according to Francis Carpenter, said that Lincoln was almost an ideal man, lacking only one thing:

> I have sometimes told him . . . that he was unfit to be intrusted with the pardoning power. Why, if a man comes to him with a touching story, his judgment is almost certain to be affected by it. Should the applicant be a *woman*, a wife, a mother, or a sister,—in nine cases out of ten, her tears, if nothing else, are sure to prevail.[1]

The pardon clerk working in the Justice Department under the Attorney General made the same point:

> My chief, Attorney Bates, soon discovered that my most important duty was to keep all but the most deserving cases from coming before the kind Mr. Lincoln at all, since there was nothing harder for him to do than to put aside a prisoner's application and he could not resist it when it was urged by a pleading wife and a weeping child.

In the first winter of Lincoln's presidency, 1861–1862, there would come to his desk an appeal for a mitigation of punishment that would seem to be just the sort of case that the tender-hearted Lincoln would find it impossible to resist. The accused—one Nathaniel Gordon—was still a relatively young man, a "respectable Presbyterian" we are told, from a "respectable sea-going family" in Portland, Maine. Being "respectable" counted for a lot in that nineteenth-century world. In the Docket of Pardon Cases in the National Archives we read: "Clemency invoked by Rev. J. W. Chickering, Portland Maine, who says the accused was once a boy in his Secondary School and his parents are members of his [the Reverend Mr. Chickering's] church."[2] The accused also had a young and, we are told, pretty wife, and we may surely infer there was weeping. *The Elmira Daily Advertiser* reported that when the accused had been sentenced to death, and was then recommitted to the notorious New York City prison, the Tombs, "he was met by his wife. An affecting interview took place." If a presumably hard-bitten reporter found a meeting between the condemned husband and his wife affecting, surely this unusually compassionate president would be deeply moved.

They had a young son: a mother and a child, appealing for the life of the father. At the climax of the case a powerful woman advocate from New York, a woman named Rhoda White, the wife of a Republican judge, himself a friend of Horace Greeley (an active advocate who had written Lincoln before), now would join in the appeal. There would be a veritable phalanx of weeping women. White would write to the president: "I would not intrude upon the sanctity of your sick room and upon your hours of grief but for the sake of *Mercy*, and for the sake of an afflicted Mother and wife who are bowed down with sorrow and look to God and to you to lift the heavy burden they are suffering under."[3]

There would be two petitions for clemency from the accused's neighbors in Portland, pages of flowing, rounded nineteenth-century signatures. One of these petitions said that the undersigned "are deeply moved by a painful sympathy for the aged and venerated mother of the convict, for his wife and only child."[4]

How could Lincoln resist?

There would, indeed, be "troops of friends" and "earnest appeals." Lincoln himself would write that he had received petitions for clemency from "a large number of respectable citizens." And after he wrote that there would be more—at one later point a petition from eleven thousand New Yorkers.

As to politicians, there would be an appeal from the Governor of New York, and a mass meeting of protest in New York City. And all that the earnest and touching appeals prayed for in the last round would not be a complete pardon, but only a commutation of the death sentence to "imprisonment for life." White would write: "His wife, an interesting woman of twenty two and his aged Mother are here, and through me implore you to commute the punishment . . ."

So what did the tender-hearted president do? He turned them all down.

It is instructive to notice how Lincoln phrased his decision: "I have felt it to be my duty to refuse."[5] His was a duty, a moral imperative, not the outcome of a calculation of contending considerations: I am constrained to turn down your appeal by a moral necessity.

And so what was the moral necessity, the duty, that interrupted Lincoln's mercy in this case? The records of the Circuit Court of the United States of America for the Southern District of New York in the Second Circuit, with flowering verbosity and magnificent redundancy put it this way:

> On the Eighth day of August in the year of our Lord one thousand eight hundred and sixty with force and arms in the River Congo on the Coast of Africa, out of the jurisdiction of any particular state of the United States of America, in waters within the admiralty and maritime jurisdiction of this court, the said Nathaniel Gordon, then and there being master of a certain vessel being a ship called the Erie . . . did piratically and feloniously forcibly confine and detain

> eight hundred negroes . . . in and on board of said vessel,
> being a ship called the Erie, with the intent of him the said
> Nathaniel Gordon to make slaves of the aforsaid eight hun-
> dred negroes . . .

Nathaniel Gordon, in other words, was a slave trader.

Gordon was the captain of the full-rigged 500-ton ship *Erie*, which had been sighted in August of 1860 at the mouth of the Congo River by the U.S.S. *Mohican* and signaled to show its colors. The *Erie* raised an American flag and shortened sail.

The *Mohican*, part of the African Squadron, had the assignment of apprehending violators of the American laws against the slave trade. The boarding party from the *Mohican* discovered 897 Africans tightly packed together below deck of the *Erie*, and arrested Captain Gordon and other officers. The Africans were released to an American agent in Monrovia, Liberia, and Gordon and the others were sent to New York for trial.

A reader today may now exclaim: A slave trader! Of course, Lincoln, or any other president, would not extend clemency to a slave trader! But in the context of the time that was by no means so clear.[6] American history up to that point had a deep ambivalence not only about slavery but even about the slave trade.

It is true that most of the founders condemned slavery.

It is true that the Philadelphia framers tied their prose in circumlocutionary knots to avoid using the actual words "slave" and "slavery" in the Constitution. Perhaps they made these rather touching little gestures in order, James Madison said, to avoid admitting in this fundamental document that there could be "property in man."

It is true that fervor of the Revolution led to the abolishing of slavery in the Northern states—all the original thirteen colonies had had at least some slaves—which in some states was not a small accomplishment.

It is true that Congress did enact—in "hot haste," Lincoln, the antislavery politician, would contend—a law prohibiting American participation in the international slave trade on the very first day that the Constitution allowed, January 1, 1808.

It is further true, as Lincoln the antislavery politician would say, "In 1820 [the South] joined the north, almost unanimously, in declaring the African slave trade piracy, and in annexing to it the punishment of death."[7]

But did the American outlawing of the slave trade and attaching the punishment of hanging to it mean that American participation in the slave trade promptly stopped?

It stopped just the way the sale of alcohol stopped with prohibition—the way the sale of drugs stops with drug laws.

Then did the continued American participation in the illegal slave trade at least lead to many arrests, trials, and hangings?

No, it did not. In the long years of its illegal but real continuation, there were many successful and profitable voyages without interference. Those who were caught were rather often given pardons.[8] And there were no hangings at all.

What does this deep ambivalence in the record of the new United States reflect? Reservations in the North about being too fierce against the slave trade.

During the century in which the United States had been a considerable participant in the entirely legal transatlantic slave trade, the center for building slave-trading ships had not been Charleston, South Carolina, or Norfolk, Virginia, but New York City, New York. And the ports from which the trade was carried on were not as much Savannah or New Orleans as Boston and Newport, Rhode Island, and Salem—the old Puritan settlement of Salem. And Portland, Maine.

Thomas Jefferson, in explaining why the tortured passage condemning slavery (blaming American slavery on the King of England) had been dropped from the Declaration of Independence, wrote not only that South Carolina and Georgia objected but also that "our northern brethren" "felt a little tender"—what a wonderful phrase—for "though their people had very few slaves themselves, yet they had been pretty considerable carriers of slaves to others."

The framers of the American Constitution, those demigods in Philadelphia, had not really distinguished themselves on the subject of slavery. They did not fight as hard on issues of slavery as Madison and Jefferson had done in Virginia on religious liberty, or Madison and James Wilson would do in that convention on small state/large state matters, or indeed the whole people of the British colonies in America would do on the touchy issues of taxation with representation—which makes us "slaves."

On the substantive issues in Philadelphia, the antislavery majority would push, but not too hard, and when (as Madison reported to Jefferson) "S. Carolina and Georgia were inflexible on the point of slaves," they made compromises with the existing reality of slavery, cloaked in euphemism. Don Fehrenbacher described the result: "It is as though the Framers were half-consciously trying to frame two constitutions, one for their own time and the other for the ages, with slavery viewed bifocally—that is, plainly visible at their feet, but disappearing when they lifted their eyes."[9]

One of the stark realities at their feet was the transatlantic slave trade, the terrible traffic that showed the monstrous institution at its worst. At first the framers proposed to allow Congress to prohibit the slave trade in 1800, but on the floor it was proposed by General Pinckney of South Carolina to move that date back to 1808, more than two decades hence. Madison protested: "Twenty years will produce all the mischief . . . So long a term will be more dishonorable to the National character than to say nothing."[10] But an off-stage bargain had been made and the revised provision passed and for the first twenty years of its history the new nation born in freedom would not only have a large, growing institution of human slavery but a flourishing and altogether legal transatlantic slave trade. During the years 1800–1808—the intervening sunset years quietly legalized on an August afternoon in Philadelphia—South Carolina imported some 40,000 new African slaves into the United States.

The Constitutional compromise, we remind ourselves, did not specify that after twenty years the slave trade must be prohibited, only that it might; what it actually did, to the contrary, was to say that for those twenty years the new federal government could not prohibit American participation in the international slave trade. The "importation" of slaves into the new nation was a matter of state decision, and from 1803 to 1808 South Carolina participated in the entirely legal transatlantic slave trade.

President Jefferson did propose in 1806, and Congress did enact—in "hot haste," as we quoted Lincoln as having said—in 1807, the law prohibiting American participation in the international slave trade commencing on the very first day that constitutional provision allowed, January 1, 1808.[11] But—thinking realistically—would that enactment just stop this lucrative trade, as with the turning off of a spigot? All of those ships, outfitted in New York, sailing from Boston, Newport, Salem, carrying on this lucrative trade—suddenly stopped? The American market was still there—expanding, in fact, with the purchase of Louisiana (with sixteen sugar plantations in 1803) and the expansion of the cotton kingdom in the Gulf states after the invention of the cotton gin. And the American market was not the largest: More of the illicit slave trade, by American carriers after 1808, supplied the slave markets of Brazil and Cuba. The prohibition of the international slave trade by American laws in 1808 had this difference from prohibition and drug laws: The markets to which the illegal traders sold their goods (slavery in the American states, in Brazil, Cuba, Jamaica, and elsewhere) were themselves altogether *legal*. Moreover, there was a domestic trade—Virginia's oversupply being sold in Louisiana and Mississippi—that was also altogether legal.

The story of the American struggle with the nefarious trade in slaves is a tale of stirring statements and laws followed by ineffectual action and enforcement, complexity, and unstated resistance. In 1820, in the midst of the contest over Missouri, Congress even went so far as to declare that participation in the slave trade was "piracy" punishable by death. Yet, no one was in fact hanged. The Act itself had to have a little reservation in it:

> If any citizen of the United States . . . or any person what-ever . . . of the crew, . . . of any ship owned . . . or navigated . . . in behalf of, any citizen or citizens of the United States, shall . . . seize any negro or mulatto not held to service or labour by the laws of either of the states . . . of the United States, with intent to make such negro or mulatto a slave, . . . such citizen or person shall be adjudged a pirate; and . . . shall suffer death.[12]

"Any negro or mulatto not held to service or labour by the laws of either of the states"—so this careful distinction has to be made.

And so did American participation in the slave trade promptly stop? Or did any of the "pirates" who continued to carry it on suffer death?

The real date when American participation in the Atlantic slave trade would end was not, as we learn in history class, 1808, but 1862.

The key fact, which Americans may now in our collective memory cover over with a fog of forgetting, was that the institution of American slavery itself was still a huge and thriving and then fiercely defended economic and social reality in 1860 and 1861, and in 1862, still entirely legal.

1808 opinions in slave-holding circles in the South about the newly illegal transatlantic slave trade would have a certain ambiguity, a tenuous quality. On the one hand, some persons in the slave-holding communities would join wholeheartedly in the condemnation of the international slave trade, with the same moral revulsion as their counterparts in the North. Or perhaps this was a kind of a surrogate or compensation for the defensiveness they were caught in with respect to the actual institution of American slavery itself by which they were surrounded. Henry Wise, a leading Virginia politician throughout the prewar period—and an energetic defender of slavery on the House floor and as Governor of the state just before the war—would, in one interlude in his career (as American minister to Brazil in the middle 1840s), become a most articulate *opponent* of the slave trade, collaborating in that undertaking, no less, with the same ambassador from Great Britain he had repeatedly attacked when he was a House member.[13]

A skeptic may point out that a Virginian (in contrast to a slaveholder from Alabama or Louisiana) could have a self-interested reason for opposing the international trade: Virginia was a state with a surplus of slaves to sell Southward, so the international trade was a competition. Nevertheless, one would not want to discount a certain amount of displaced and concentrated moral revulsion even in the states whose social order still rested on the results of that trade.

As the tensions over slavery sharpened after the Mexican War, and in the 1850s the swaggering invocations of Southern "honor" grew, and the "right" to spread the institution to new territory was adamantly insisted upon, how could the defenders of slavery condemn the slave trade? Part of the argument that slavery was a positive good was that it was good for the African—bringing him the benefits and comforts of "Christian" civilization. So the traders buying slaves on the West African coast to transport them to a raw land cannot have been doing anything evil, could they?

There even came to be, in the 1850s, a body of opinion in the South proposing the reopening of the Atlantic slave trade. For though the Constitution of the Confederate States of America of February 1861 did have a clause forbidding the international slave trade, there was strong firebrand opposition to that clause. And the states' rights interpretation of it was so complete as to make it altogether possible, according to W. E. B. DuBois, that a successful Confederate States of America would have reopened the African slave trade for individual Confederate states.[14]

Under these conditions affecting public sentiment, what would you expect the enforcement of the ban on American participation in the slave trade to have been? The enforcement was lax. And what would you expect the punishment of offenders to have been? The punishments were light.

To enforce the law would require a squadron of ships patrolling the waters off African ports, and such a squadron would require appropriations from a Southern-dominated Congress and executive action by administrations all of which (except for the four years of John Quincy Adams) had strong political ties to the slave states. Conviction of those apprehended would require proof that the accused was an American citizen (so one could be shifty about citizenship) or that the vessel was American-owned (so one could be shifty about ownership and flags). The law required that the slave-trading pirate be arrested by American officers; capture by the much more diligent British did not count. Only seafarers could be charged, not the owners gathering in the profits back on dry land. And then if successfully held to trial, the prosecution had to persevere and the jury to convict, neither of which was easy given the history and atmosphere described. To some juries it seemed altogether too severe to hang an American who had not harmed any fellow American, but only Africans who had been enslaved by fellow Africans.

The largest failing had to do with the American unwillingness to cooperate with the British in patrolling for and capturing slavers. The British, having once been the most extensive national participants in the transatlantic slave trade, became, beginning early in the nineteenth century, the primary actor against the trade. But although other nations cooperated with the Royal Navy in its role as constable of the seas, capturing slave traders, the United States did not.

England was—it is difficult for later generations to remember—almost an established U.S. enemy in the early years. The two countries had fought two wars, and in the early 1840s almost fought another. The sore point in the War of 1812? Capturing slavers: A British ship stopped, boarded, and searched a ship flying an American flag. The Americans, with their historic sensibility about impressment of American sailors (and perhaps the imposition of Royal power on colonial smuggling) would not allow that. So ironically, in the period 1808–1862, flying an American flag became a certain protection for a slave ship, because it meant that you were vulnerable only to the thinly spread and rather half-hearted American patrol, and could not be boarded by the effective enforcers of the international laws against the slave trade, the British Navy.

The date of the effective end of American participation in the slave trade is 1862 rather than 1808, not only because that is the year of the climax of the Gordon case but also because the Lincoln administration negotiated with the British a treaty to suppress the African slave trade, the Seward-Lyons treaty (Lord Lyons was the British ambassador) that Congress ratified in July of 1862. Now vessels of both nations would patrol, and could stop and board, suspected slavers of either, and take them to new special courts in New York, Sierra Leone, and the Cape of Good Hope.

Lincoln had always clearly detested the slave trade. At the outset of the Lincoln administration scattered federal efforts to suppress the slave trade were consolidated under the Secretary of the Interior and new assistant George C. Whiting. In his first annual message President Lincoln said of the African slave trade: "It is a subject of gratulation that the efforts which have been made for the suppression of this inhuman traffic, have been recently attended with unusual success."[15] Whiting and Secretary of the Interior Smith reported to Lincoln in their first report the capture of five slavers. But the larger contribution of this new administration, the decisive one, was the Seward-Lyons treaty in 1862, effectively ending American participation in the Atlantic slave trade three years before American slavery itself was ended by constitutional amendment.

In the long years (1808–1862) of its illegal but real continuation, however, the story of captures and prosecutions was as our summary would suggest: dismissal of charges; ineffectual prosecutions; deadlocked juries; acquittals; forfeiting of bail; escapes; nominal fines; short jail sentences served (rarely); rather often—full pardons.

Until 1854, in all the years during which American slave trading was a crime punishable by hanging (that is, since 1820) *none* of the captured American slavers had been even convicted as a slave-trading pirate under American law, subject to capital punishment—let alone actually found guilty and executed. In that year one James Smith, master of the brig *Julia Moulton*, into which had been packed 664 Africans ("lying on their right sides, to be sure, so their heart action would be as easy as possible") was caught.[16] He tried to shuffle his citizenship to indicate he was not an American citizen and to claim his vessel also was not of American ownership, but he was brought to trial, prosecuted, and found guilty by a jury after only an hour's deliberation. He was the first American to be convicted as a slave-trading pirate and therefore subject to execution by hanging. But Smith was calm, and as it proved not without reason. His skilled lawyer (later to defend Jefferson Davis) made no effort to present Smith as an innocent led astray but assiduously worked the technicalities, got a mistrial, and eventually a plea bargain that brought Smith's punishment all the way down from hanging to two years in jail and a fine of $1,000. Smith served his term and applied to President Buchanan for a remission of the fine; in May of 1857 President Buchanan granted to the first man ever convicted of being a slave-trading pirate under American law a full pardon. The *New York Tribune* commented acidly that presumably President Buchanan "thinks it a pity, . . . now that the slave-trade is so brisk, that Captain Smith should not have an opportunity to re-engage in his favorite employment."[17]

Given this history, it is not surprising that Gordon and his sea-going family and his friends in the busy port of Portland, Maine, did not expect that he would ever face the hangman, or perhaps any severe punishment at all.

In fact, he, or perhaps his father (also named Nathaniel), had had brushes with these laws before, to no serious damage: In 1838, a Nathaniel Gordon, presumably the father, master of the brig *Dunlap* of Portland, had been charged with importing a Negro slave.

Moreover, ten years later, in 1848, in the streets of Rio a ship named the *Juliet*, rumored to be a slaver, was boarded, searched, and reluctantly let go when the boarding party could find nothing decisive, and was later rumored to have returned carrying a cargo of slaves—now under Brazilian management. The registry of the *Juliet*, before this sleight-of-hand, had been Portland, Maine, and the captain a Nathaniel Gordon.

Three years later Gordon turned up in Rio again, commanding a ship called the *Comargo*, also suspected of being a slaver. When Brazilian authorities arrested members of the crew, the American consul talked with two of them and learned the story of the earlier ship, the *Juliet*: Evading the African squadron, the ship had gone all the way around to the East coast of Africa (a rare trip in the transatlantic slave trade), had taken on board 500 Africans, had come back around the long voyage back to Brazil, had landed the Africans and the crew in another secluded spot, and then—this was the particularly striking point—was then deliberately set on fire and burned. The profits from one successful voyage so far outweighed the value of the ship that it might be prudent (especially, one might surmise, in the case of a vessel already suspect like the *Juliet*) to destroy the evidence.

None of these brushes with the law led to any conviction of any of these Nathaniel Gordons.

So when in August of 1860 this Captain Nathaniel Gordon was arrested in the mouth of the Congo River now on his ship the *Erie*, with a cargo of 897 Negroes, he certainly would not have feared— the 1820 law notwithstanding—for his life.

But Gordon this time had the bad luck that while he waited for trial in the Tombs—the notorious jail in New York City—the American nation elected its first full-fledged antislavery administration. So the newly appointed district attorney who would prosecute him, a man named E. Delafield Smith, would mean business.

When the first trial, in June of 1861, ended in a hung jury— seven to convict, five to acquit—District Attorney Smith did not give up or plea bargain, but filed for a new trial, and found witnesses who had not testified in the first trial.

Of course Gordon had shrewd lawyers and of course they tried all the dodges and technicalities that had worked in other cases. Gordon's lawyers claimed that the *Erie* (rather suddenly—like the *Juliet*) had ceased being an American vessel because it had been sold to foreigners. They even made the particularly ingenious argument that *Gordon himself* might not be an American, because his mother sometimes accompanied his father on his voyages and thus might have been born at sea. They also argued that the crime had been committed so far into the mouth of the Congo as to have been *Portuguese* water, therefore outside American jurisdiction.

Finally—it was common for a slave ship captain when caught suddenly to claim irresponsibility: "No, no, I am not in command of this ship; I am just a passenger. The commander is that Spaniard over there." And that, of course, is what Gordon's lawyers did: He was no longer in charge of the *Erie*, they said, once some Spaniards came aboard.

The Judge dismissed the first three of these and witnesses contradicted the fourth.

District Attorney Smith's witnesses at the second trial testified that they had a confrontation with Gordon about the purpose of the voyage. As sometimes happened, the whole crew had not been fully informed at the outset. The *Erie* had been detained by a wary United States consul in Havana, but Gordon had given a sworn affidavit that his ship was chartered for a legal voyage to the coast of Africa. (Trade with the African coast in many other items of course was fully legitimate, offering further opportunities for subterfuge.) But when the Africans were taken aboard in the Congo, and members of the crew challenged Gordon, he offered each of them a dollar per head (so the witnesses now testified) for every African landed in Cuba.

Republican District Attorney Smith presented a particularly pungent episode, one of those lightning-flash glimpses of the horrors of the slave trade. While the crew from the capturing ship the *Mohican* was sailing the *Erie* to Monrovia, they brought the Africans on deck for water, and then found they had been so tightly packed they could not get them back in place. Gordon himself (certainly the man in charge) showed them "the manner of doing it, which was by spreading the limbs of the creatures apart and sitting them so close together that even a foot could not be put upon the deck."

The jury this time deliberated for only twenty minutes and returned with a verdict of guilty. The judge, William D. Shipman, hearing his first slave-trade case, gave a stern condemnation of the "wickedness" of the slave trade, sentenced Gordon to be hanged on February 7, 1862, and told him that "you are soon to pass into the presence of that God of the black man as well as the white man."[18]

However—Gordon and his lawyer still did not think he would have any such confrontation just yet. There was a fallback plan: that power to pardon which the framers had bestowed upon the nation's chief executive.

So now Gordon's counsel, a former judge named Gilbert Dean, hurried to Washington and presented all of his arguments to this president.

What arguments for mitigation of Gordon's punishment would be made, by Dean and White and others?

First—that the law under which Gordon had been found guilty had never been enforced before—so it ought not to be enforced now. Nobody has been hanged; few punished at all. Dean wrote to Lincoln: "Far more than forty years the statute under which he has been convicted has been a dead letter."[19] The placard posted around New York had the same metaphor: "Captain Nathaniel Gordon is under sentence of execution for a crime which has been virtually a dead-letter for forty years. Shall this young man be quietly allowed to be made a victim of fanaticism?"[20]

In one of his arguments Dean made affirmations of the value of human life that have a deeply ironic ring, when you remember Gordon's crime. The issue was a technical one, about greater care having been taken with property cases than with this case. At the end of a paragraph deploring the allegedly greater technical care for titles to property than with Gordon's possible execution, Dean wrote, without evident consciousness of the irony, "human life is of less consequence than Bales of Cotton or Boxes of Dry Goods"—no doubt thinking of Gordon's life, not the 897 Africans packed solid in the hold of the *Erie* like bales of cotton or boxes of dry goods.

One of Dean's more ingenious arguments built on a judicial interpretation of the 1820 statute that went like this: "That a person having no interest in, or power over the negroes, so as to impress on them the character of slaves and only employed in their *transportation* is not guilty of the capital offense." Now, *there's* an argument. They were already slaves in Africa when I picked them up, somebody else sells them in Brazil, Cuba, or South Carolina—I'm just in the *transportation* business!

Some of the arguments took account of the surrounding scene of Civil War. Dean noted the "forgiveness" and "amnesty" offered to some Confederates and "Pirates" (meaning blockade runners) but not to his client: "While the prison doors are opening to Convicted Pirates and acknowledged Traitors, the Gallows is being erected for

Gordon, and why? Is the moral crime of which he is guilty greater than those of you are releasing?" White expressed that view of Gordon's supporters that the rules had abruptly changed when she said (with some truth) that "Mr. Gordon was engaged in the slave trade at a time when many *then* in power upheld it, and engaged in it." And then she added with emphasis: "*Not since the war began.*" (To be sure, Gordon was arrested in August of 1860 and so had not really been in a position to engage in the trade since the war began.)

One last argument on behalf of Gordon is particularly revealing, as it parallels arguments made by the antislavery politician Lincoln out in Illinois in the 1850s—only in reverse. Dean, explaining why the statute has been for forty years a dead letter, explained it thus: ". . . because the moral sense of the community revolted at the penalty of death imposed on an act when done between Africa and Cuba, which the law sanctioned between Maryland and Carolina."

And here now is the point in Dean's most pungent sentence: "It was, nay it is, lawful to carry a child born in Virginia to Louisiana and there to sell him into perpetual slavery. . . . is it an offense then deserving death to bring a barbarian from Africa to the same place?"

So the Gordon case came to President Lincoln, one of his first major pardon cases.

As a rising Illinois politician, he had made clear his judgment that slavery was a "monstrous injustice," a "vast moral evil," an "odious institution." And he had made arguments that *assumed* in his hearers his own moral revulsion at the slave trade.

Why is it—he asked in his first great speech in the autumn of 1854—that you will not shake hands with a slave trader, or let your children play with his children? And as to the moral abomination of the *transatlantic* slave trade he asked: Why did you join, in 1820, almost unanimously, in making the African slave trade punishable by hanging? You never thought of hanging men for catching and selling wild horses.

And he made the same comparison that Dean would make, between the domestic and the international trade, to a contrasting moral conclusion. Dean said: Since it resembles the domestic slave trade, the transatlantic trade is not so bad as to be punishable by death. Lincoln the antislavery politician had said: since the domestic trade resembles the abominable international trade, do not *expand* this abomination into new territory.

One place Lincoln made this comparison was in his satire on Stephen Douglas's use of the word "sacred" in the phrase "*sacred right of self-government*"—meaning the right to take slaves into the territories.

> If it is a *sacred* right for the people of Nebraska to take and hold slaves there, it is equally their *sacred* right to buy them where they can buy them cheapest; and that undoubtedly will be on the coast of Africa; provided you will consent to not hang them for going there to buy them. You must remove this restriction too, from the *sacred* right of self-government. I am aware you say that taking slaves from the States to Nebraska, does not make slaves of freemen; but the African slave-trader can say just as much. He does not catch free negroes and bring them here. He finds them already slaves in the hands of their black captors, and he honestly buys them at the rate of about a red cotton handkerchief a head. This is very cheap, and it is a great abridgement of the *sacred* right of self-government to hang men for engaging in this profitable trade![21]

The heavy sarcasm from Lincoln, the rising politician, assumed that his audience knew that the transatlantic slave trade was a moral abomination—and now was bringing them to see the parallel wickedness in extending the slave trade to new territories.

So now the politician who had made those arguments was President of the United States, and had before him a real live transatlantic slave trader.

There were petitions, arguments, pleas for mercy of the sort to which he was, usually, quite responsive. All anyone was asking at this point was commutation of the death sentence to life imprisonment. Lincoln did, at least, ask his Attorney General for his response to lawyer Dean's arguments.

Lincoln in his use of the pardon power was usually merciful to individuals caught up in something beyond their control in which they run afoul of legal judgments—to farm boys who fall asleep on sentry duty, to Union soldiers who left camp to go make sure their girlfriend had not taken up with a rival, to ordinary citizens on the Confederate side because of where they lived, to German speakers who did not understand what they had been told. He was inclined to be compassionate later on, against Stanton's strong protest, to a confused old fellow named Yocum who turned an escaped slave back to his master. Stanton said that was as bad as a slave trader. Lincoln did not think so.

Nathaniel Gordon was something else.

Lincoln cast his decision in the plainest moral terms: "I felt it my duty to refuse."

He refused any mitigation of the death penalty for this blatant captain and owner of a slave trader.

No mercy this time.

Well, almost no mercy.

He did make one little concession—quite interestingly. He knew that Gordon never imagined that he actually would be executed. And there was that word "reprieve" in the Constitution. He asked Bates whether he could grant a "respite of his sentence without relieving him altogether of the death penalty." Bates answered affirmatively: That power to grant a "reprieve" does not "annul" the sentence; it only "prolongs the time."[22] So three days before the scheduled hanging Lincoln issued a formal "stay of execution" full of whereases, one of which was: "'whereas, it has seemed to me probable that the unsuccessful application made for the commutation of his sentence may have prevented the said Nathaniel Gordon from making the necessary preparation for the awful change that awaits him' now, therefore, I President Lincoln grant him a 'respite' until February 21."

The "said Nathaniel Gordon" was given an extra two weeks, to prepare for the awful change that awaited him.

But still Gordon and his lawyers were not yet ready to make preparation for that awful change. Gordon's energetic counsel tried the Supreme Court, tried again at the Circuit Court with another technical argument, tried again to persuade President Lincoln by bringing not only Gordon's wife but also his mother and White, and the petition from now *eleven thousand* New Yorkers. The governor of New York made yet another last-minute appeal to Lincoln.

What do you suppose would be the most interesting argument now made when Lincoln postponed Gordon's execution so that it was to come on February 21—an argument made both by a speaker at the mass protest meeting in New York and by Dean, trying everything? They now argued: Don't desecrate the period of Washington's birthday with a hanging!

Dean wrote: "do not, I beseech you allow . . . the eve of the preparation for solemnizing the Anniversary of the 22nd February to be marred by the creaking of the gallows—or saddened by the report of the dying groans and struggles of a human being sacrificed to appease the spasmodic virtue of men."

On February 21, there was a protest rally at the Merchant's Exchange and an armed guard of eighty United States marshals' men surrounding the gallows at the Tombs, the city prison. Inside the prison someone had smuggled the well-connected Gordon some cigars soaked in strychnine, but he succeeded only in making himself ill and accelerating his punishment. The authorities moved the execution from two o'clock up to noon.[23] He was then placed "beneath the fatal beam" and hanged, the only slave trader ever executed under American law.

In granting the two weeks respite Lincoln had said "it becomes my painful duty to admonish the prisoner that, relinquishing all expectation of pardon by human authority, he refer himself alone to the common God and Father of 'all men.'"

Surely it is significant that Lincoln, in stating his refusal to do anything more, referred to the common God of all men. In this case, justice for the 897 Africans crammed into the slave deck of the *Erie* and the perhaps 500 Africans on the last voyage of the *Juliet*, and the hundreds, perhaps thousands of Africans on the other Nathaniel Gordon voyages that Gordon brought in chains across the Atlantic on the *Comargo* and how many other vessels, and all the other damage that the nefarious trade did to the common life, outweighed the claim of even a limited mercy to this man.

Except for one little Lincolnian touch: A two weeks' reprieve, to get his soul in shape. Otherwise, no mercy, no pardon for this slave trader by human authority in the person of Lincoln. Mercy, if at all, would come from the God he would now have to face, the God of the black man and the white man.

CHAPTER 10

Abraham Lincoln and Ulysses S. Grant

Jean Edward Smith

WHEN JUDGE WILLIAMS ASKED ME TO COMPARE PUBLIC PERceptions of the Lincoln and Grant presidencies, I am afraid I accepted too quickly, and I have been at a loss as to what to write. Having just looked over what I prepared, I am afraid I resolved my uncertainty by writing nothing. This will take approximately twelve pages.

While preparing this essay, I was thinking of the unwisdom of speaking too frequently and the wisdom of restraining oneself. Some of you may recall that wonderful remark of Benjamin Disraeli when a callow, young member of the House of Commons came to him and said, "Prime Minister, I've just come to the House; do you think it would be well if I participated actively in debate?"

And the Prime Minister looked at him appraisingly for a moment and said, "No, I think it would be better if you did not. I think it would be better if the House wondered why you didn't speak rather than why you did."

I wish I could treat my subject with humor, but I'm afraid 1860s humor is hard to come by. The Southerners were particularly sanctimonious. General Robert E. Lee was given two bottles of whiskey by an old friend when the war began for medicinal purposes. When Lee surrendered at Appomattox, the bottles were still in his kit unopened. That would not have happened with General Grant!

Unlike Lincoln, Jefferson Davis was particularly somber, although he could be hilarious unwittingly. After General William T. Sherman captured Atlanta, Davis proclaimed a Southern victory and asserted the Union army would be destroyed on its retreat just as Napoleon's had been in Russia.

"Who's going to furnish the snow?" Grant quipped.

Actually, Lincoln and Grant shared a native frontier humor. I'm sure most of you are familiar with an episode early in the war when a group of Protestant clergymen visited Lincoln in the White House. "Mr. President," said the leader, "I had a vision from the Lord last night, and I want you to know that the Lord is on the side of the Union."

"That's mighty fine, Reverend," Lincoln replied, "but what I need is Kentucky."

Not all Southerners were humorless. My favorite is General George Pickett, who was asked in 1868 why the South lost the war. "I think the Yankees had something to do with it," said Pickett.

General Philip H. Sheridan always had a robust sense of humor. After the war, Sheridan was military governor of Texas and Louisiana. A newsman asked him how he liked Texas.

"If I owned Texas and Hell," said Sheridan, "I'd live in Hell and rent Texas out."

Comparing the presidential reputations of Lincoln and Grant presents a paradox. During most of his years in the White House, Lincoln was reviled by major segments of the population, ridiculed by the intelligentsia, and could rarely count on unified national support. With the succession of Union victories in late 1864 his standing improved, and after his assassination he was canonized. Grant, on the other hand, enjoyed the applause of most of the nation during his entire eight years as president, and was reelected in 1872 with the largest popular majority of any candidate since Andrew Jackson. But after Grant's death in 1885, and for the next hundred years, his presidency was savaged, first by the American historical establishment, and then in popular memory. One president, denigrated in life, was deified after death; the other, revered while alive, was relegated to the bottom of the presidential pyramid after he was gone.

Why the contrast? It has a lot to do with the treatment of African-Americans. Lincoln has been rightly praised for eradicating slavery and saving the Union. But he was spared the agony of Reconstruction. Grant picked up the burden and fought for Black equality with the same tenacity that held the Union line at Shiloh. But by the late 1880s and 1890s, equality for African-Americans and the noble aims of Reconstruction took a back seat to reconciliation with the white South, racial segregation, and the systematic denial of the franchise to the Negro. In short, Grant was a casualty of white supremacy, the legacy of which endures to this day.

Before drawing the contrast between presidential reputations, let me emphasize the common ground on which Lincoln and Grant stood. For both men the conflict in 1861 was not a civil war, much less a war between the states, but a rebellion: a rebellion against the authority of the United States. Both Lincoln and Grant rested their case on the constitutional view of sovereignty established by the Marshall Court. It was the people who were sovereign, said Chief Justice John Marshall, not the states. It was the people who promulgated and ratified the Constitution, not the states. And it was the people who made it perpetual and indissolvable.

We say in linguistic shorthand that Lincoln saved the Union. But in a constitutional sense, what he and Grant did was suppress the rebellion against the authority of the United States Government in the Southern states, which remained part of the Union. President Lincoln, under his authority as commander in chief, and his responsibility to "take care that the laws be faithfully executed," was merely insuring that the will of the people expressed in the Constitution continued to prevail in all sections of the country.

To see the Lincoln and Grant presidencies in perspective, it is essential to understand the constitutional principle underlying the conflict—and to contrast that to the historical revisionism that transformed the War of the Rebellion into the war between the states. That transformed treason, slavery, and rebellion into a just cause, led by Christian heroes, fighting for a way of life blessed with aristocratic virtue. In that sense, let me suggest that there is nothing more pernicious to the cause for which Lincoln and Grant fought than the reenactment spectacles that have swept the country, the discussion groups so absorbed with military tactics that they overlook the causes and consequences of the war, and the interpretation of battlefields that treat the Southern cause with implicit legitimacy while ignoring the treasonous underpinnings of the conflict. Aside from the glorification of war, which some might contend contributes to a mind-set conducive to military adventures abroad, these endeavors obscure the fact that the Civil War was a rebellion against the United States. And if I may, just to drive this point home, let me remind you that the Civil War cemeteries maintained by the United States government, with but one or two exceptions, do not contain the bodies of Confederate dead—that honor denied those who raised their weapons against the established authority of the nation.

Now, for Lincoln and Grant. Our thinking about Lincoln has been shaped to some extent by what his friends and supporters wrote, magnified by victory in 1865 and the tragedy of his assassination. With Grant it has been just the opposite. William Hesseltine, a 1930s biographer, attributed the denigration of Grant's presidency to the fact that his enemies wrote better than his friends. "Consciously or unconsciously," said Hesseltine, "they stuffed the ballot boxes of history against Grant."[1]

Delightful as that analysis may be, the reasons lie deeper in the corpus of American historiography. And so what I would like to do is briefly sketch the reputation of Lincoln during his presidency and afterward, and contrast that to Grant.

I am sure many of you are familiar with J. G. Randall's often quoted article of the early 1940s, "The Unpopular Mr. Lincoln,"[2] and the rejoinder presented by Hans L. Trefousse from this platform several years ago.[3] Rather than join that debate, let me simply restate the record of the first Lincoln administration and compare it to Grant's two terms in office. Events proved Lincoln wiser than his critics, but that does not diminish the opprobrium heaped upon him, or ameliorate his deplorable relations with Congress.

Republicans in Congress were particularly critical of the president. One can argue that party leaders were more comfortable in opposition; that many had made their reputation attacking Presidents Pierce and Buchanan; and that Lincoln was seen as merely another one-term resident of the White House who could be safely ignored. But that should not obscure the fact that Lincoln's pragmatic moderation offended the radicals of his party without satisfying the conservatives. Former Supreme Court justice Benjamin Curtis of Massachusetts (the great dissenter in the *Dred Scott Case*), visiting Washington in January 1863, was struck by the general agreement among all he met on the president's "utter incompetence."[4] Two months later, Richard Henry Dana, another Massachusetts man come to Washington, found "the most striking thing" about the capital was "the absence of personal loyalty to the President. It does not exist," wrote Dana.

Conservative Republicans believed Lincoln had unnecessarily converted a war for the Union into a crusade against slavery; that he had suppressed free speech, censored the press, arbitrarily arrested dissidents, suspended the writ of *habeas corpus*, and defied the chief justice of the United States.[5]

Radicals on the other hand blamed the president for moving too slowly against slavery as well as his failure to understand that the entire political and social structure of the South needed to be rebuilt. Contempt for Lincoln was so great that Thaddeus Stevens came within an eyelash of introducing a motion of censure against the administration in 1863. And the Committee on the Conduct of the War, "the spearhead of the radical drive against the administration," as T. Harry Williams called it, was precisely the device to wrest control of the war from the president.

In the mid-term elections in 1862, five key states—New York, Pennsylvania, Ohio, Indiana, and Illinois—all of which had gone for Lincoln in 1860, voted Democratic. Even Lincoln's renomination in 1864 was in doubt, certainly in the president's own mind. Without stringing together one disparaging quotation after another, let me simply cite James Gordon Bennett's lead editorial in the New York *Herald* of February 19, 1864:

> President Lincoln is a joke incarnate. His election was a very sorry joke. The idea that such a man should be president . . . is a joke. His inaugural address was a joke. His cabinet is and has always been a standing joke. All his state papers are jokes. His intrigues to secure a renomination and the hope he appears to entertain of a re-election are, however, the most laughable jokes of all.[6]

After the passage of almost 150 years, those words and many similar criticisms are all but forgotten. What remains is the image of the great emancipator, martyred at the moment of victory, safe in the knowledge that his utmost goal, the preservation of the Union, was secure. Merrill Peterson argues with great eloquence that "in his magnificent humanity Lincoln transcended the war. . . . for many . . . his person and his character constituted the chief glory of the war; and as its colors faded into the past, the memory of Lincoln became the most treasured legacy of that conflict."[7]

Lincoln's name was coupled with Washington's. Funeral banners proclaimed "Washington the Father, Lincoln the Savior." Initially,

Lincoln was a sectional hero, adored in the North, all but ignored in the South. But with the passage of years, the moderation of feeling, and the unprecedented prosperity of the United States, Lincoln's place in the pantheon of presidents became secure. The magnitude of his achievement combined with the drama of his death has etched his memory permanently in the national consciousness.

Lincoln was initially a minority president. Andrew Johnson was an accidental president. By contrast, Grant was swept into office in 1868 on an electoral tidal wave. Nominated unanimously by the Republican Party on the first ballot without any opposition whatever, Grant trounced his Democratic opponent 3:1 in the electoral college. In 1872, Grant was again nominated unanimously on the first ballot, and stomped Horace Greeley in the general election by almost 800,000 votes—the largest plurality received by any presidential candidate until 1900.

Grant finished his two terms as president at the peak of his popularity. "No American has carried greater fame out of the White House than this silent man who leaves it today," wrote James Garfield.[8] For the next two and a half years, Grant toured the world, received everywhere by heads of state and adoring crowds. He returned to face a groundswell urging him to run for a third term, and came within a whisker of being awarded the Republican nomination, though he did nothing to encourage it. Afterward he entered the investment banking business in New York, only to suffer a humiliating bankruptcy when a corrupt partner brought down the firm of Grant and Ward in 1884. Penniless, and without a pension or other means of support, Grant turned to writing, and in the last year of his life, fatally ill with cancer, wrote the *Memoirs* that not only rescued his family from poverty, but established his reputation as one of the finest writers in the English language. Within a year of publication, Grant's *Memoirs* sold over 250,000 sets (500,000 volumes), and became the greatest best seller in America to that time, a remarkable accomplishment that testifies to his place in popular esteem.

Given Grant's stature as the nation's preeminent citizen from the mid-1860s until his death in 1885, why has his reputation been so tarnished? Let me suggest that Grant was condemned for what he stood for. As president, Grant was indelibly linked with Reconstruction. And for four generations of white Americans, particularly white Southerners, Reconstruction was anathema. As commander in chief, Grant used every means at his disposal—the Army, the courts, and his personal prestige on Capitol Hill—to insure that the verdict of Appomattox was not frittered away and that African-Americans in the South were able to enjoy the rights granted them under the Constitution. By the 1880s that view was no longer fashionable. Jim Crow replaced Reconstruction. And for almost a hundred years, mainstream historians, unsympathetic to Black equality, brutalized Grant's presidency.

These were not Lost Cause historians or rebel irreconcilables, but the core of the American historical establishment: James Ford Rhodes of Ohio, Herbert Baxter Adams at Johns Hopkins, and above all, John William Burgess and William A. Dunning at Columbia and the dozens of graduate students who studied with them— particularly white young men from the South—and who then returned home and rewrote the history of Reconstruction.

David Herbert Donald, who hails from Mississippi, described the work of the Dunning School as follows:

> Researched from primary sources, factually accurate, and presented with an air of objectivity, these dissertations were acclaimed as triumphs of the application of the scientific method to historiography, and indeed they still provide our basic knowledge of the political history of the South during the post war years. Yet, with every conscious desire to be fair, these students of Dunning shaped their monographs to

accord with the white Southerner's view that the Negro was innately inferior. . . . Consequently, the Dunning students condemned Negro participation in Southern Reconstruction governments, even while they condoned white terrorist organizations such as the Ku Klux Klan.

Professor Donald's comments are in his introduction to Dunning's *Essays on the Civil War and Reconstruction*, a work replete with references to "barbarous" freedmen committing "the hideous crime against white womanhood."[9]

The Dunning School was the historical mainstream. Dunning edited the *Political Science Quarterly* for sixteen years, and is the only person to have been elected president of both the American Historical Association and the American Political Science Association. These were the prevailing views of the time, reinforced by the United States Supreme Court when it struck down the Ku Klux Klan Act;[10] eviscerated the Fifteenth Amendment;[11] overturned the Enforcement Act of 1870;[12] nullified the Civil Rights Act;[13] and in 1896, with only John Marshall Harlan of Kentucky dissenting, promulgated the doctrine of "separate but equal," giving the Court's constitutional blessing to racial segregation.[14] These decisions were widely applauded. Charles Warren, Harvard's great legal historian, restated the national consensus: "Viewed in historical perspective," wrote Warren, "there can be no question that the decisions in these cases were most fortunate. They largely eliminated from National politics the negro question which had so long embittered Congressional debates."[15]

That was the country's attitude, and Grant's reputation suffered accordingly. But the negative assessments of Reconstruction overlook the unprecedented accomplishments of the Grant administration in foreign affairs, in bringing peace to the Great Plains, in arresting inflation, in crushing terrorist violence in the South, in combating corruption, in postal and civil service reform, the creation of the national park system, and perhaps above all, in providing the nation with peace, order, and stability after eight years of war and upheaval.

Without going into detail, let me remind you that Hamilton Fish, Grant's secretary of state, served for the entire eight years that Grant was in office and proved to be one of the greatest secretaries of state in American history. Or that George S. Boutwell and Benjamin H. Bristow did outstanding jobs at Treasury. Or that Ebenezer Rockwood Hoar and Amos T. Ackerman proved implacable enemies of corruption and racial terrorism as attorneys general. Or the total reorganization that Postmaster General John A. J. Creswell effected in the nation's mail service. To head the Bureau of Indian Affairs, Grant named the first Native American (Ely S. Parker); and to ease the bitterness of defeat, on his first day in office he appointed General James Longstreet collector of customs in New Orleans—the second-highest-paying post in federal service.

As president, Grant steered the United States onto the world stage. He avoided war with Spain over Cuba, reversed the downward spiral in Anglo-American relations, settled the *Alabama* claims, established the precedent for international arbitration, resolved a long-standing boundary dispute with Canada over the Strait of Juan de Fuca, and rewrote the law of nations pertaining to the obligations of neutrals. And like President Dwight D. Eisenhower one hundred years later, Grant enjoyed the international prestige to accomplish this.

In domestic affairs, Grant crushed the Ku Klux Klan, sent the leaders to prison, routed white terrorism in the South, suppressed the mutiny against federal authority in Louisiana, and defended the rights of African-Americans to political and legal equality. No other president has carried on such a determined struggle, against such hopeless odds, to protect the freedmen in the exercise of their constitutional rights.

So too with Native Americans. What historians call Grant's peace policy eventually brought peace to the Great Plains, broke the corrupt ring of Indian agents who had profited at the expense of Native Americans, and paved the way for assimilation and eventual citizenship for the nation's original inhabitants.

Always overlooked by those intent on trashing the Grant administration is that it was Grant who established the first Civil Service Commission. It was Grant who inaugurated the National Park system with the establishment of Yellowstone in 1872. And it was Grant who in 1875 tamped down the raging controversy over religious influence in the public schools. "Leave the matter of religion to the family circle, the church & the private school support[ed] entirely by private contribution," said Grant. "Keep church and state forever separate." Grant was ahead of his time in urging that the tax exemption for church property be rescinded, but there is no question this was an issue about which he felt strongly.

The economic accomplishments of the Grant administration laid the foundation for the incredible growth of the American economy in the late nineteenth century. Grant weaned the country from the greenback inflation lingering from the Civil War, and established a sound currency that made the dollar one of the world's most respected mediums of exchange. In Grant's own mind, his 1874 veto of the Inflation Bill followed by passage of the Resumption Act the following year—returning the United States to the gold standard—were the two greatest achievements of his eight years in the White House.

But above all, Grant steadied the nation. His rocklike presence in the White House comforted the country and hastened the return to normalcy. And as he prepared to leave office, his calming influence reassured the nation during the Hayes-Tilden election crisis of 1876. Grant stepped in, called the parties together, fashioned the formula for adjudicating the results, and rammed it through a hopelessly divided Congress. And the country trusted Grant to do so.

Lincoln and Grant deserve the nation's credit for saving the United States, eradicating slavery, and striving to provide equality for the freedman. One could not have succeeded without the other. And while Lincoln set the course, it was Grant who sailed the ship. Lincoln lost his life before the work was finished. Grant left office with the task incomplete. Justice and equality for African-Americans, indeed, for all hyphenated Americans, were slow in coming. But inexorably, implacably, relentlessly, like Grant moving South in 1864, the long march of equality has come near to fruition. Reconstruction is being reevaluated, and with it, let me suggest, the reputation of President Grant will be salvaged.

CHAPTER 11

Motivating Men: Lincoln, Grant, MacArthur, and Kennedy

Geoffrey Perret

WHEN FRANK WILLIAMS ASKED ME TO WRITE ABOUT ABRA-
ham Lincoln, Ulysses S. Grant, Douglas MacArthur, and John F.
Kennedy, I wondered, is it possible to tie them together? The one
thing they had in common was leadership, obviously, but there had
to be something more, something else. I've written a biography of
Dwight D. Eisenhower, but he isn't included. So what was I missing? I appealed to Frank for a different topic, but the judge turned
down my appeal.

For a while, I felt I was living out an old Irish joke about a young
man from New York who journeys to Ireland to explore his roots.
Let's call him Kevin. As Kevin searches for the village where the
family home is located it is getting dark and there are no road signs to
help him. He is close to despair when an Irish farmer—tweed cap on
his head, shillelagh under his arm, and a dog trotting at his heels—
steps out onto the road from a field. Kevin lowers a window and calls
out, "Excuse me, please, but how would you get to Skibereen?"

The farmer adjusts the cap, shifts the shillelagh from one hand
to the other and looks at the dog. Then he looks at Kevin and shakes
his head slowly. "I wouldn't start from here."

Well, here is where I am starting from and the first element of this essay is in the title, "Motivating Men," because that describes what they were, what they did and how they were perceived. Between them, these four cover almost every variety of leadership: in peace and war, the moral as well as the physical, the highly wrought and the understated, leadership of the word, and leadership of the deed.

And as I thought about them I realized just what it was that made the difference: Lincoln, Grant, MacArthur, and Kennedy had all been on campaign. Eisenhower never did. He deeply regretted never having been shot at in World War One and was almost apologetic about it. As the Supreme Commander in World War Two he was exposed to danger in various ways at various times, but that was not the same as being a combat commander.

Lincoln had served in the Black Hawk War of 1832 as both an officer and an enlisted man. He later made fun of his military service, saying the only blood he shed for his country was what the mosquitoes took. When he said that, it was during the Mexican War, a conflict that he opposed. This self-mockery should not be taken at face value; Lincoln scored political points this way. The truth was in what he told a friend shortly before he became president—that the most satisfying experience of his life had been to command a body of infantry.

Combat experience and physical courage give an added dimension to leadership; cloak it with an unimpeachable authority. That was the something else: what made the difference in the example of leadership these four provided.

Having realized that, I felt that I had solved a problem, but if I left it there, this would hardly amount to an essay. So what else was there that linked these four men? More than I had ever imagined.

For one thing, all were masters of the word. Lincoln, Grant, MacArthur, and Kennedy all had a writer's imagination, that faculty of being completely involved in an intense experience, yet all the while a part of one's consciousness seems to be standing over to one side, looking on.

No one could doubt that they could turn feelings and desires into words. In Lincoln, that writer's imagination shows up mainly in his speeches and correspondence. He was such a phrasemaker that not only is Lincoln the most quoted—and misquoted—of presidents but may also be more frequently quoted than all of his predecessors and successors combined.

In Grant's case, his words are there not only in his memoirs, a classic work that has never been out of print, but in his orders. Von Moltke the Elder had what he called "The First Law of Operations." This law said that any order that could be misunderstood would *be* misunderstood. No one ever misunderstood a Grant order.

This was a tremendous achievement in the age before modern staff schools. During World War One, Billy Mitchell kept a captain on his staff who was as dumb as a stump. Whenever Mitchell wrote an order, he would hand it to the captain and ask if he understood it. If the captain said he did, the order went out, but if the captain said he didn't, Mitchell rewrote the order.

Although MacArthur was renowned for his oratory, he was also a fine writer of prose. His autobiography, called *Reminiscences*, is superb and, unlike many a general's memoir in our time, he actually wrote it.

In the 1930s, when MacArthur was serving as Chief of Staff of the Army, an ambitious young officer asked MacArthur what he could do to advance his career. MacArthur had some simple advice: learn to write well. That writing talent had helped Grant and Mac-Arthur reach the top. It was crucial, too, in the rise of Eisenhower, who was assigned to MacArthur's staff in the 1930s.

It is hardly surprising that with the writer's imagination at work in Lincoln, Grant, MacArthur, and Kennedy there is also an appreciation of poetry. In the world of literature, it is poetry that occupies the summit. All other literary forms, including biography, are to be found in the foothills or, at best, on the upper slopes.

Lincoln loved poetry of a sentimental nature and memorized huge amounts of it. Grant, too, found comfort and inspiration in poetry. At his first battle in Mexico what came to his mind as he saw the Mexican army deploy? Here was an army of brilliant uniforms patterned on those of Napoleon's army and it looked magnificent. These are the words that came to his mind, from Byron:

> The Assyrian came down like a wolf on the fold
> And his cohorts were gleaming in purple and gold
> And the sheen of their spears was like stars on the sea . . .

MacArthur believed in poetry so much that one of his first actions when he became superintendent at West Point was to make the cadets write it. Kennedy did not write it, but he regularly turned to it for encouragement and inspiration. He limited himself mainly to hortatory verse and it came naturally to him to tell the people around him that he and they were "these few, these happy few, this band of brothers." When he and Jackie returned to Hyannis from their honeymoon in Acapulco, Kennedy stood on the steps of their new house before they entered it for the first time. He told her there was something she needed to know. Then he recited a poem by Allan Seeger, a young Harvard graduate who had died in an attack on a German-held village in France on July 4, 1918. This is how it begins,

> I have a rendezvous with Death
> At some disputed barricade . . .

He recited the poem, flawlessly, to its uncompromising conclusion:

> And I to my pledged word am true,
> I shall not fail that rendezvous.

As is often the case with writers, all four men were highly strung. They were attuned instantly to whatever emotional or psychological current ran through themselves, the people around them, and the world at large. That does not mean they were necessarily guided by it, but they were profoundly aware of it.

All four had a strong and singular sense of self, one that manifested overtly, in a unique dress sense. There were dozens of tall men in frock coats and stovepipe hats in the 1860s, as we can see from photographs of the time. Not one of them looks remotely like Lincoln. He knew his ungainliness made him stand out, and it does not seem to have troubled him. If anything, his casualness only added to it, and he was almost certainly aware of that.

Grant, the most modest of men in some ways, made himself stand out from other commanders by wearing a private's blouse with a general's stars. The cigar, too, was a useful and instantly recognizable prop.

As for MacArthur, when he served on the Western Front in World War One, he wore an eight-foot scarf knitted by his mother. It reached to his knees. He also took the grommet out of his cap, creating a fashion for the "crush cap" later made famous by World War Two bomber pilots.

Between the wars, the Class A uniform included a black silk tie. Yet MacArthur as chief of staff wore a purple satin tie. When he was criticized in the press for this he responded indignantly. He had fought in the uniform of his country, he declared, and intended to be buried in it. Out of uniform? Never!

Kennedy dressed like a college student even after he was elected to Congress. He did not dress like other politicians. It was a sign, one that advertised not only his youth but his view of himself as being different from them, not just now but for always.

When he was reelected to the Senate in 1958, he changed his look completely, because he was running for the White House. Even so, he did not look like a politician—he dressed like a movie star. Kennedy adopted the Frank Sinatra look. From the way he dressed, Kennedy looked like the East Coast representative of the Rat Pack.

It was not only the way they looked that signaled their distance from the typical politicians or generals of their age. What absorbed all four was not the acquisition of power, even if there were moments when they took a deep pleasure from exercising the power they possessed. Their core ambition was not power but the force that transcends power and ultimately redeems it—leadership.

Power for power's sake, power for ego's sake, power as compensation for some fundamental flaw, such less laudable drives were never what pushed them to the top of the military and politics. In all of them there was a yearning for moral purpose big enough to redeem great risk and sacrifice.

I think that's obvious in the case of Lincoln, Grant, and MacArthur, but what about Kennedy, the promiscuous playboy, a man who rejected bourgeois notions of morality? Well, that moral yearning was as strong in him as in any of the others. He was a paradox, not a hypocrite.

Someone remarked the other day that Lincoln was the only president to sacrifice party advantage in order to promote racial equality. I think Kennedy qualifies, too.

Kennedy spent much of his political career, and nearly all of his brief presidency, trying to avoid involvement with the civil rights movement. He was prepared to make the token gesture, such as inviting black leaders to the White House, but nothing more. The bedrock of Democratic support was the Solid South, unbreakable since the Civil War. Almost any gesture toward the civil rights movement risked cracking the Solid South.

Yet in the closing months of his life, he not only identified his administration with the Civil Rights movement but also sent a voting rights bill to Congress that outraged opinion across the South. He did so for the best reason possible—it was the right thing to do.

There was something else at work, too, at least as far as Lincoln, MacArthur, and Kennedy were concerned. All three were trying to cheat death through fame. In Grant, there was a different impetus, a rare combination of desires—yearning for adventure while yearning not to be noticed. This is the anti-heroic temperament far ahead of its time. A twentieth-century man in an age still bathed in the Romantic ideals unleashed by the Enlightenment, ideals in which heroes acted on the grand scale, was flamboyant and noticed.

Robert E. Lee was the personification of the Romantic idea of the military hero, and at Appomattox two ages, two temperaments came face to face, not just two men. The one harkened back to a landed aristocracy, with gracious ways and an impressive pedigree; the other pointed ahead to an age when the Common Man despite his matter-of-fact ways and humble origins would rise, and by merit alone.

All four come to us as marmoreal figures, marble men, each helping to define the age in which he lived. Yet this marmoreal quality in death, underlining their importance beyond the grave, leads us away from the plasticity of life as it is really lived, taking us away from the man that each knew himself to be.

How, then, do we grasp what they mean to later generations? To say they were men of their time yet ahead of their time has become something of a truism in discussing the great dead. Nor can they all be approached in the same way.

What Lincoln and Kennedy really represent is what in poetry is called a caesura. It indicates a sudden and marked shift in sensibility. Let me provide an illustration, from a poem that I'm sure most people here will recognize.

"Oh, Captain! My captain! Our fearful trip is done,
The ship has weather'd every rack, the prize we sought is won,
The port is near, the bells I hear, the people all exulting,
While follow eyes the steady keel, the vessel grim and daring.
But, oh, heart! heart! heart!
The bleeding drops of red . . ."

With "heart! heart! heart!" the whole feeling of Whitman's poem changes. It shifts in a way that makes it impossible to go back to the mood established in the first four lines. Something similar can happen in a nation's psychology.

With the presidencies first of Lincoln and later of Kennedy there came just the kind of fundamental change in temper that shivers a culture and makes way for new possibilities. In Lincoln's case, it was a shift to something deeper; in Kennedy's, to something broader.

Perhaps it was only a coincidence, but it is also possible that in some obscure, hard-to-see way there is a close connection between that and the fact that Lincoln and Kennedy could only find their truest selves in the presidency. It was only in the White House that they, and the country, realized what truly exceptional men they were.

This was unlike Grant's experience. For him the White House was but an extension of a previous life, which is also how it was for Eisenhower. Grant needed to command an army, not a nation, to find himself. And MacArthur . . . who knows? I suspect, though, that he lacked the ability to compromise that politics demands.

All four grasped early the secret of a successful life—courage (in both its parts, the physical and the moral) is the first requirement. Without it, no man can hope to be complete or demand courage of any kind from others. In the end, they became leaders who blazed so brightly they could ignite fires—or sparks at least—in other men.

All four brought to their careers a sense of superiority over nearly everyone around them. They knew their worth. That did not mean they were arrogant even if, in MacArthur's case, he appeared to be so. They did not see themselves as being better than other people. What they saw was that they had been blessed with abilities few others possessed. To be true to themselves they had to put those abilities to use.

All were extremely sensitive to press criticism. When Lincoln read newspaper attacks on himself or his administration he was likely to throw the paper on the floor and say, "I know more about it than they do!" Kennedy did the same. MacArthur was so thin-skinned a word could cut like a knife. Grant, too, picked up newspapers with a certain wariness. Yet like Lincoln, MacArthur, and Kennedy, there were always a few favored journalists who were part of his circle. The writer's temperament again. They could enjoy the company of newspapermen, while distrusting newspapers.

They were all fascinated by History. In order to make history, they studied how others had done it, much as a painter might study the Old Masters or a young composer might study Mozart or Bach.

The four of them were restless spirits yoked to ambitious natures. The only road they felt comfortable on went up. And wherever they found themselves, they had an eye on somewhere else.

Lincoln probably spent more time in the White House than in any dwelling other than his parents' log cabin. Grant was too restless to stay anywhere for long. It seems almost inevitable that given the chance to travel around the world he did so once he departed the White House: A two-and-a-half-year peregrination ended only because Julia told him she'd had enough. There was something symbolic and fitting to the fact that Grant died in a rented cottage.

MacArthur was an army brat. His earliest memory, he claimed, was the sound of bugles. It only inflames any adventurous spirit to move from place to place; never more so than when a move brings a major challenge, such as fighting a war or creating an army.

As for Kennedy, he was restless to a degree that borders on the manic. He could not sit still. Forever tugging at his socks, tapping his teeth, patting his head, fidgeting with a pencil or pen, Kennedy had more nervous energy than he knew what to do with. He loved speed and he loved being in motion. As someone who worked for him remarked, "Jack would take an airplane to cross the street if he could." First as a student, later as a politician, and finally as a president, Kennedy had various homes and moved regularly between them. Before he became president, he visited more than fifty countries. Convinced that he would die young, this obsession with movement became a form of defiance, for movement is life.

No one reaches the top of a profession or achieves immortal fame without a love of competition that goes beyond mere winning. For men such as these, competition is not a means to an end but a pillar holding up one's identity. Everyone faces the existential challenge of answering: Who am I? What am I? Why am I here? For Lincoln, Grant, MacArthur, and Kennedy, one way to find out was by testing themselves against other men. The aim was not the cheap satisfaction of victory over others, however, but a stronger, sharper sense of themselves and the world.

I am not talking here about winning. No one wins every time. Besides, only those who try to go too far find out how far they can go. What is truly instructive is what happened when they lost. For all of them, every defeat was turned into fuel that was fed into the fire of a self-consuming commitment to something greater than self.

As they projected themselves on the world, they were expected to make resounding statements, to be orators. And were they? Lincoln, beyond any doubt. The Gettysburg Address alone justifies his fame. And no one can think of MacArthur without remembering, "Old soldiers never die" and "There is no substitute for victory." MacArthur was probably the last of the great nineteenth-century orators.

Only toward the end did Kennedy turn into a great public speaker. Before he became president he was, by his own admission, inept at delivering a major speech. Yet always there hung over him the shadow of his hero, Winston Churchill, one of the greatest orators in modern history. So long as he fell short of the Churchillian standard, Kennedy felt he was failing in some fundamental sense. In his inaugural address he consciously aimed for something Churchillian, and hit the target. After that, he hardly ever failed as a public speaker.

Which brings us to Grant, whose best-known utterance—"Let Us Have Peace"—is mediocre. Grant was no orator, which was his loss, and ours. We respond to great speakers and great speeches, not to great non-speakers such as Grant, no matter how masterly their silence. To Grant, a speech was merely words. A man, a soldier especially, makes himself known through his deeds.

While reviewing the forces that drove them to become great, it is impossible to ignore the question of whether or not they met the most important of life's challenges. Did they find true love and happiness? Grant, without a doubt. His marriage to Julia was a romance from the day they met to the day he died, and even beyond it. MacArthur, yes, but the second time around. Kennedy, definitely no. Jackie was not the great love of his life. Love, if you aren't careful, will take over your life. He simply had too much to do and life, in his case, was literally too short. And Lincoln? He's a maybe.

The security of the state is the first business of government and all four had something to offer. Lincoln, for example, was the first Commander in Chief to know what comes almost naturally to successful generals but to few politicians. As a French general once expressed it, "All great battles are decided along the joins of the staff maps." Meaning, it's the things you don't see on the battlefield that determine its outcome—logistics, intelligence, organization, plans. Grant knew that, as did MacArthur, and Kennedy, like Lincoln, was quick to grasp it.

It is striking that all had trouble with the military high command: Kennedy and MacArthur did not trust the Joint Chiefs of Staff, if for different reasons and while fighting different wars. Lincoln had nothing but trouble, first with Scott, who provided Lincoln with the right strategy for fighting and winning the Civil War, something that Lincoln rejected. He had trouble getting George B. McClellan to fight and with getting Henry W. Halleck to be anything more than a clerk. Grant, too, found Halleck almost impossible to deal with, whether in the West or the East.

Even earlier, Grant had found the War Department impossible to deal with. First, when money belonging to his regiment was stolen in Mexico and he was expected to make good the loss. And again, when he was among the handful of officers, such as Lee and Bragg, to be recommended for a third brevet promotion in Mexico. The War Department lost the paperwork and the brevet never came through.

All four lived with threats and risks of assassination. Two died at an assassin's hand; MacArthur was the victim of a failed attempt in Tokyo. His response was to have the putative assassin brought to his office for tea and a chat. He saw their encounter as a chance to learn first hand what ordinary Japanese thought of him and of the occupation. After that, he had the man released. Thereafter there was probably no one in Japan who was a greater admirer of MacArthur than the would-be assassin.

When I was researching my biography of Grant, I came across dozens of death threats among the Grant papers at the Library of Congress: plenty of crudely drawn gallows and nooses; a few handguns; several large knives with drops of blood falling from them drawn in red ink. All of them relate, of course, to Grant's efforts to push Reconstruction. There were so many that for a time I was tempted to write a short article called "Death Threats in the Library of Congress."

Another striking discovery, for me at least, was that while all four held a strong belief in God, they shared a more tenuous belief in religion. These were all men who knew the limits of organizations.

All of them bore responsibilities that on occasion seemed too great for them to bear. Both Lincoln and Kennedy said several times they were ready to quit. Grant could hardly wait to leave the White House. And MacArthur deliberately provoked his own dismissal from command in Japan and Korea. Had he remained, he would have been engaged in prolonged negotiations with the Chinese and North Koreans for a ceasefire, a task he would have found demeaning. That responsibility went to his successor, Mark Clark, who later described it as the worst experience of his life.

The strain of high office left Lincoln depressed much of the time; living proof that a man can be guided by a strong sense of mission and still have to fight off despair. It would be too much to call Lincoln's life a passion play, but that's what his presidency was. It was a transfiguring ordeal, pain beyond words, suffering beyond comprehension. Yet there is, too, a Buddhist belief that says spiritual agony can lead toward an understanding of beauty. There is certainly a discovery of the world, and of the self, to be had, one deep enough to balance against suffering. Whatever nonphysical pain can teach, Lincoln learned it. And whatever physical pain can teach, Kennedy mastered.

As they strove to offer leadership to a nation in times when the need for strong leadership was almost palpable, these four reached across generations and inspired one another. Lincoln was encouraged by Grant's strength and intelligence, saying "He's the first general I've had" and "There's a man in it!" Grant was equally moved by Lincoln's greatness of spirit and mind. MacArthur had Lincoln's picture on his office wall. Wherever he went, from France to Manila, Lincoln was constantly in his field of vision. Kennedy, too, was inspired by Lincoln, not least by the Gettysburg Address, a speech that comes close to inspirational verse.

In the end, though, the fundamental reason they were able to motivate others was that they had learned to motivate themselves. And they could do this despite physical pain, depressed spirits, three a.m. doubts, crushing responsibilities, powerful enemies, and the moral burden of knowing that they were making life or death decisions on the basis of information that was biased, incomplete, or wrong.

Philip Larkin memorably wrote, "Man hands on misery to man / It deepens like a coastal shelf." True. The proof is in the newspaper nearly every day and played out on television screens nearly every night. Yet there is something else that's true—Man hands on courage to his fellow man. And it too rises like a coastal shelf.

The conclusion I reached as all these points of comparison came to mind was that maybe Frank was right after all. It doesn't really matter where you start from—once you start talking about leadership, all roads lead to Lincoln.

CHAPTER 12

Lincoln and His Admirals

Craig L. Symonds

IN 1952, T. HARRY WILLIAMS PUBLISHED A BOOK THAT HAS since become a classic in Civil War military history, and which remains in print to this day. It is titled *Lincoln and His Generals*, and in it Williams posits that Abraham Lincoln was, in his words, "a great natural strategist, a better one than any of his generals." Those generals, incidentally, do not come off particularly well in Williams's book. Though he has some good things to say about Ulysses S. Grant and William T. Sherman, Williams has mostly scorn for the likes of Ambrose Burnside, Joseph Hooker, William S. Rosecrans, and Don Carlos Buell, and he reserves his most vitriolic prose for George B. McClellan. In part, of course, this is because McClellan is such an easy target, but also it is because, of all Lincoln's generals, McClellan was the most dismissive of the president, whom he referred to in private letters as "the original gorilla."[1]

Williams admits that Lincoln had a steep learning curve as a military strategist, especially in the first few months of the war. Issues such as grand strategy and especially military tactics and doctrine were all new to him. And, inevitably, he made mistakes. But

Williams insists that Lincoln was a good judge of men, and that he had a profound commonsense grasp of strategy. In particular, Lincoln's persistent effort to get his generals to see the importance of attacking the enemy *army* rather than occupying strategic *locations* was a centerpiece of Lincoln's strategic vision, and he struggled for years before he finally found a field commander who embraced it. Likewise, Lincoln understood almost instinctively that because the Union had a four-to-one manpower advantage over its opponent, the logical thing to do was attack simultaneously across a broad front so that the outmanned Confederates could not concentrate their armies against each Union force one at a time. A simultaneous advance by all Union armies would force the Confederates to choose which advance to contest, and meanwhile the other Union armies could move forward largely unopposed, thus achieving what some strategists have labeled a "concentration in time." Or, as Lincoln later phrased it to Grant in a much-quoted, and typically Lincolnesque, aphorism: "Those not skinning can hold a leg."[2]

Williams's book went a long way to strengthen Lincoln's reputation among military historians. Williams's Lincoln was not merely a gentle, awkward man who could turn a fine phrase, who bore malice toward none, who freed the slaves and then sought to bind up the nation's wounds. He was all that, perhaps, but he was also a pragmatic and insightful grand strategist who understood, or at least who came to understand, the military art.

But what about naval warfare? Did Lincoln understand the admirals in the same way he understood the generals? Did he understand sea warfare as fully as he came to understand land warfare? As was the case in his early efforts to understand land warfare, Lincoln had a few early stumbles. The somewhat arcane world of naval warfare was both less pressing and marginally more complex than the problems of land warfare, and Lincoln's initial forays into the realm of Neptune were marked by confusion and even bungling. But in the end, Williams's conclusion might just as easily be applied to Lincoln as a naval strategist. While he had a steep learning curve, and committed a number of blunders at the outset, he was a great natural naval strategist, as good as, if not necessarily better than, his admirals, and he was the final architect of victory at sea as well as on land.

Two things made him successful in this endeavor: The first was his almost uncanny insight as a judge of men. As in his dealings with his generals, Lincoln offered his trust and support to his leading naval commanders until they proved themselves worthy or unworthy. Those he deemed worthy he supported against all opposition; those he deemed otherwise he did not hesitate to dismiss. While necessarily weighing the political aspect of every appointment, in the end he measured each naval commander by his contribution to the war effort.

The second factor in his success was his determination to learn. The same ambition that drove him to absorb as much information as he could in his life-long self-education was evident in his unending effort to learn the elements of grand strategy and naval operations. Aware of his own lack of specialized knowledge about sea warfare, he bowed to the experts early on. But he learned, and as he did so, he brought to this aspect of his role as Commander in Chief the same elements that made him a successful prosecutor of land warfare: a keen understanding of human nature, a pragmatic and flexible approach to problems of every kind, and a vision that allowed him to see past the immediate issue at hand through to the long term consequences.

This essay will examine Lincoln's relationship with two of his admirals: David Dixon Porter and Samuel Francis Du Pont. Such an examination yields a useful comparison. One man started off on as bad a footing with Lincoln as can be imagined, but then overcame his bad start to earn Lincoln's approbation and support. The other started out with every possible advantage, but disappointed Lincoln and eventually found himself dismissed.

Lincoln met Porter during the first days of his administration in rather unusual, and hardly auspicious, circumstances. At the time, the new president was attempting to find a way out of the Fort Sumter crisis. In Charleston Harbor, Major Robert Anderson's garrison was virtually under siege. In his inaugural address, Lincoln had pledged himself to "hold, occupy, and possess the property, and places belonging to the government," a clear reference to Fort Sumter (which Lincoln consistently spelled "Sumpter"). Lincoln could not begin his administration by backing down on such a pledge. But could Fort Sumter be held? More to the point, could Anderson be resupplied? Even if a fleet managed to fight its way into Charleston Harbor, Lincoln feared that it would cast the Government in the role of aggressor, would cause Virginia to secede, and lead to civil war. Holding the border states in the Union was still the centerpiece of Lincoln's policy in these critical weeks.[3]

Nevertheless, in the last week of March, Lincoln decided he must act. His secretary of the navy, Gideon Welles, asserted that the navy *could* mount a relief expedition to resupply and reinforce Anderson, and Lincoln thereupon ordered him to prepare one, but told him as well to make no "binding engagements." He wanted to keep his options open.[4]

Not everyone in the Lincoln administration thought an expedition to Sumter was a good idea. Secretary of State William H. Seward, in particular, believed that Sumter's location in the middle of Charleston Harbor made any resupply attempt impossible. The fort, he was convinced, would have to be given up. He hoped to mute the appearance of irresolution that such a decision would encourage by dispatching a naval expedition off the coast of Florida to hold Fort Pickens.

Indeed, Seward seemed to be full of ideas that week. On April 1, he delivered to Lincoln a curious document entitled "Some thoughts for the President's consideration." In it, he suggested that so long as Fort Sumter was the focus of public attention, it would be impossible to divert the national question from one of slavery versus non-slavery to one of union versus non-union. He even suggested conjuring up a foreign crisis to reunify the nation. Most astonishing of all, perhaps, was his off-hand suggestion that Lincoln "devolve" the responsibility for managing the crisis onto some member of his cabinet—meaning, of course, himself.[5]

While Lincoln was still digesting this missive, Seward arrived with a bundle of orders concerning naval matters. Among other things, they instructed U.S. Navy ship captains to concentrate the Home Fleet in the Gulf of Mexico off Vera Cruz. That should have sounded a warning bell, but convinced by Seward's assurances that these were routine matters, Lincoln signed the whole batch of papers, unaware that in doing so he had effectively scuttled the Fort Sumter expedition. When Welles received copies of the signed documents, he dashed to the White House and burst in on the president. Lincoln looked up to see the bewhiskered navy secretary bearing down on him under a full head of steam with a sheaf of papers clutched in his hand and an expression so confrontational that Lincoln impulsively blurted out: "What have I done wrong?" Welles showed him, and Lincoln immediately countermanded Seward's order.

But Seward wasn't yet ready to give up. His next gambit was a kind of appeal to authority. He sent for Colonel Montgomery C. Meigs, the engineering officer who was supervising the construction of the capitol dome, and forty-eight-year old navy Lieutenant David D. Porter. Porter was a member of a renowned navy family. The son of David Porter, a hero of the War of 1812, he was also the brother of William Porter, who was a navy commander, and foster brother of David Glasgow Farragut. Despite this lineage, Porter had considered leaving the navy until the outbreak of war. His presence in Washington that spring was fateful, for it led to his entanglement in Seward's scheme.[7]

Seward queried Meigs and Porter about the practicality of a relief expedition for Fort Pickens. They both agreed that such an

expedition was entirely feasible, and Porter outlined the steps that
he thought would be necessary to execute it. Seward then jumped
up from his couch and ordered both men to accompany him to the
White House. At the executive mansion, Lincoln listened respectfully as Meigs and Porter outlined an impromptu plan to ensure the
security of Fort Pickens. Lacking military or naval expertise himself, Lincoln was eager to hear from the experts. Porter told him
that the security of Fort Pickens could be assured by an expedition
made up of only one armed steamer carrying six companies of infantry. And because of the geography of the site, such an expedition
was unlikely to provoke a confrontation with local authority. Porter
suggested that the U.S.S. *Powhatan*, then at the Brooklyn Navy
Yard, might be the most appropriate vessel for such a mission.[8]

Lincoln was certainly aware that Seward was running his own
game here. He must have wondered if this visit was not, in fact,
part of a ploy by Seward to sabotage the Fort Sumter expedition in
exchange for one to salvage Fort Pickens. He therefore consulted
the list of ships that General Scott had put together detailing the
vessels that would take part in the planned Sumter expedition. The
Powhatan was not among them. Even so, he did not want to get
into more trouble with Welles. "What will Uncle Gideon say?" the
president asked. Seward waved off that detail. "I will make it all
right with Mr. Welles," Seward replied.[9]

Lincoln thereupon gave his consent to organize an expedition to
Fort Pickens, and Meigs and Porter went into the next room to
write out orders. Porter wrote his own orders, giving himself command of the *Powhatan*, and another authorizing the ship to be fitted
out and prepared for undisclosed sea duty. Presumably for reasons
of security, or perhaps for more sinister reasons, those orders also
cautioned the commandant of the New York Navy Yard, Andrew H.
Foote, that "under no circumstances" was he to "communicate to
the Navy Department the fact that she is fitting out."[10]

In fact, of course, the *Powhatan* was one of the ships that Welles
had designated for the Sumter expedition, and Foote had already

received orders from Welles to hold the ship in readiness for that expedition. Moreover, despite his assurances to Lincoln, Seward did not "make it all right with Mr. Welles," who remained ignorant of the Seward-Meigs-Porter scheme to use the *Powhatan* to relieve Fort Pickens. The State and Navy Departments were working at cross purposes.[11]

When Porter showed up on board the *Powhatan* with his orders signed by Lincoln, Foote was skeptical. He wanted to confirm the orders with Welles, but the orders Porter carried explicitly forbade him from doing so. He did all that he thought he could do under such curious circumstances. He wrote to Welles saying that he had received orders "to have certain preparations made" and that he was proceeding as ordered. Welles, of course, assumed this was a reference to the Sumter expedition and told him to go ahead.[12]

This scenario reveals just how ad hoc, even haphazard, Lincoln's naval policy making was in the early days of his administration. Not until April 5 did all the parties involved in this convoluted drama begin to read off the same script. Seward learned that Welles had ordered the *Powhatan* to prepare for an expedition to Sumter, and suspecting that "Uncle Gideon" was trying to steal the ship away for his own expedition, he stormed over to the navy secretary's home, woke him up from a sound sleep, and demanded to know why he was meddling in Porter's command of the *Powhatan*.

Surely there is some mistake, Welles told him. Porter had no command, and the *Powhatan* had been detailed to be the flagship of an expedition to relieve Fort Sumter. Each man claimed a prior right to the use of the ship. Only one person could break the tie, and together the two cabinet secretaries drove over to the White House to wake up Lincoln.

Lincoln wasn't asleep. He heard both sides, and he agreed at once with Welles that Sumter was the more important objective. He told both men that he had approved of the *Powhatan* for the Pickens expedition only because it was not listed on the roster of ships to go to Sumter. Now that he knew better, he told Seward to relieve Porter from his command and return the *Powhatan* to Welles's control. His plot undone, Seward dutifully wrote the order. That night in his diary, Welles dryly observed that "Mr. Seward remarked to me that, old as he was, he had learned a lesson from this affair, and that was, he had better attend to his own business and confine his labors to his own Department. To this I cordially assented."[13]

Porter's orders were cancelled. But as it happened, the order came too late. At about 2:30 in the afternoon on April 6, even as Lincoln, Seward, and Welles talked in the White House, the *Powhatan* put to sea bound for Fort Pickens. A few hours later, Seward's recall order arrived at the Brooklyn Navy Yard. Foote sent a fast tug in pursuit of the *Powhatan* to recall her. Porter was already well out to sea when the dispatch vessel overhauled him and its skipper handed him a terse telegram from Seward ordering him to give up the *Powhatan*.

Porter now had to do some swift thinking. If he returned to port, Colonel Meigs's six companies of infantry, already en route, would arrive at Fort Pickens without their naval support. Moreover, their artillery was stowed below deck on board the *Powhatan*. Besides, Porter told himself, he had orders in his pocket (orders which he had written himself) that were signed by Lincoln, and this recall order came from Seward. Seward's orders were more recent to be sure, but did orders from the secretary of state supersede orders signed by the president? Porter decided to proceed. He penned a quick note to Seward, the complete text of which was: "I received my orders from the President and shall proceed and execute them." Then he gave orders to the engine room to go ahead full and he sped away as fast as possible in order to avoid a second recall.[14]

The *Powhatan*'s arrival at Fort Pickens helped ensure that it remained in Union hands. Nevertheless, Porter had taken much upon himself: He was swimming with the big fish now, making decisions that were well above his pay grade. Welles suspected him of disloyalty; Foote told him, "You ought to have been tried and shot." It is hard to imagine a naval officer getting off to a worse start with his commander in chief.[15]

Lincoln was remarkably ill served by his cabinet in this crisis, and he had every reason to blame the misunderstandings and confusion on others. Instead, he characteristically took all the blame upon himself. He disliked commanders who found fault with others to justify their own errors, and never did so himself. Welles noted in his diary that "Lincoln never shunned any responsibility and often declared that he, and not his Cabinet, was in fault for errors imputed to them, when I sometimes thought otherwise."[16]

Even so, Lincoln had to have harbored a certain amount of skepticism, if not outright distrust, of Porter who had been Seward's apparent collaborator and who, in the end, had defied orders to charge off on a mission of his own. The president had to wonder if Porter was a man who could be trusted.

If Lincoln's initial dealings with Porter were discouraging, his initial contacts with Captain Du Pont seemed to hold great promise. Du Pont was a decade older than Porter, and he was a full captain— the highest rank then available to naval officers. There were naval officers who were senior to Du Pont, but most of them, like the septuagenarian William Shubrick, were so senior that it seemed problematic they could undertake an active role in the war. Of course Shubrick had the added disadvantage of being a native of South Carolina. Du Pont was himself a scion of the slave state of Delaware, but his loyalty, like that of Tennessee-born Farragut, was not in question.[17]

When, despite Seward's efforts, the Fort Sumter crisis ended with the exchange of gunfire that marked the onset of war, it was to Du Pont that Lincoln turned for professional naval advice, just as he turned to Winfield Scott for professional military advice. Of first consideration was the implementation of the naval blockade that Lincoln declared on April 19, only a week after Fort Sumter. In making this declaration, Lincoln created some legal and diplomatic problems for himself.

First of all, a blockade declaration implied a de facto recognition of the belligerent status of the Confederate nation. Lincoln (and Welles) tried to get around this by asserting that the purpose of the declaration was merely to close the ports. Domestic unrest, so the argument went, made the collection of duties in certain ports difficult, so that until the unrest was overcome, the ports would be temporarily closed to trade. But such a legal construction did not authorize the capture of ships at sea that attempted to run the blockade so that in the end, Lincoln had to settle for the name, as well as the fact, of blockade.[18]

A second problem was that international agreements had recently held that so-called "paper blockades" were nonbinding. If Lincoln expected other nations to respect his blockade declaration, the United States would have to station squadrons off the entrance of every Southern port. And that was a gargantuan task. The U.S. Navy in 1861 consisted of some eighty or so ships, only forty-two of them in commission; and the Southern coastline was 3,500 miles long and pierced by 189 ports and navigable inlets. Transforming the blockade declaration into a reality would be an enormous administrative task. To oversee this task, Lincoln needed a naval expert. He picked Du Pont.

As head of the so-called "Strategy Board," Du Pont recommended the establishment of four blockade squadrons: the North and South Atlantic Squadrons, and the East and West Gulf Squadrons. Within each zone, a naval base would be wrested from the enemy to serve as a headquarters and supply depot for the blockading squadrons.

Pleased with his work on the Strategy Board, Lincoln authorized Welles to offer Du Pont command of the entire Atlantic Fleet. Du Pont declined that honor, but he did accept command of the most important of the four blockading squadrons: the South Atlantic

Squadron, and in that capacity he won the first important naval victory of the war when he captured Port Royal Sound in November 1861, where he established the squadron headquarters in conformance with his overall strategic plan for the blockade.

By 1862, Du Pont, more than Farragut, and certainly more than Porter, was the navy's fair-haired boy. His squadron increased dramatically in size from a dozen warships to several score. With large squadrons off Savannah, Georgetown, and most important of all, Charleston, his vessels conducted a ceaseless vigil over the rebel shore.

It was not enough. At least it was not enough as far as Secretary Welles was concerned. By this time, Welles had assimilated two important pieces of information about naval operations against the enemy shore: First, he noted that Du Pont's wooden ships had successfully battered the Confederate forts guarding Port Royal into surrender; and second, he was positively giddy about the evident superiority of ironclads over wooden warships demonstrated in Hampton Roads in March when the U.S.S. *Monitor* faced down the Confederate *Virginia* (or *Merrimack*), a circumstance which suggested that ironclads were even more effective than wooden warships. He approved a gigantic building program that eventually produced some fifty-two monitors. Surely, Welles reasoned, when Du Pont had some ironclads available, he could steam into Charleston Harbor—that citadel of the rebellion—smash the forts there into submission, and capture the city. Moreover, it was important from Welles's point of view that Du Pont do so without involving the army. He no doubt imagined the headlines that would result from a navy-only seizure of the cradle of the rebellion. In the midsummer of 1862, Welles's assistant secretary, Gustavus Fox, wrote Du Pont that he had two goals: "first, to beat our southern friends; second, to beat the Army."[19]

Du Pont was skeptical. Monitors, he knew, were strong defensive weapons: they could resist repeated pounding from heavy caliber guns; but since each monitor carried only two guns, they had little offensive power. Welles sent Du Pont two monitors, then four, then six, but Du Pont asserted that this was not enough. Eventually he got a total of eight, but even eight monitors carried only sixteen guns, while the forts ringing Charleston Harbor mounted five times as many. Loyal subordinate that he was, Du Pont had no option but to do his best, but he was not hopeful. In phrasing eerily reminiscent of the kind of thing that McClellan wrote to his wife before the peninsular campaign, Du Pont wrote his own wife that "It seems to be my fate [to] have the eyes of the nation and the government upon me and expectant, when the national heart is sore and impatient for a victory." Du Pont informed his wife that "Old Welles said the attack must be made whether successful or not."[20]

On April 7, 1863, Du Pont led his squadron into Charleston Harbor as ordered. And, as he had predicted, he got clobbered. In the two hours that Du Pont's ironclad fleet engaged the forts in Charleston Harbor, the eight monitors got off a total of 159 shots, fifty-five of which struck their target. On the other hand, each of the monitors was pounded by a hail of heavy shot from the forts: The *Patapsco* was hit forty-seven times; the *Nantucket* fifty-one times; and the *Weehawken* fifty-three times. Worst hit of all was the *Keokuk*, a new-design ironclad with two non-revolving turrets. It was hit ninety times and began taking on water at an alarming rate. The next day it turned turtle and sank. Du Pont called off the attack.[21]

When he did so, he had every intention of renewing the assault the next day. But after consulting with his ship captains and learning the extent of the damage they had suffered, Du Pont decided to call off a second attack. Tactically he was entirely correct; politically he was committing suicide. Welles had convinced himself that monitors were the magic bullet of the naval war—that wherever they went, the enemy would be helpless. He could not credit any reason beyond a lack of will that would justify Du Pont's decision.

Lincoln, too, was disappointed. He had hoped that even if Du Pont failed to capture Fort Sumter, he would at least be able to run past it and take up a position in the inner harbor, thus closing the port to trade. Such an expectation was unrealistic, for, as Du Pont put it, correctly, "there is no running by" the Charleston Forts, "the harbor is a bog or a cul de sac." But Lincoln had a second reason for urging Du Pont to stay close. He was concerned that without a credible threat from Du Pont's ironclads, P. G. T. Beauregard might be tempted to dispatch reinforcements from Charleston to Vicksburg where Grant's campaign was just getting under way. When Lincoln heard that Du Pont had been repulsed, he immediately wired the Admiral instructions: "Hold your position inside the bar near Charleston, or, if you have left it, return to it, and hold it until further orders." He did not order Du Pont to renew the attack; he was willing to allow his admiral discretion in that regard. But he wanted him to stay close and keep Beauregard guessing.[22]

A few days later, Lincoln followed up his telegram with a letter in which he assured Du Pont that "no censure" toward him was intended, but he repeated the earnest hope that "the demonstration [be] kept up for a time, for a collateral and very important object." He repeated the order not to leave the inner harbor "till further orders from here." Too late. Du Pont had already pulled his squadron back from Charleston Harbor to Port Royal and had no intention of returning. When John Hay delivered this second letter to Du Pont, he noted that the admiral was "in very low spirits about it." Those low spirits were evident in the letter that Du Pont wrote to Welles: "I am, however, painfully struck by the tenor and tone of the President's order which seems to imply a censure." Privately he was angered by the implied rebuke. To his wife he wrote: "I cannot trust myself even to you to comment."[23]

It therefore came as no surprise when Du Pont was relieved of his command. What triggered his fall from grace, however, was not simply that he had failed to win, or even that he was unwilling to make a second attempt. A few weeks after the failed attack on Charleston, Du Pont was angered when he read a critical report of his assault in a Northern newspaper; he demanded that Welles allow him to publish his own official report to counter the public criticism. Welles refused his request, mainly because he did not want the weakness of the monitors made public. Du Pont replied defensively, argumentatively, and confrontationally.[24]

By this time, Lincoln was beginning to perceive in Du Pont characteristics that he had come to associate with his more difficult generals—and in particular, McClellan. Here was a man of undisputed administrative talents, a man who had orchestrated the entire blockade program, but who constantly called for reinforcements, and who had an apparent unwillingness to come to grips with the enemy. Already Du Pont's repeated requests for more monitors had provoked Lincoln to tell a joke in the cabinet about the monkey who kept asking for a longer and longer tail. Privately, he told Welles that Du Pont's complaints and excuses reminded him of McClellan. A century later the historian Clarence Macartney would assert boldly that "Du Pont was the McClellan of the Navy." If the analogy was not exactly perfect, it was close enough to make Lincoln uncomfortable.[25]

By June, Lincoln was ready to accede to Welles's suggestion that Du Pont should be dismissed, and the Delaware aristocrat was relieved from his duties, and replaced by John A. Dahlgren, an ordnance specialist whose experiments with naval guns had fascinated Lincoln, and who had become a kind of unofficial naval aide to the president.

Du Pont's crime was not that he had failed to capture Charleston. Lincoln did not demand that every operation be an unqualified success; he forgave Burnside for Fredericksburg and Grant for Cold Harbor. The president's disappointment stemmed from two things. First, he was influenced by Welles, who was convinced that Du Pont had never given the operation against Charleston a fair try. Welles simply could not imagine why the eight monitors could not fight their way *past* Sumter into the inner harbor; when reality did not live up to his vision, he held Du Pont accountable. Second, and perhaps more to the point, Lincoln was disappointed with Du Pont because the admiral seemed to be more interested in justifying the correctness of his decisions than he did in prosecuting the war. As Welles put it in his diary, Du Pont "thinks of himself more than of the country and the service." Such an attitude was all too familiar. Du Pont's aristocratic demeanor and bristly response to criticism also undermined his cause. In the end, it was less for his failure on April 7 than for his apparent contrariness that Lincoln agreed to let Welles replace him.[26]

Thus by the spring of 1863, Lincoln had concluded that Du Pont, of whom so much had been expected, was little more than a nautical version of McClellan, and like little Mac, Du Pont found himself outside looking in.

If Du Pont's star was on the descent, Porter's was now very definitely on the rise. On April 7, the very day that Du Pont steamed into Charleston Harbor to initiate his ill-fated attack, Porter wrote to Secretary Welles from his cabin on board the river ironclad *Black Hawk* to explain his plans for attacking the Confederate citadel of Vicksburg. "I am preparing to pass the batteries of Vicksburg with most of the fleet," he wrote. "General Grant is marching his army below and we are going to endeavor to turn Vicksburg." Almost exactly two years after Porter had shanghaied the *Powhatan* to Fort Pickens, thus upsetting Lincoln's plan for a relief expedition to Fort Sumter, Porter was a Rear Admiral in command of the most important squadron, save perhaps Du Pont's, in the U.S. Navy.[27]

The transformation had come about slowly. Following the *Powhatan* imbroglio, Porter had spent a lengthy tenure as the commander of Farragut's mortar flotilla. He had been present during his foster brother's run past Forts Jackson and St. Philip below New Orleans, and in the run upriver to Vicksburg. By this time—the late summer of 1862—Lincoln was having a great deal of trouble finding a satisfactory commander for the Mississippi River Squadron, nearly as much trouble as he did finding a satisfactory commander of the Army of the Potomac. Foote (who had once suggested to Porter that he should be shot) had performed well enough, cooperating with Grant in the capture of Forts Henry and Donelson in February and with Pope in the seizure of Island Number 10 in April. But Foote had been forced to retire due to ill health. To replace him, Lincoln wanted a man who was both a fighter by instinct, and who was inclined to cooperate with the army in joint operations.

The seizure of the Mississippi River was a key element in Lincoln's strategic plan. Moreover, with the same instinct that compelled him to lecture his generals about targeting the enemy army rather than strategic places, he understood that a riverine campaign would necessarily require a cooperative venture by the army and the navy. But relations on that front had always been fraught with difficulty. One of the problems was Secretary Welles's ongoing determination to engineer navy victories without the cooperation of the army, which he considered a rival.

Moreover, even if the will to cooperate had been present, there was no protocol in place for determining command and control of joint operations. Heretofore, navy captains had been responsible for maneuvering their ships, while army generals had full control of their troops ashore. When cooperation had been necessary, such as in the landing at Vera Cruz in the Mexican War, the commanders would consult. But voluntary consultation was a thin reed on which to hang command responsibility.

This had become evident when Farragut seized New Orleans in April of 1862. Although the Union warships successfully ran past the forts, brushing aside the small Confederate flotilla, and steamed upriver to New Orleans itself, Farragut could not take physical possession of the city without a landing force. While he fumed helplessly, the Confederates continued to run trains out of the city, evacuating important military equipment. Almost as bad, when Far-ragut and Porter subsequently moved upriver to Vicksburg, it be-came evident that although the Union navy could command the river, it could do little against that city atop the bluffs.[28]

Lincoln was mulling over the problem of Vicksburg when he received a visit from Porter in August 1862. Welles, it seems, had just given Porter a set of orders casting him into administrative limbo as the aide to an aged desk-bound commodore in St. Louis. Porter had come to the White House to appeal for active service. Lincoln had not seen the heavily-bearded naval officer since the *Powhatan* incident; if he harbored any latent suspicions about Por-ter's role in that episode, he did not let it show. Instead, aware of Porter's role in recent operations on the Mississippi, and ever eager to learn more about operations in distant theaters, Lincoln took the opportunity to grill Porter about Vicksburg: Why exactly was it so difficult a place to capture?

Porter dutifully described the particular geographic characteris-tics of the city that made it so daunting. In doing so, he emphasized the importance of army-navy cooperation. Earlier, Porter had writ-ten that "It is to be regretted that a combined attack of army and navy had not been made" at Vicksburg. Commonsensically, he noted that "Ships and mortar vessels can keep full possession of the river, . . . but they can not crawl up hills 300 feet high."[29]

After this conversation, Lincoln had a much clearer notion of what was likely to be needed at Vicksburg, and he also had a clearer sense of Porter's strengths as a commander. Soon after Porter left, the president sent for Gustavus Fox to talk to him about it. Fox subsequently championed Porter's cause, and within a few weeks, Porter had new orders: He was astonished to find himself promoted from navy commander to acting rear admiral in a single step, skip-ping over the rank of captain altogether. Moreover, he was jumped over the heads of every captain in the navy and assigned to the command of the Mississippi River Squadron.[30]

Almost certainly Porter's remarkable rise to prominence was due in part to Lincoln's intervention. Porter certainly believed that to be the case. And it was a crucial decision, for it is hard to imagine the success of Grant's 1863 campaign against Vicksburg without the key element of Porter's willingness to run past the Vicksburg batteries in support of Grant's operations. As much as anyone, it is due to Lincoln that the winning team of Grant and Porter had the opportunity to turn the tide in the Western theater.[31]

On April 16, nine days after Du Pont's failed attack on Charleston, Porter ran his flotilla past the Vicksburg batteries, and then subsequently transported Grant's army across the river. He then cooperated with Grant in the siege of the city. It fell on July 4. Five months later, in December of 1863, Lincoln nominated Porter for promotion to the permanent rank of Rear Admiral to date from July 4.[32]

If the president decided that Du Pont was a nautical McClellan, he also overcame his initial skepticism about Porter to conclude that his nautical Sherman was indeed Porter.

Lincoln's relationship with these two officers, Porter and Du Pont, reveals several important characteristics about Lincoln's management of men, and ultimately his management of war. First, he was willing—even eager—to solicit the advice of experts. He listened carefully to Du Pont's plan for the blockade of the Southern coast, and even after others had raised questions about Porter's loyalty, he listened just as carefully to that officer's assessment of the situation at Vicksburg. Knowing he was not an expert, Lincoln was conscientious in soliciting the views of those who were. He let them play the role of teacher while he adopted that of the student. In the end, of course, he graduated with honors.

Second, Lincoln could forgive errors. If he ever suspected that Porter had behaved badly in steaming off to Fort Pickens with the *Powhatan*, he never articulated his suspicions. Porter was able to overcome his poor start, and in the end it was partly because of Lincoln that Porter was promoted to admiral, in which capacity he played a key role in opening the Mississippi and sundering the Confederacy in half. It is noteworthy, however, that Lincoln much preferred men who made mistakes of commission rather than errors of omission. Porter went charging off in the *Powhatan* to accomplish a purpose—the salvation of Fort Pickens; by contrast, Du Pont's petulant obstreperousness contributed nothing to the prosecution of the war. If you are going to make a mistake, Lincoln's actions seemed to imply, make them in trying to accomplish something, not in iterating the obstacles and difficulties that are in the way.

Third, Lincoln did not like to intervene in the details of military or naval operations. He was no micromanager. He did not tell Porter or Du Pont what to do, only what he hoped they would accomplish. He defined the *objective* and allowed his subordinates to define the *means* they would employ to achieve it. Men like Porter and Farragut, or, for that matter, men like Grant and Sherman, grasped the essence of Lincoln's directions, and applied their professional expertise toward the accomplishment of those goals, and they did so without whining, or complaining, or asking constantly for reinforcement.

In the end, Lincoln was successful because he was able to manage the people who eventually got the job done. Seward, Welles, Fox, Du Pont, and Porter hardly represented a harmonious team. Under a different commander in chief they might have spent all their time (instead of only part of their time) tugging in opposite directions. Instead, Lincoln ensured that each man contributed what he could toward a goal that was bigger than any of them. And that, in the end, is the essence of a successful strategy.

CHAPTER 13

After Emancipation:
Abraham Lincoln's Black Dream

Michael Vorenberg

MORE THAN 140 YEARS AGO AT GETTYSBURG, ABRAHAM LIN-coln helped bury thousands of soldiers—and the Constitution as it was. By invoking the framers of the Declaration of Independence rather than the framers of the Constitution at his Gettysburg Address, and by declaring a "New Birth of Freedom," Lincoln, in a move so well described by Garry Wills almost a decade ago, told the nation that the Constitution that had sanctioned slavery could no longer guide a nation that was fighting for freedom. Or, as Lincoln put it so eloquently in his December 1862 message to Congress, "the dogmas of the quiet past are inadequate to the stormy present."

Yet the Gettysburg Address, for all of its poetry, was incomplete. Its terms were vague; not one of the three words so often used by Lincoln—Union, Constitution, and Slavery—were to be found in the speech. Nor was there any direct call for a specific measure to give legal, constitutional force to the "new birth of freedom" that he proclaimed. Worse, Lincoln himself conceded that the Emancipation Proclamation itself, signed on January 1, 1863, could be outlawed by the Supreme Court or Congress, or be rescinded by his successor if he were defeated for reelection, and thus have no effect at all once the war was over. Lincoln's omission during the Gettysburg Address of a specific measure to guarantee freedom makes sense—he stayed away from specifics during the speech—but one wonders if Lincoln had in mind the idea of amending the Constitution to abolish slavery, a proposal that was gaining popularity at the moment that he delivered the speech. If such a measure was on Lincoln's mind, he kept shut-mouthed about such desires, and for a long time. Not until June 1864, seven months after the amendment had been introduced in Congress, eight months after the Gettysburg Address, and eighteen months after the Emancipation Proclamation, did Lincoln finally endorse the antislavery amendment in public. Indeed, there is no evidence that he supported the measure even in private during this time. Of course later, after he had been renominated and reelected, Lincoln threw his full weight behind the amendment, and helped to secure congressional passage of the resolution, sending the amendment to the states for ratification. But why had he maintained such silence early on?

That question is part of a larger constellation of criticisms of Lincoln all of which revolve around the notion of him as a reluctant emancipator. Most of this criticism focuses on the pre–Emancipation Proclamation Lincoln and all but ignores Lincoln's handling of black freedom after the Proclamation. Because of this focus on the early presidential years, historians, especially those who hold to the notion of Lincoln as reluctant emancipator, tend to neglect the evolution of Lincoln's views on race and slavery during the *whole* period that he resided in the White House.

This essay takes up the subject of what Lincoln learned and did not learn during the war. First, it examines the subject of Lincoln's effort to colonize African-Americans outside the United States, a subject that I have written about before, though my views have since changed. Then the essay turns to the large subject of Lincoln's attitudes toward the intellectual capacities of African-Americans. Finally, and in a move that I admit is anachronistic, the essay poses the question: How might Lincoln's attitudes toward African-Americans in the post-Proclamation period inform our understanding of the wisdom, necessity, and possible process of some modern system of restitution for the crime of American slavery?[1]

First—colonization. Always dominating the writing on Lincoln and colonization is the question: "When, if ever, did Lincoln give up the idea of colonizing African-Americans abroad?" The last documented time that we hear Lincoln talking of colonization is to General Benjamin Butler in the spring of 1865. As most historians know, Professor Mark E. Neely showed that Butler's account of this meeting was a fabrication, thus getting Lincoln off the hook. Then there is the record of John Hay, who, in his diary at July 1, 1864, wrote that Lincoln had finally "sloughed off" that idea of colonization. Many had read that passage as evidence that Lincoln held onto colonization until *at least* July 1, 1864. But Hay's entry allows for the possibility that the secretary believed that Lincoln had given up the idea well *before* July 1, 1864, and this is more likely what Hay did believe. Hay simply mentioned Lincoln's view of colonization on this particular date because a bill rescinding funds for colonization had just crossed his desk. So it is possible to argue, as I did argue, that Lincoln gave up on colonization as soon as he had signed the Emancipation Proclamation and that he had held onto the notion only to make emancipation more palatable to himself and to conservatives in the North and upper South. Moreover, he could not really consider colonization practicable or politically acceptable once African-Americans had served with such success in battle in early and mid-1863. Thus it makes sense that he failed to support the colonization mission to Île à Vache after it had left in the spring of 1863.

On deeper reflection, however, it seems that these efforts to guess at what Lincoln thought and when he thought it are not very valuable. Yes, Lincoln could not have spoken to Butler on the day that Butler said. Yes, he probably did not say to Hay on July 1, 1864: "Today, and only today, I have given up on colonization." With detective work and a positivist method that assumes hard digging can reveal all the answers that matter, we historians thus make advances. But maybe what we are really doing is providing distractions. After all, isn't it possible that Butler and Lincoln did have a conversation some time in late 1864 or early 1865, that Butler remembered the date incorrectly, that Butler told Lincoln his various schemes for using African soldiers abroad, and Lincoln nodded approvingly, perhaps because he liked the idea, or more likely because he wanted to end the conversation with a general whom he did not much like.

Regardless of if and when Lincoln spoke to Butler toward the end of the Civil War, the fact remains that Lincoln never did think that immediate abolition was preferable to gradual abolition. Only the circumstances of war and politics forced him toward immediate abolition. Over and over during the period after he signed the Proclamation, Lincoln expressed his concern that the former slaves would become "a laboring, landless, and homeless class" if they were immediately emancipated. According to Alexander Stephens, the vice president of the Confederacy, Lincoln told Stephens at Hampton Roads that if he were in the Georgian's place, he would persuade the governor of his state to assemble the legislature and instruct the newly elected body to recall the state's troops, elect members to Congress, and ratify the antislavery amendment "*prospectively, so as to take effect—say in five years.*"[2] At least part of Stephens's story is dubious. Surely Lincoln would have doubted the constitutionality of prospective ratification. Also, he knew that no program of gradual emancipation could exist in the face of a constitutional amendment declaring that "neither slavery nor involuntary servitude . . . shall exist." Yet the essence of Stephens's account—

that Lincoln regretted that abolition was to occur immediately rather than gradually—is entirely believable. He supposedly told an Alabama man a few days before his death that if it were up to him, he might allow "gradual emancipation, say running through twenty years," to take place, but the matter was out of his hands because of the constitutional amendment "now before the people."[3] Perhaps at Hampton Roads, Lincoln made a similar statement to Stephens, who twisted it to make Lincoln sound as if he believed gradual emancipation and the abolition amendment were compatible—something Lincoln surely could not have believed.

In the same way, it is possible that Lincoln *privately* believed that the best future for most African-Americans would be one in which they lived separately, outside of the country, even though, as president, he knew that he had to work toward a different, biracial future. When he met with his Cabinet in February 1865, he again made his plea for funds to pay compensation to loyal slave-owners for the loss of their freed slaves, a plea that was summarily rejected. But tellingly, he did not make a plea for colonization, even though, in the past, colonization and compensation had always been joined in his policies. Clearly, by at least early 1865, he knew that colonization was a hopeless, unworkable, and unpopular cause, but his desire for a compensation program for former slave-owners suggests that he had not yet relinquished his preference for gradual emancipation.

Consider the following wildly improbable scenario. Imagine that on the evening before that Cabinet meeting of February 1865, a Martian came to Lincoln at the White House and told him the following: that there were unlimited funds to colonize African-Americans abroad, that a group of well-meaning Martians had created a large, new continent in the central Atlantic filled with rich land, easily reachable, with many ports, navigable rivers and canals, roadways, and railroads. The Martians would present this land to the

United States on the condition that it would be only for people of African descent, and they would pay the way for any African-American who wanted to go. As part of the deal, they would even reunite African-American families separated under slavery and by the war and do their best to transplant them as groups to the new land. What would Lincoln have said? It would be a remarkable defender of Lincoln who believes that Lincoln would have told the Martian to take his business elsewhere, that he believed the country would be better if the races were to associate with each other, to mix and mingle.

Of course, this is an exercise in hypothetical history, perhaps the worst sort of such exercise, for it calls for an outside actor so extraordinary as to be extraterrestrial. But the Martian question has the advantage of exposing in a flash the textures of Lincoln's practical views on race. Yes, Lincoln would have said yes to the Martian, but unlike the speculative historian, he would never have wasted his time on such hypotheticals. He was ever immersed in practical matters and never took the luxury of fantasizing about situations beyond the real or at best the possible. The Martian question may be interesting—but it is entirely our question; it could never have been Lincoln's. His vision of the future of African-Americans was shaped and constrained by his acceptance of the fact that whites and blacks would have to find a way to live together in the country. Perhaps he did dream of a White America, but he kept the dream *as* a dream, never working to implement it as policy to the detriment of some higher cause such as Union. And that point must preface any discussion of Lincoln's dream, white or otherwise. He dreamt, yes; he even spoke of his dreams in rare moments. But when he acted as president, he left the dreams behind.

So, what then, was Lincoln's waking dream? That is, what realistic vision of the future for African-Americans did he have in mind in the months after the Emancipation Proclamation? Was he the White Supremacist or the Racial Egalitarian? For a moment, let us put all labels that strictly involve race aside and simply call Lincoln, instead, a Whig. The notion of Lincoln as a Whig in the White House is not a new one: more than forty years ago, David Herbert Donald used the Whig model to characterize Lincoln's style of presidential leadership. Since the time of Donald's essay, the Whig mentality has been the subject of much excellent study, especially in the work of Daniel Walker Howe. The Whig mentality, aside from governing Lincoln's administrative behavior, as Donald described, also influenced his social sensibilities as president, including his attitudes toward race.[4]

Let us put aside the debate about whether Lincoln saw himself more as a Whig or a Republican, or whether he hoped the Whig party would some day be reborn. Instead, let us acknowledge that he had been a Whig for almost thirty years before joining the Republican party, and he undoubtedly still identified with Whig ideology, even if he no longer identified with the defunct party.

First, as a Whig, Lincoln held an optimistic vision of a positive, though limited, role of the federal government in promoting social reform. He came to the White House with the belief that federal authorities should encourage but seldom compel the state and local authorities to help the nation achieve its glorious mission.

Second, as a Whig, Lincoln believed that all people were inherently equal but that, through years of racial oppression, the moral and intellectual development of African-Americans was stunted, posing an almost insurmountable obstacle to their achieving equality with whites. Here Lincoln's thinking was much in line with the thinking of most Democrats, including Thomas Jefferson. But Lincoln diverged from the Jeffersonian tradition regarding blacks. Lincoln believed that blacks, like whites, were capable of improving themselves, though such improvement might take some time. This guarded optimism distinguished Lincoln from his contemporaries among the Democrats, almost all of whom believed that the slaves, once freed, would wither away into extinction. One Democrat,

Samuel Barlow (General George B. McClellan's advisor and political manager), penned a statement that captured perfectly his party's
thinking on black freedom: "Freedom of the blacks must lead to a
speedy annihilation of the race," he wrote. "Perhaps this is necessary." Continuing, he speculated:

> Perhaps it is wise that they shall be freed from the restraints
> as well as the duties which are now enforced by their mas-
> ters and be allowed to follow in the footsteps of the red
> man, be allowed to reap the inevitable consequences of in-
> feriority of race, surrounded by a civilization the advantages
> of which they cannot share and under the vices of which
> they must succumb.[5]

Barlow's sentiment was shared also by many former Democrats who
had joined the Republican party, including the crusty old Jacksonian
Francis P. Blair, Sr., who wrote to William Lloyd Garrison in 1864
that there was no "better hope of the amalgamation of the Africans
with our race" than there was of the amalgamation of the Indians
with the white race.[6]

Certainly, Lincoln retained his own doubts about the African-
American potential for success right up until the end of the war.
At the Hampton Roads conference in February 1865, when the
Confederate commissioner Robert M. T. Hunter argued that the
emancipation of the slaves would lead to the ruin of the South and
the decimation of the African-American race, the president tried to
lighten the mood by giving his own version of what would happen
to the freed people. As usual, he made his point by way of a story,
in this instance the well-known story of farmer Case of Illinois. Case
had found an economical way of feeding his hogs by planting potatoes and letting the animals root them out for themselves. In this
way, the hogs were fed, and the potatoes harvested. But what would

happen, asked a neighbor, when the ground froze a foot deep during the winter. "Well," stammered Lincoln's farmer, "it may come pretty hard on their *snouts*, but I don't see but that it will be 'root, hog, or die!'"[7] "Root, hog, or die" later became the catch phrase of Reconstruction-era conservatives who demanded that the federal government not concern itself with the fate of African-Americans (the "Liberal Republicans" made it their slogan in the 1872 election). For Lincoln in 1865, the phrase reflected a similar fatalistic attitude toward the future of the freed people, but it also revealed that Lincoln, unlike many of his political opponents, had become convinced that some of the blacks would, to use his metaphor, root successfully. This was the narrow scope of Lincoln's progressive vision: he did not foresee all blacks locked into the same dismal future, but instead believed that some of them would flourish.

The key to the African-American future, believed Lincoln—and here was the final way in which Whig ideology infused his racial vision—was education. Lincoln embraced the Jeffersonian notion that a successful democracy depended on a well-educated electorate, but he went beyond Jefferson in suggesting that blacks—at least some blacks—were as capable as whites of becoming educated citizens. If Lincoln at first resisted black suffrage, he did so not because of blind white supremacism but rather because he held to the traditional Whig fears of an uneducated electorate that could be manipulated by dangerous enemies, domestic or foreign.

For Lincoln, it was education, much more than race, that defined a person, and a nation. As a young boy, he scribbled in one of his school books, "Good boys who to their books apply / Will all be great men by and by."[8] In his first political campaign, running for the Illinois state legislature in 1832, he called education "the most important subject which we as a people can be engaged in," and he spoke of a future when learning could be extended to all: "I desire to see the time," said Lincoln, "when education, and by its means, morality, sobriety, enterprise and industry, shall become much more general than at present."[9] Lincoln came to define himself by his education. In the two autobiographical sketches he prepared during the year preceding the 1860 election, he paid particular attention to his schooling. His father, he gratuitously pointed out, was uneducated, but young Abraham was determined to improve himself intellectually. His autobiographies reflect a humility and even a humiliation at having to contend with political opponents like Stephen Douglas and William Henry Seward, who had attended private academies or colleges. Lincoln wrote of himself, "He regrets his want of education, and does what he can to supply the want."[10] Yet in his self-deprecation he helped to ingrain education into the Lincoln myth: Whereas history would come to see Andrew Jackson, the quintessential Democrat, as the self-*made* man, Lincoln, the quintessential Whig, would become known as the self-*taught* man.

Education, then, became the focus of Lincoln's vision of a successful African-American future. Before the war, especially in his debates with Stephen Douglas, Lincoln had frequently shared with Douglas doubts about what Lincoln called the "moral and intellectual endowment" of blacks.[11] His concern that Southern blacks had intellects that were, in his words, "clouded by Slavery," led him to believe, as he told a delegation of black leaders in 1862, that the race had little future in America.[12] It was in that speech that Lincoln recommended colonization abroad to the black delegation as a solution to their intellectual shortcomings. It was natural, then, that once the war-time experiments in free black labor began to prove successful, Lincoln would emphasize education as the key to African-American self-sufficiency. "Education for young blacks," wrote Lincoln to General Nathaniel Banks in the summer of 1863, should be included in Louisiana's reconstruction, and in his Reconstruction Proclamation in December of that year, Lincoln encouraged all Southern states to provide for the education of the freed people. By 1865 the president was handing out compliments to those military officials in the South who had helped foster what he called the "moral and physical elevation" of the newly freed African-Americans.[13]

Yet Lincoln knew that more was needed than white philanthropic efforts at educating blacks in order to ensure a successful future for both races. He knew that for real success, blacks would need the self-motivation to educate themselves. Prior to becoming president, Lincoln probably was skeptical of African-Americans' desire for education. Life as president in Washington, D.C., during the Civil War changed that prejudice. In Washington, Lincoln had the first opportunity of his life to see just how self-motivated African-Americans could be in acquiring education. Lincoln's model for self-education among African-American was, of course, Frederick Douglass. Self-directed and self-taught, Douglass, by his very existence, must have shattered whatever was left of the president's preconceptions of the former slave as morally and intellectually destitute. Lincoln trusted Douglass's political savvy as well as his moral code, and he read the abolitionist's speeches and sought his advice three times during the war: The president and the abolitionist conferred in 1863 about equal pay for black soldiers, in 1864 about the emancipation issue in the presidential election, and in 1865 about Lincoln's Second Inaugural.

In a way, Douglass even delivered his own Gettysburg Address, although his talk came about one hundred miles to the east, in Philadelphia, and about two weeks after Lincoln's more famous address. In his speech, Douglass used words much like Lincoln's at Gettysburg: "What business . . . have we to fight for the old Union?" asked Douglass. "We are not fighting for it," he answered. "We are fighting for something incomparably better than the old Union. We are fighting for unity; unity of idea, unity of sentiment, unity of object, unity of institutions, in which there shall be no North, no South, no East, no West, no black, no white, but a solidarity of the nation, making every slave free, and every free man a voter."[14] Aside from Douglass's explicit mention of the issue of black suffrage, the words could just as well have been Lincoln's. And if we are willing to concede that Lincoln's racial views changed through his relationship with Douglass, and that the president's attitudes grew closer to Douglass's as the war's end approached, we might also accept the possibility that Lincoln, had he lived, would have made black suffrage not just a suggestion but a mandate.

Douglass was not the only educated African-American that Lincoln met during the war. In his daily life at home he had constant dealings with educated black servants such as Elizabeth Keckley, his wife's dressmaker, and his valet William Johnson, who accompanied him to Gettysburg. In his official capacity as president, Lincoln had the opportunity to meet powerful black abolitionists like Sojourner Truth and Martin Delany, people who had simply been names on a page during his years in Illinois. The president's position exposed him to black ministers, black educators, and even black officials from the newly recognized Republics of Haiti and Liberia. In fact, it was his meeting with two highly educated leaders of the black community in New Orleans that probably did more than anything else to convince him that at least some Southern blacks should be granted the ballot. These men, Jean Baptiste Roudanez and Arnold Bertonneau, presented Lincoln on March 12, 1864, with a petition demanding black suffrage in Louisiana. The petition had been signed by over one thousand literate African-Americans, some of whom had fought under Andrew Jackson at the Battle of New Orleans in 1815.[15] Impressed by Roudanez, Bertonneau, and the people they represented, Lincoln sat down the next day to write his now famous though then private letter to Governor Michael Hahn suggesting that intelligent blacks and black veterans be allowed to vote. It was the president's face-to-face contact with black educated elites, as well as his favorable impression of African-American soldiers, that allowed him, for the first time in his life, to consider blacks as potential actors on America's political stage.

Lincoln's newfound appreciation of black self-determination during the war helped convince him of what is obvious to us today: Most blacks were just as eager for self-education, if not more so, as Lincoln had been as a young man. He expressed his guarded optimism about the potential for black self-improvement to African-Americans directly only once, in a speech that he made to a group of Washington African-Americans who came to serenade him after Maryland voted to free its slaves in the fall of 1864. In response to the serenade, Lincoln congratulated the blacks on Maryland's edict of freedom, and he added a final word of advice: "I hope that you, colored people, who have been emancipated, will use this great boon which has been given you to improve yourselves, both morally and intellectually."[16] Clearly, the president still held to a vestige of his belief that freedom was something given to rather than sought by the slaves, and he still carried with him an assumption that most African-Americans were largely ignorant. But at least he was ready to acknowledge an "ambition for education," to use the words he once used to describe himself, on the part of African-Americans.[17] Lincoln's speech on this occasion stands in sharp contrast to his speech of two years before—the only other speech in which he addressed African-Americans directly—when he implored blacks to leave the country. Now the president was willing to entertain a biracial vision of the country, a vision that depended on blacks maintaining an aspiration for education.

Speculation and disagreement about what might have happened had Lincoln survived the assassin's bullet will never end, but it is fair to assume that, at the very least, Lincoln would have supported government funding of African-American education. Most likely, he would have preferred that the state governments play the major role and the federal government the minor role in funding education for blacks, much as happens today in all education programs. However, in his effort to make the federal army an instrument of bringing education to African-Americans, he made clear his desire to use the federal government as a resource for African-Americans to use as they sought to improve themselves.

That approach on Lincoln's part is ironic when one considers the effort among some activists and lawyers today to secure so-called reparations for slavery. If one can get past all the misconceptions about the reparations movement that are spouted by poorly informed members of the press meaning to whip up public debate or by vocal, vain conservatives trying to use the issue to get their voice heard, one sees a reasonable proposal by most advocates of reparations. Although some activists seek specific damages in civil suits against private corporations, far more seek funding for black education. In other words, if there is a consensus among those who believe that there should be reparations for slavery, it is that money should be paid by the government for black education as compensation to a people who were denied education for so long because of the institution of slavery.[18]

Would not Lincoln have agreed with this position? He would not have seen the matter in terms of compensation for slavery, but he certainly would have believed that something was owed to those of African descent for the horrors wreaked upon them. He said as much in his Second Inaugural of March 1865:

> If we shall suppose that American Slavery is one of those offences which, in the providence of God, must needs come, but which, having continued through His appointed time, He now wills to remove, and that He gives to both North and South, this terrible war, as the woe due to those by whom the offence came, shall we discern therein any departure from those divine attributes which the believers in a Living God always ascribe to Him? Fondly do we hope—fervently do we pray—that this mighty scourge of

war may speedily pass away. Yet, if God wills that it continue, until all the wealth piled by the bond-man's two hundred and fifty years of unrequited toil shall be sunk, and
until every drop of blood drawn with the lash, shall be paid
by another drawn with the sword, as was said three thousand years ago, so still it must be said "the judgments of the
Lord, are true and righteous altogether."[19]

Here was as powerful a statement in favor of reparations as ever
was made. Reparations here meant war and mass death as payment
for slavery. Surely Lincoln would have preferred the less bloody
and less expensive alternative of government funding of black education as payment for slavery. In this very limited way, might Lincoln not have smiled upon efforts by African-Americans today to
educate themselves in any way possible, including using the law,
one of Lincoln's favorite instruments, to get the money to educate
themselves?

Yet, paradoxically, Lincoln's emphasis on education for the freed
people may have helped sow the seeds of failure during the Reconstruction era, and funding for African-American education today
may again do only half the work that is needed. While emphasizing
education for blacks, the president said almost nothing during the
war about the need to educate *whites* for a biracial society. There is
something unsettling about Lincoln standing on the porch of the
White House and telling newly freed African-Americans that they
were not ready for freedom, that they must educate themselves for
freedom. The enslaved blacks were ready for freedom, and they had
been ready for freedom since the guns had fired in Charleston Harbor four years before. It was the whites who had yet to be educated
for black freedom. And it was Lincoln's failure to see this basic truth
that represents a genuine failing. His dream of an educated society
rested on the wrong assumption that only blacks required special
education in order to create multiracial harmony in the future. He

might have considered, and today's advocates for reparations might also consider, how public monies might be used to fund education for whites as well—specifically, for programs where whites and Americans of all races can be educated about what it means to live with others of different races. We should not expect Lincoln to have been ahead of the game in realizing the need for multicultural education. But perhaps he could have had a better understanding that the proper waking dream was not a purely white dream *or* a black dream, but rather a dream of a society adopting Lincoln's model of self-education and educating itself, all of its members, to search for new ways to learn to live in harmony with one another.

CHAPTER 14

The Second Inaugural Address: The Spoken Words

Ronald C. White, Jr.

I AM HONORED TO BE PART OF THE LINCOLN FORUM AND CON-
vene a conversation about the text of Abraham Lincoln's Second
Inaugural—both the meaning of Lincoln's words and the skill of his
artistry with words. For a while now, I have been asking Americans
in different parts of the country to recall their thoughts and feelings
upon visiting the Lincoln Memorial and reading the Second Inaugural. I ask you to do the same. Whether their visit or your visit was
thirty years ago or three months ago, the word that I have heard
most often is "awe." But awe is not the same thing as
understanding.

Lincoln's Second Inaugural Address was delivered on March 4,
1865. The text of the Second Inaugural consists of seven hundred
and three words. Lincoln arranges his words in twenty-five sentences in four paragraphs. Five hundred and five words in the address are of one syllable. Many of us know this address primarily

This chapter is a revised and expanded treatment of a subject the author introduced in *Lincoln's Greatest Speech: The Second Inaugural* (New York: Simon &
Schuster, 2002).

because of the opening lines of the last paragraph, "With malice toward none; with charity for all." There is much more to know. In this brief address Lincoln mentions God fourteen times, quotes scripture four times, and invokes prayer three times.

Eleven days later, in response to a congratulatory letter from Thurlow Weed, New York Republican boss, Lincoln stated, "I expect the latter to wear as well as—perhaps better than—any thing I have produced." Lincoln then added these words, "but I believe it is not immediately popular."[1]

If Lincoln believed the Second Inaugural was his finest address, it has usually not been so remembered. Both the Gettysburg Address and the Second Inaugural Address are enshrined at the Lincoln Memorial, but I suggest that the Second Inaugural has most often lived under the shadow of the Gettysburg Address.

My purpose in lifting up the Second Inaugural is not to diminish the Gettysburg Address. I stand in awe of both its meaning and its artistry. Today I would like to offer some brief remarks comparing the context of the two speeches and then some extended comments on the meaning and rhetorical artistry of several aspects of the Second Inaugural.

The dramatic context of the Gettysburg Address is well known. We know the story of the decisive battle of July 1–3, 1863. We may know something of the circumstances behind the invitation to Lincoln to offer "dedicatory" remarks on November 19, 1863. I trust we recognize that he did not write the address on the flap of an envelope. Everything about this story is filled with drama and pathos. Millions each year visit the battlefields, walk reverently among the grave sites, and ponder Lincoln's two and a half minute address. The Gettysburg Address was invoked, yet again, this past September on the occasion of the one-year remembrance of 9/11.

Our appreciation and analysis of the Second Inaugural begins with the recognition of a dramatic context that has either been forgotten or is unknown. Lincoln had every reason to be hopeful as inauguration day, March 4, approached in 1865. The Confederacy was splintered if not shattered. On February 1, General William Tecumseh Sherman led 60,000 troops out of Savannah. Slashing through South Carolina, they wreaked havoc in the state that had been the seedbed of secession. At the same time, Union General Ulysses S. Grant was besieging Petersburg, twenty miles south of Richmond. Despite Confederate General Robert E. Lee's previous record for forestalling defeat, it was clear that the badly outnumbered Confederates could not hold out much longer. Everything pointed toward victory.

Apprehension intruded upon this hopeful spirit. Rumors were flying about the capital that desperate Confederates, now realizing that defeat was imminent, would attempt to abduct or assassinate the president. Secretary of War Edwin M. Stanton took extraordinary precautions. All roads leading to Washington had been heavily picketed for some days and the bridges patrolled with "extra vigilance." The problem was greatly complicated by the presence of large numbers of Confederate deserters who now roamed the capital. Stanton posted sharpshooters on the buildings that would ring the inaugural ceremonies.

After four years as a war president, Lincoln could look ahead to four years as a peace president. With no congress in session until December to hamper him, he would have free reign to do some peacemaking on his own.[2]

Gamblers were even betting that the sixteenth president would be inaugurated for a third term in 1869. The president, who had been battered by critics in Congress and the press for much of the war, was finally beginning to receive credit for his leadership. Many were suggesting that the stakes were about to get higher. How would Lincoln, the resourceful Commander in Chief in war, guide a reunited nation, during what was beginning to be called "Reconstruction"?

As the day for his second inauguration drew near, everyone wondered what the president would say. No one seemed to know anything about the content of Lincoln's second inaugural speech. A
dispatch from the Associated Press reported that the address would
be "brief—not exceeding, probably, a column in length." It was
recalled that he took thirty-five minutes to deliver his First Inaugural Address. There was great curiosity about the substance of this
president's address.[3]

If reports about the length of the address were correct, how
could Lincoln deal with so many multiplying issues? Would he use
his rhetorical skills to "take the hide off" his opponents in the South
and North? Was the Confederate States of America to be treated as
a conquered nation? How did one demarcate between the innocent
and the guilty, between citizens and soldiers? What would Lincoln
say about the slaves? They had been emancipated, but what about
the question of suffrage?

Just beneath the outward merrymaking lay a different emotion.
A weariness of spirit pervaded the nation. Government officials
were fatigued from four long years of war. The agony of battle took
its toll on families everywhere. Many citizens were as filled with
anger as with hope. Even the anticipation of victory could not com-
pensate for the loss of so many young men, cut down in death or
disabled by horrible wounds just as they were preparing to harvest
the fruits of their young lives.

Washington, which had been transformed into an armed camp
in the early days of the war, now had become a gigantic hospital.
White buildings and tents dotted the city. Many hospitals were new
structures like the Stanton Hospital at New Jersey Avenue and I
Street. Others, such as the Douglass Hospital, had taken over former private mansions on Minnesota Row. Many of the forty or so
hospitals were makeshift single-story wooden sheds. All were
crowded. Often hundreds, sometimes thousands, of wounded soldiers lay in adjoining beds.

March 4 dawned with incessant rain. Carriages were in great demand. Premium prices were being offered to ride to the proceedings. Police estimates placed the crowd between 30,000 and 40,000. The *Philadelphia Inquirer* reported that the arriving throng was present "in force sufficient to have struck terror into the heart of Lee's army (had the umbrellas been muskets)."[4] The streets oozed with soft mud, described by locals as "black plaster." The Corps of Engineers surveyed the scene to determine the practicality of laying pontoons on Pennsylvania Avenue from the Capitol to the White House. They found the bottom too unstable to hold the anchors of the needed boats. The project was abandoned. During the early morning hours gale winds whipped through the city uprooting trees.

Selden Connor, a Union soldier from Michigan who had arrived in Washington only the day before, was overwhelmed by the size of the gathering. He wrote to his mother, "there was a crowd almost numberless."[5] Maggie Lindsley, twenty-four, had been a supporter of the Union cause in Nashville, a view not shared by most of her friends. Encountering the crowds heading for the Inaugural, she wrote later that day in her diary, "We were on the edge of a great surging ocean of humanity."[6] As visitors and residents walked toward the Capitol, they encountered military patrols on horseback at every major intersection.

The ceremonial procedures would not differ substantially from Lincoln's first inaugural. Yet, there were differences. Instead of the small clusters of soldiers present in 1861, large numbers of military could be observed throughout the city. The soldiers were marked by their wounds. Amputation had become the trademark of Civil War surgery. According to federal records, three out of four operations were amputations. Too often the surgery had to be repeated again. Many visitors professed shock at the sight of so many young men with amputated legs or arms.

Black soldiers changed the composition of the army from 1861 to 1865. The use of black troops prompted protests both in the

North and in the South, but one hundred seventy-nine thousand black soldiers and ten thousand sailors would serve in the Union forces before the end of the war. The presence of so many blacks in the inaugural crowds particularly struck the correspondent for *The Times* of London. "It was remarked by everybody, strangers as well as natives, that there never had been seen such crowds of negroes in the streets of the capital. At least one-half of the multitude were coloured people."[7]

Noted Washington camera artist Alexander Gardner was poised to record the event for posterity. The Second Inaugural Address would be the only occasion in which Lincoln is photographed delivering a speech.

In front of the president, in the crowd, Lincoln recognized Frederick Douglass, the articulate African-American abolitionist leader, reformer, and newspaper editor. Lincoln's First Inaugural Address had dismayed Douglass. He had found Lincoln's words much too conciliatory toward the South. Douglass visited Lincoln in the White House in 1863 and again in 1864 to speak with the president about a variety of issues concerning African-Americans. Today Douglass had come to hear what Lincoln would say as the end of the war was in view.[8]

Up behind the right buttress stood the actor John Wilkes Booth. Lincoln had seen Booth perform at Ford's Theatre the previous November. Booth came to the Second Inaugural for his own dark motives. He must have wanted to know what this "false president" would say.

When Lincoln was introduced, the crowd exploded in expectation. The applause and cheers rolled towards those in the farthest reaches of the crowd. Lincoln rose from his chair and put on and adjusted his steel-rimmed eyeglasses. He stepped from underneath the shelter of the Capitol building and out past the magnificent Corinthian columns. At fifty-six, he looked older than his years. Lincoln held in his left hand his Second Inaugural Address printed in two columns. The handwritten draft of the address had been set in type. The galley proof was clipped and pasted in an order to indicate pauses for emphasis and breathing.[9]

Lincoln prepared to speak.

Lincoln's opening words, "At this second appearing," are not a throwaway line. Lincoln almost did not have a second.

In the midst of the elation of Lincoln's second inauguration, many could remember back not many months to a quite different mood. For much of Lincoln's first term, political pundits had predicted that he would be another of the one-term presidents that had become customary in the middle years of the nineteenth century. In a federal government that was only seventy-six years old, American as well as foreign newspapers commented that this would be the first time in thirty-two years that a president would be inaugurated for a second term.[10]

A year after the decisive summer victories of 1863 at Gettysburg and Vicksburg, the summer of 1864 witnessed campaigns that brought disappointment, even despair, throughout the North. In early May 1864, Grant began the year's Eastern campaign by confidently leading nearly 100,000 men against Lee's 65,000 soldiers in the Battle of the Wilderness. In the fighting that lay ahead, at Spotsylvania and at Cold Harbor, Grant would suffer almost 60,000 casualties, nearly the equal of the troops Lee put in the field. By the end of seven weeks of battles and skirmishes, the Northern public began to ask if victory was worth the swelling cost in human lives.

With no major victories now for more than a year, weariness seemed to be winning out. Some Democrats began to press for a negotiated settlement to end the carnage. Even as the North was getting used to finding new generals to lead the war effort, some Republicans began to suggest it was time to find a new candidate for the presidential election coming in November 1864.

In the summer of 1864 Lincoln was receiving pessimistic reports from his advisors about his prospects for reelection. Henry J.

Raymond, founder of the *New York Times*, convened the Republican National Committee at the Astor House in New York on August 22. After canvassing the situation with members representing all the states, Raymond sat down to write the president. He told Lincoln that even if an election were "to be held now in Illinois we should be beaten." Raymond cited Simon Cameron who reported, "Pennsylvania is against us." Raymond in turn declared that New York "would go 50,000 against us to-morrow."[11] In sum, Raymond told Lincoln, "the tide is setting strongly against us."[12]

Lincoln became resigned in August that he could not be re-elected. On August 23, 1864, six days before the Democratic convention would select his opponent, he wrote a private memorandum expressing his feelings. "This morning, as for some days past, it seems exceedingly probable that this Administration will not be re-elected. Then it will be my duty to so co-operate with the President-elect as to save the Union between the election and the inauguration; as he will have secured his election on such ground that he can not possibly save it afterwards."[13]

Lincoln began his address in a subdued tone. In the highly charged atmosphere of wartime Washington, with soldiers everywhere, it is as if he wanted to lower anticipations. In the first, third, and fifth sentence of this first paragraph Lincoln lowered them with the key words: "less . . . little . . . no."

He started more like an observer than the main actor. The language of the first paragraph is impersonal. Yes, he uses the pronouns, "I" and "myself," but the ethos of the paragraph was unemotional. Lincoln directed the focus of his remarks away from himself by speaking in a passive voice. After this first paragraph, he will use no more personal pronouns.

Lincoln dispenses one by one with the usual contents of such an address. In the first sentence he says that this is not the occasion for "an extended address." In the second sentence he reiterates why a detailed "statement" was proper four years before, but not today.

In the third sentence he reminds the audience that on many other occasions they had heard "public declarations" on "every point and phase" of the war, implying that he would not make such a declaration on this occasion. The audience surely would have relished the Commander in Chief giving a report on "the progress of our arms," but he would not do that. After Lincoln told the audience everything the speech would not be, he concluded the first paragraph by announcing he was offering "no prediction" about the end of the war.

There seems to be nothing in Lincoln's beginning paragraph that would arouse the passions of the audience. The opening, unlike the Gettysburg Address, contains no dramatic language. When we first hear or read Lincoln's beginning words of the Second Inaugural, they may even come upon us as awkward if not ungraceful.

In the second paragraph, Lincoln began the shift in content and tone that would give this address its singular meaning. In a paragraph of five sentences, he employed several rhetorical strategies that work to guide and aid the listener.

First, Lincoln's central overarching strategy was to emphasize common actions and emotions. In this paragraph he used "all" and "both" to be inclusive of both North and South. Lincoln was here laying the groundwork for themes that he would develop more dynamically in paragraphs three and four.

Notice the subjects and adjectives in three of the five sentences in the second paragraph.

Sentence one: *All* thoughts were anxiously directed to an impending civil-war.

Sentence two: *All* dreaded it—*all* sought to avert it.

Sentence four: *Both* parties deprecated war.

Second, Lincoln used one of his favorite rhetorical devices: alliteration. He used "d" as the beginning letter in eight vital words: directed, dreaded, delivered, devoted, destroy, dissolve, divide, and deprecated. The use of alliteration, present in every sentence but the four-word last sentence, promoted connection within the paragraph. Alliteration accented the rhythmic pacing of language. Finally, the repetition enhanced the cadence of Lincoln's words.

Third, Lincoln used the word "war" seven times. The image of war is actually present nine times in the ninety-nine words of the paragraph, as "war" is understood twice in the second sentence in two pronouns; I believe he repeats the image of war both for emphasis and movement.[14] The centrality of war is magnified because the word is voiced in every sentence. The tension mounts throughout the paragraph, building to a crescendo in the three parts of the forceful third sentence: (1) Both . . . deprecated war; (2) one . . . would make war; (3) the other would accept war.

In lifting up the word war, Lincoln was preparing his audience for more profound questions. Up until now, war was being described as the direct object, both grammatically and historically, of the principal actors. As he now recounts the complex motivations that led to war, Lincoln was beginning to suggest that neither side was fully in control. War was about to become the subject rather than the object.

"And the war came." The second paragraph of the Second Inaugural concludes with an astounding sentence. Four words. Four syllables. So much is suggested in so little.

In this brief, understated sentence, Lincoln acknowledged that "the war came" in spite of the best intentions of the political leaders of the land. "And the war came" in spite of the determination of the president himself. As Lincoln looked back from the perspective of four long years, he saw that all along the war had a life of its own.

This sentence is both a transition and a foreshadowing. The audience doesn't know it yet, but "And the war came" will lift the conflict beyond mere human instrumentality. Lincoln wants his listeners to understand that this war cannot be understood simply as the fulfillment of human plans.

How did Lincoln speak that final sentence: "And the war came"? Did he say it loudly, as the culmination of the crescendo? This is possible. But I think not. I believe he spoke it softly, mournfully: "And the war came." And it was a bloody war of biblical proportion.

In fact, when the decision was made to consecrate the ground at Gettysburg, a monumental task lay ahead. There were left behind more than fifty thousand Confederate and Union dead, wounded or missing soldiers. About 6,000 dead, half Union, lay on the battle-field. How were these soldiers to be buried before Edward Everett, Lincoln, and other dignitaries arrived for the dedication of the battlefield and cemetery in November?

A major assignment was to sort the possessions of the soldiers who lay there. Clothing was searched. Belongings were labeled and stored so that family members would be able to recover them— pocket diaries, letters, and photographs, as well as money, watches, and jewelry.

What chiefly survived were Bibles.[15] An overwhelming number of the soldiers, North and South, carried Bibles. Most often the Bible was a pocket New Testament. "Both sides read the same Bible."

When Lincoln introduces the Bible into the Second Inaugural, we enter new territory in presidential inaugural addresses. Before Lincoln, there were eighteen inaugural addresses delivered by fourteen presidents.[16] From George Washington to James Buchanan, each president referred to God or the deity. These references almost always came in the last paragraph. The mention of God or a Divine Being was in the form of the need for reliance on or guidance from the "Parent of the Human Race" (George Washington), the "Patron of Order" (John Adams), "Infinite Power" (Thomas Jefferson), "Almighty Being" (James Madison and Andrew Jackson), "Almighty God" (James Monroe), and "Divine Providence" (James Buchanan).[17]

The Bible was quoted only once in those eighteen addresses. John Quincy Adams quoted from the Psalms: "except the Lord keep the city the watchman waketh but in vain."[18] The lack of precedent did not deter Lincoln. In the 340 words remaining in the Second Inaugural, Lincoln will quote or paraphrase four biblical passages.

The introduction of the Bible signals Lincoln's determination to think theologically as well as politically about the war. "Both read the same Bible, and pray to the same God" is filled with multiple meaning.

By one reading, Lincoln is acknowledging the universal use of the Bible and prayer by soldiers throughout the war. By extension, he is including his inclusive spirit in language that surely means the people of the South as well as the people of the North read the Bible.

By another reading, Lincoln goes forward to probe the appropriate use of the Bible when he adds: "and each invokes His aid against the other." Lincoln, who always had an ambivalent relationship with religion, suggests that the Bible and prayer can be used as weapons to curry God's favor for one side or the other. Both before and during the war Lincoln observed directly opposite readings of the Bible. On one side stood those who read a Bible that they steadfastly believed sanctioned slavery. On the other side were those who understood the Bible as encouraging the abolition of slavery.[19]

According to the Letter to the Hebrews in the New Testament, "the word of God is living and active, sharper than any two-edged sword." Lincoln liked to wield the Bible as a sword, using one edge to affirm and the other to question. Or, as the same verse continues, to use the other edge of the sword "to judge the thoughts and intentions of the hearers" (Hebrews 4:12 KJV).

On this second reading, Lincoln judges "the thoughts and intentions" of those who use or misuse the Bible or prayer for partisan purposes. Lincoln offers here not only affirmation, but interrogation. The last part of the sentence, "and each invokes His aid against the other" is not framed grammatically as a question, but it is clear that Lincoln now begins a section where he asks questions both about human actions and God's actions.

Lincoln is asking how it is possible for one side to ask God's aid against the other side. He is not only asking a question. He is inveighing against a tribal God who takes the side of a section or party. He is building a case for an inclusive God. Lincoln, who had been discontented with the sectarianism of the churches, was not happy with talk of a God who was captive to North or South. He had become troubled by those who came to him to say God is on our side. In his Second Inaugural Lincoln speaks instead of an inclusive God. This God, as Lincoln would explain, is inclusive both in judgment and reconciliation.

Lincoln pressed this point by invoking the first of four biblical passages. He employed words from Genesis in which God tells Adam and Eve that because they have disobeyed God, their lot of their daily life will be that "By the sweat of your face you shall eat bread" (Genesis 3:19). Here God was judging human beings.

Lincoln used these words, surely familiar to his hearers, to start his case for the judgment of slavery. Lincoln had experienced this kind of religion in an interview just three months before the Second Inaugural. In early December 1864, two women from Tennessee called upon the president to ask for the release of their husbands who were being held as Confederate prisoners of war. Lincoln heard their story and asked them to come back the next day.

The following day one of the women pleaded with Lincoln that "her husband was a religious man." Lincoln objected. "In my opinion, the religion that sets men to rebel and fight against their government, because, as they think, that government does not sufficiently help *some* men to eat their bread on the sweat of *other* men's faces, is not the sort of religion upon which people can get to heaven!"[20] Three months later this interview was surely in Lincoln's memory as he prepared his Second Inaugural. Certainly he worked with the same text from Genesis as he pursued pretentiousness in both South and North.

As Lincoln buttressed his moral aversion toward the South's embrace of slavery by quoting from the Old Testament, he balanced judgment with mercy by quoting from the New Testament. "Let us judge not that we be not judged" (Matthew 7:1, Luke 6:37).

These words come from the Sermon on the Mount in which Jesus advocates an ethic rooted in humility and compassion. "Blessed are those" who do not follow the way of the world, in this case judgment, but the new way of grace and mercy.

The searing light of Lincoln's moral judgment is refracted through a justice that is evenhanded. Lincoln, whose religion has often been depicted as Old Testament in character, here uses a teaching from the New Testament Sermon on the Mount that offers explicit contrast to a legal understanding of human relationships. This verse enjoins the hearer to practice mercy and humility.

This second biblical quotation is central. How we would like to hear Lincoln's tone as he quoted these words of Jesus. A speaker could employ such words just as a fencer might make a return thrust following a parry. Understood as a retaliatory sally, the intent of Lincoln's words is undermined. These words retain their integrity when used, as Lincoln does here, in humility and confession. Lincoln had earned the right to say these words by his own conduct over the course of four years of war.

The trajectory of this remark was toward the North. Northern politicians, press, and people had been harsh in their judgment of the South. Lincoln's struggle with the abolitionists was with the moral pretentiousness of their rhetoric. His dispute with the radical Republicans of his own party was over their intention to punish the South. His struggle with the churches was with their self-righteousness.

"The Almighty has His own purposes." With these words Lincoln brings the idea of God to the rhetorical center of his Second

Inaugural Address. After discussing different actors, Lincoln concentrates on God as the primary actor. In quick strokes Lincoln describes God's actions: "He now wills to remove," "He gives to both North and South, this terrible war," and "Yet, if God wills that it continue."

This affirmation about God points both backward and forward. The assertion points backward because it places in new light statements made early in the address about the purposes of different parties. It points forward to certain "divine attributes" of a "Living God."

In Lincoln's much-loved Shakespeare one needs to progress to Act III in order to understand the events and dialogue in Act I. Just so, Lincoln was preparing his audience for his dramatic introduction of the purposes of a "Living God" by an earlier litany of human purposes in paragraphs one and two. We are now able to see that in Lincoln's first two paragraphs much more was taking place than historical description. Lincoln wanted his audience to understand the limitations of human purposes.

With deft strokes Lincoln had painted the motivations and actions of different parties. He did not exclude himself. He was one of those who had "looked for an easier triumph." Each side believed its cause to be just. Neither side seemed willing to admit the partiality of its vision. The litany is meant to prepare us for a larger purpose.

Though praising the inscrutable intentions of God in his Second Inaugural Address, Lincoln did not retreat to agnosticism about the specific content of those purposes. He focuses those purposes in the Second Inaugural by invoking a fiery Biblical quotation. In his brooding he has discerned that the purposes of God can also bring judgment, which we hear in a third passage from the Bible. "Woe unto the world because of offences! for it must needs be that offences come; but woe to that man by whom the offence cometh!" (Matthew 18:7 KJV).

246 RONALD C. WHITE, JR.

When Lincoln speaks the word "offences," he shifts the tone of his address. The feeling tone of "offence" jolts us. As Lincoln defines American slavery as one of those offences against God, he broadens out the historical and emotional range of his address.

Lincoln had long believed that slavery was evil at its core because one person held another in bondage. He arrived more slowly at the conclusion that slavery was evil in its circumference for it propagated still other evils. Whereas for a long time he had been willing to contain slavery politically and geographically, he had come to the conclusion in the midst of the Civil War that its moral implications could not be contained. Slavery made a lie of democratic principles.

"If we shall suppose that American Slavery is one of those offences." What was there and then in the Bible had become here and now in American Slavery. In utilizing this second passage from the Gospel of Matthew, Lincoln employs the sanction of scripture to initiate his indictment of slavery and ultimately his formal charge against the American people.

Lincoln does not say Southern slavery. By saying American slavery, Lincoln asserts that North and South must together own the offence. He is not simply trying to set the historical record straight. He is thinking of the future. Lincoln understood, as many in his own party did not, that the Southern people would never be able to take their full places in the Union if they felt that they alone were saddled with the guilt for what was the national offense of slavery.

Lincoln offers a biblical and theological sanction for declaring that slavery must *now* come to an end. Starting in 1854 he began to appeal to Thomas Jefferson's words in the Declaration of Independence, "all men are created equal" as a warrant for advocating certain rights for blacks. Now, in 1865, Lincoln appeals to Jesus' words in the Bible as a warrant that the time for slavery had *now* come and gone.

As the address builds toward its final paragraph, Lincoln makes an unexpected political and rhetorical move. Speaking on the eve of military victory, when many expected him to celebrate the successes of the Union, he called upon his audience to recognize a perilous evil in their midst. Instead of self-congratulation, he asks his fellow citizens for self-analysis. No president, before or since, has so courageously pointed to a malady that resides at the very center of the American national family. Lincoln had come to believe that where there was evil, judgment would surely follow.

Lincoln carried to his speech the scales of justice. He did so knowing that Americans had always been uncomfortable facing up to their own malevolence. We might think that the Civil War forced such an encounter, but evil in any war always seems to be relegated to the other side. Many in the North felt quite righteous in criticizing the South for rebellion and slavery. Most in the South believed they were acting in the spirit of the freedom of 1776 in severing ties with a tyrannical and hypocritical federal government. Now Lincoln concentrated a discussion on the problem of evil, weighed on the scales of divine justice.

As Lincoln examined the consequences of evil, he placed his judgments within two large historical contexts. In prosecuting the nation for the offence of slavery, Lincoln reached back beyond the nation's birth as he recalled "two hundred and fifty years of unrequited toil." Lincoln was reminding his audience that the stain of slavery was enmeshed in the fabric of American history from its beginnings. In invoking "the judgments of the Lord," Lincoln placed his remarks within the psalmist's words uttered "three thousand years ago."[21] "The judgments of the Lord are true *and* righteous altogether" (Psalm 19:9).

Lincoln shared with his contemporaries a belief in the special destiny of America. Where he distinguished himself was in his willingness to confront its ambiguities. Brooding over the honor and dishonor in his nation's actions, he was unwilling to reduce political rhetoric to national self-congratulation.

The first eight words of Lincoln's last paragraph proclaim a timeless promise of reconciliation. "With malice toward none; with charity for all." Lincoln begins his final exhortation by asking us to enter a new era, armed not with enmity but with forgiveness. These words immediately became the most memorable expressions of the Second Inaugural. After his assassination, as they were printed on mourning ribbons, they came to represent Lincoln's legacy to the nation.

"With malice toward none; with charity for all" became some of our sacred words. Other words of his, from the Gettysburg Address— "of the people, by the people, for the people"—endure because they forever define America.[22] "With malice toward none; with charity for all" describe Lincoln's vision for a post–Civil War America. They also define Lincoln's legacy as a leader and as a speaker.

As Lincoln began this final paragraph, he had been speaking for barely five minutes. Surely he would continue his discussion of the war and slavery. The audience was waiting for him to speak about his policy and plans for Reconstruction. But now, in an address filled with surprises, he turned briskly to his unexpected conclusion.

Lincoln must have trusted that by now he had forged a bond with his audience. Well aware of the feelings of both hope and despair, he was about to ask his listeners for acts of incredible compassion. He would summon them to overcome the boundary of sectionalism and come together again in reconciliation.

Lincoln ends his Second Inaugural Address with a coda of healing: "to bind up . . . to care for . . . to do all which may achieve and cherish a just, and a lasting peace, among ourselves, and with all nations." Portraits of widows and orphans now balance the images of blood and swords.

Lincoln had defined the signposts toward winning the peace by achieving reconciliation. In this final paragraph he declares that the true test of the aims of war will be how we now treat those who have been defeated. If enmity continues after hostilities cease, the war will have been in vain.

These are no maudlin words crafted for emotional effect. His words are directed to the tough, practical-living actions that must replace retribution with charity.

In this final paragraph Lincoln offers the ultimate surprise. Instead of rallying his supporters, in the name of God, to support the war, he asks his listeners, quietly, to imitate the ways of God.

CHAPTER 15

Abraham Lincoln and Civil Liberties: Then and Now

Frank J. Williams

RECENT ACTS OF TERRORISM HAVE YET AGAIN RAISED TEN-sions between American security and civil liberty. The forces of both Al Qaeda and Saddam Hussein have created a heightened awareness of, and increased desire for, national security. This is not the first time. President George W. Bush is treading the same waters as Abraham Lincoln, and both have been accused of forsaking civil liberties. Many times in this nation's history, our leaders have been criticized for taking extra-constitutional measures, and upon close examination of the situation that faced Lincoln, many parallels can be drawn to the current atmosphere in this country. If Lincoln failed to uphold all the provisions of the Constitution, he faced possible condemnation regardless of his actions, assailed not only by those who genuinely valued civil liberty, but also by enemies and opponents whose motive was criticism itself. Whatever criticism Lincoln faced for pushing his power to the limits of the Constitution, far harsher would have been his denunciation if the whole experiment of the democratic American Union failed, as seemed possible given the circumstances. If such a disaster occurred, what benefit would have been gained by adhering to a fallen Constitution? It was a classic example of the age-old conflict: Do the ends justify the means? In the end, the verdict of history is that Lincoln's use of power did not constitute abuse. Many surveys of historians rank Lincoln as number one among the great presidents.[1]

Nearly one hundred and fifty years later, President Bush is facing a need to take extra-constitutional measures in the face of the first serious threat to our country in at least fifty years. Like the criticism Lincoln faced, there is enormous opposition to his post–September 11 policies and his decision to engage Iraq in war.

In June 1863, Lincoln composed a justly famous reply to Albany, New York, Democrats who had accused him of forsaking civil liberties. This "reply to Erastus Corning and others" was widely reprinted at the time and has been frequently cited by historians since—usually as an example of Lincoln's deft handling of critics.[2] The less-often cited letter that inspired the response, and the rebuttal to Lincoln's reply, make clear that the upstate New York Democrats believed deeply that Lincoln had gone too far in denying constitutional guarantees and that the opposition animus was hardly limited to New York. Antiwar Democrats from around the nation shared these concerns.

Lincoln's critics were inspired by a variety of extra-constitutional decisions. In facing emergencies during the Civil War, Lincoln found himself in a difficult political position. In the words of historian James G. Randall: "No president has carried the power of presidential edict and executive order (independently of Congress) so far as he did. . . . It would not be easy to state what Lincoln conceived to be the limit of his powers."[3] It has been noted how, in the eighty days from the April 1861 call for troops to the convening of Congress in special session on July 4, 1861, Lincoln performed a whole series of important acts by sheer assumption of presidential power. He proclaimed not "civil war" in those words, but the existence of "combinations too powerful to be suppressed by the ordinary course of judicial proceedings." He called forth the militia to "suppress said combinations," which he ordered "to disperse, and retire peaceably" to their homes.[4] Congress is constitutionally empowered to declare war, but suppression of rebellion has been recognized as an executive function, for which the prerogative of setting aside civil procedures has been placed in the president's hands.[5]

For over a year and a half, our country has been involved in a war in Iraq. The war has not been formally declared. While Lincoln's acts were placed within the power of the executive by declaring them a suppression of rebellion, President Bush has couched the warlike effort in Iraq as a movement to liberate Iraqis from their dictator. But however warlike Bush's executive actions are in Iraq, Lincoln did more.

To suppress the "rebellion," he proclaimed a blockade, suspended *habeas corpus* rights, increased the size of the regular army, and authorized the expenditure of government money without congressional appropriation. He made far-reaching decisions and commitments while Congress was not in session, and all without public polls.

By the time of his inauguration on March 4, 1861, seven Southern states had already seceded from the Union. But Lincoln played a waiting game and made no preparation for the use of force until he sent provisions to Fort Sumter in Charleston Harbor a month later, which precipitated its bombardment by the rebels.

Then began Lincoln's period of executive decision. Congress would not meet until the special session of July 4, and it was basic to the Whig-Republican theory of government that Congress was vested with the ultimate power—a theory with which Lincoln, as both Whig and Republican, had long agreed. As a former member of Congress, four-term legislator, and for twenty-four years a lawyer, Lincoln respected the traditional separation of powers. But by then, Lincoln could not bring himself to believe that "the framers of [the

Constitution] intended, that in every case, the danger should run its course, until Congress could be called together."[6]

The border state of Maryland was, by 1861, seething with secessionist views that were at times more violent than those in some Southern states that did secede. Events in Maryland ultimately provoked Lincoln's suspension of the writ of *habeas corpus*. The writ of *habeas corpus* is a procedural device by which a prisoner can request an appropriate court to review his imprisonment. If the imprisonment is found not to conform to law, the individual is entitled to immediate release. With suspension of the writ, this immediate judicial review of the imprisonment becomes unavailable. This suspension triggered the most heated and serious constitutional disputes of the Lincoln Administration.

Lincoln's defenders argued that "events" had forced his decision. On April 19, the Sixth Massachusetts Militia arrived in Washington after having literally fought its way through hostile Baltimore. On April 20, Marylanders severed railroad communications with the North, almost isolating Washington, D.C., from that part of the nation for which it remained the capital. Lincoln was apoplectic. He had no information about the whereabouts of the other troops promised him by Northern governors, and Lincoln told Massachusetts volunteers on April 24, "I don't believe there is any North. The Seventh Regiment is a myth. R. Island is not known in our geography any longer. *You* are the only Northern realities."[7] On April 25, the Seventh New York Militia finally reached Washington after struggling through Maryland. The right of *habeas corpus* was so important that the president actually considered the bombardment of Maryland cities as a preferable alternative to suspension of the writ; he authorized General Winfield Scott, Commander of the Army, to bombard the cities if "necessary," but only "in the extremest necessity"[8] was Scott to suspend the writ of *habeas corpus*.

In Maryland, there was at this time a dissatisfied American named John Merryman. Merryman's dissent from Lincoln's charted course was expressed in both word and deed. He spoke out vigorously against the Union and in favor of the South. He recruited a company of soldiers for the Confederate Army and became their Lieutenant Drillmaster. Thus, he not only exercised his constitutional right to disagree with what the government was doing, but engaged in raising an armed group to attack and attempt to destroy the government. This young man's actions precipitated legal conflict between the president and chief justice of the United States, Roger B. Taney. On May 25, 1861, Merryman was arrested by the military and lodged in Fort McHenry, Baltimore, for various alleged acts of treason. Shortly after Merryman's arrest, his counsel sought a writ of *habeas corpus* from Chief Justice Taney, alleging that Merryman was being illegally held at Fort McHenry. Taney, already infamous for the *Dred Scott* decision, took jurisdiction as a Circuit Judge. On Sunday, May 26, 1861, Taney issued a writ to fort commander George Cadwalader, directing him to produce Merryman before the Court the next day at 11:00 a.m. Cadwalader respectfully refused on the ground that President Lincoln had authorized the suspension of the writ of *habeas corpus*. To Taney this was constitutional blasphemy. He immediately issued an attachment for Cadwalader for contempt. The marshal could not enter the Fort to serve the attachment, so the old justice, recognizing the impossibility of enforcing his order, settled back and produced the now famous opinion, *Ex parte Merryman*.[9]

Notwithstanding the fact that he was in his eighty-fifth year, the chief justice vigorously defended the power of Congress alone to suspend the writ of *habeas corpus*. The Chief took this position in part because permissible suspension was in the section of the Constitution describing congressional duties.[10] He ignored the fact that it was placed there by the Committee on Drafting at the Constitutional Convention in 1787 as a matter of form, not substance. Nowhere did he acknowledge that a rebellion was in progress, and that the fate of the nation was, in fact, at stake. Taney missed the crucial point made in the draft of Lincoln's report to Congress on July 4: The whole of the laws which were required to be faithfully executed, were being resisted, and failing of execution, in nearly one-third of the states. Must they be allowed to finally fail of execution, even had it been perfectly clear, that by the use of the means necessary to their execution, some single law, made in such extreme tenderness of the citizen's liberty, that practically, it relieves more of the guilty, than of the innocent, should, to a very limited extent, be violated? To state the question more directly, are all the laws, *but one*, to go unexecuted, and the government itself go to pieces, lest that one be violated?[11]

By addressing Congress, Lincoln had ignored Taney. Nothing more was done about Merryman at the time. Merryman was subsequently released from custody and disappeared into oblivion. Two years later, Congress resolved the ambiguity in the Constitution and permitted the president the right to suspend the writ while the rebellion continued.[12] Lincoln's handling of Merryman could be said to have been out of "the extremest necessity," and may have saved our country from destruction, yet imagine the reaction of our fellow American citizens today if a militant antiwar demonstrator was treated as Merryman was in 1861.

Nevertheless, five years later (after the Union victory and with a Lincoln appointee—Salmon P. Chase—now serving as chief justice) the Supreme Court reached essentially the same conclusion as Taney in a case called *Ex parte Milligan*: "The Constitution of the United States is a law for rulers and people, equally in war and in peace. . . . The government, within the Constitution, has all the powers granted to it, which are necessary to preserve its existence."[13] *Habeas corpus* could be suspended, but only by Congress; and even then, the majority said that civilians could not be held by the Army for trial before a military tribunal, not even if the charge was fomenting an armed uprising in a time of civil war.

Lincoln never denied that he had stretched his presidential power. "These measures," he declared, "whether strictly legal or not, were ventured upon, under what appeared to be a popular demand, and a public necessity; trusting, then as now, that Congress would readily ratify them."[14] Lincoln thus confronted Congress with a *fait accompli*. It was a case of a president deliberately exercising legislative power, and then seeking congressional ratification after the event. There remained individuals who adamantly believed that in doing so he had exceeded his authority.

The constitutional questions—the validity of the initial war measures, the legal nature of the conflict, Lincoln's assumption of war power—came before the Supreme Court in one of the classic cases heard by that tribunal. The decision in the *Prize Cases*[15] was issued in March 1863, though the specific executive acts had been performed in 1861. The particular question before the Court pertained to the seizure of vessels for violating the blockade, whose legality has been challenged since it was set up by presidential proclamation in absence of a congressional declaration of war. The issue, however, had much broader implications, since the blockade was only one of the emergency measures Lincoln took by his own authority in the "eighty days."

It was argued in the *Prize Cases* that Congress alone had the power to declare war, that the president had no right to institute a blockade until after such a declaration, that war did not lawfully exist when the seizures were made, and that judgments against the ships in lower federal courts were invalid. Had the high court in 1863 decided according to such arguments, it would have been declaring invalid the basic governmental acts by which the war was waged in its early months, as well as the whole legal procedure by which the government at Washington had met the 1861 emergency. The matter went even further and some believed a decision adverse to the president's excessive power would have overthrown, or cast into doubt, the legality of the whole war.

Pondering such an embarrassment to the Lincoln Administration, the distinguished lawyer Richard Henry Dana, Jr., wrote to Charles Francis Adams: "Contemplate . . . the possibility of a

Supreme Court, deciding that this blockade is illegal! . . . It would end the war, and how it would leave us with neutral powers, it is fearful to contemplate!"[16]

Given these circumstances, the Lincoln Administration was enormously relieved when the Court sustained the acts of the president, including the blockade. A civil war, the Court held, does not legally originate because it is declared by Congress. It simply occurs. The "party in rebellion" breaks allegiance, "organizes armies, and commences hostilities." In such a case, it is the duty of the president to resist force by force, to meet the war as he finds it "without waiting for Congress to baptize it with a name." As to the weighty question whether the struggle was an "insurrection," or a "war" in the full sense (as if between independent nations), the Court decided that it was both.[17]

The Court then held Lincoln's acts valid. The blockade was upheld, and the condemnation of the ships sustained. But it was a narrow victory. The decision, handed down on March 10, 1863, was five to four, with Chief Justice Taney among the dissenters. Again, Lincoln was not Don Quixote: he could count judicial votes as well as congressional and popular votes. He had stacked the Court in his favor and his appointments cast the deciding votes. The three Lincoln appointees—Noah H. Swayne, Samuel F. Miller, and David Davis—joined Justice Robert C. Grier, who wrote the majority opinion, as did the loyal Justice James M. Wayne of Georgia.

Another illustration of Lincoln's legal and political astuteness with constitutional issues relates to emancipation. The problem was prodigious. Nothing in the Constitution authorized the Congress *or* the president to confiscate property without compensation. When the preliminary Emancipation Proclamation, issued on September 22, 1862, declared slaves in the states still in rebellion to be free on January 1, the legal basis for this action seemed obscure. Lincoln cited two acts of Congress for justification.[18] Although reference to the two acts occupied much of the proclamation, they actually had little to do with the subject, indicating that Lincoln had not really settled in his own mind the extent of his power and on what authority to issue the Proclamation. But, by the time of the final Emancipation Proclamation on January 1, 1863, Lincoln had concluded his act to be a war measure taken by the Commander in Chief to weaken the enemy.

> Now, therefore I, Abraham Lincoln, President of the United States, by virtue of the power in me vested as Commander-in-Chief, of the Army and Navy of the United States in time of actual armed rebellion against authority and government of the United States, and as a fit and necessary war measure for suppressing said rebellion, do . . . order and declare that all persons held as slaves within said designated States, and parts of States, are, and henceforward shall be free; . . .[19]

The Proclamation may have had "all the moral grandeur of a bill of lading," as historian Richard Hofstadter later charged,[20] but the basic legal argument for the validity of Lincoln's action could be understood by everyone. African-Americans in the North and Union-occupied South reacted with exhilaration when the proclamation was signed on January 1, 1863, and more than 180,000 went to serve in the Union forces.[21] And the time was ripe. To a critic, James Conkling, the president wrote:

> You dislike the emancipation proclamation; and, perhaps, would have it retracted. You say it is unconstitutional—I think differently. I think the constitution invests its commander-in-chief, with the law of war, in time of war. The most that can be said, if so much, is, that slaves are property. Is there—has there ever been—any question that by the law of war, property, both of enemies and friends, may be taken

when needed? And is it not needed whenever taking it, helps us, or hurts the enemy?[22]

This is the Lincoln who consistently took the shortest distance between two legal points. The proposition as a matter of law may be argued. But it is not the law being analyzed, but rather Lincoln's political *and* legal approach to it. Lincoln saw the problem with the directness with which he dissected most problems: the Commander in Chief may, under military necessity, take property. Slaves were property. There was a military necessity. Therefore, Lincoln, as Commander in Chief, took the property. Not only could Lincoln count votes, he could reason clearly during a constitutional crisis.

Clement Laird Vallandigham, the best known antiwar Copperhead[23] of the Civil War, was perhaps President Lincoln's sharpest critic. An Ohioan, this "wiley agitator,"[24] as Lincoln once obliquely described him, found many supporters for his views in New York State. Active in politics throughout most of his life, he was elected to Congress from Ohio in 1856, 1858, and 1860. Before he was defeated for the 38th Congress in 1862, he returned to Ohio to seek the Democratic nomination for governor. While in Congress he made a bitter political speech on July 10, 1861, criticizing Lincoln's inaugural address and the president's message on the national loan bill. He charged Lincoln with the "wicked and hazardous experiment" of calling the people to arms without counsel and authority of Congress, with violating the Constitution in declaring a blockade of Southern ports, with "contemptuously" setting at defiance the Constitution in suspending the writ of *habeas corpus*, and with "cooly" coming before the Congress and pleading that he was only "preserving and protecting" the Constitution and demanding and expecting the thanks of Congress and the country for his "usurpations of power."[25]

In his last extended speech in Congress on January 14, 1863, Vallandigham reviewed his lifelong attitude on slavery and espoused the extreme Copperhead doctrine, saying:

> Neither, sir, can you abolish slavery by argument. . . . The South is resolved to maintain it at every hazard and by every sacrifice; and if "this Union cannot endure part slave and part free," then it is already and finally dissolved. . . . But I deny the doctrine. It is full of disunion and civil war. It is disunion itself. Whoever first taught it ought to be dealt with as not only as hostile to the Union, but an enemy of the human race. Sir, the fundamental idea of the Constitution is the perfect and eternal compatibility of a union of States "part slave and part free;" . . . In my deliberate judgment, a confederacy made up of a slaveholding and non-slaveholding States is, in the nature of things, the strongest of all popular governments.[26]

Later that year, on March 25, 1863, Union General Ambrose E. Burnside took command of the Department of the Ohio with headquarters at Cincinnati. Burnside, who earlier had succeeded George B. McClellan in the command of the Army of the Potomac, had failed miserably before Lee at Fredericksburg. Smarting from his defeat, he was eager to repair his military reputation. The seat of the Copperhead movement was located within the area of his new command. Wholesale criticism of the war was rampant there and this particularly irked Burnside. On March 21, the week after Vallandigham's return from Washington and four days before Burnside took command of the Department of the Ohio, Vallandigham had made one of his typical anti-Administration speeches at Hamilton, Ohio. On April 13, General Burnside, without consultation with his superiors, issued his famous General Order No. 38 in which he announced that all persons found within the Union lines committing acts for the benefit of the enemies of the country would be tried as spies or traitors, and, if convicted, would suffer death.[27] The Order enumerated the various classes of persons falling within its scope and stated that the habit of declaring sympathy for the enemy would not be allowed in the Department and that persons committing such offenses would be at once arrested with a view to being tried or banished from the Union lines.[28]

Learning that Vallandigham was to speak at a Democratic mass meeting at Mt. Vernon, Ohio, on May 1, Burnside dispatched from his staff two captains in civilian clothes to listen to Vallandigham's speech. One of the captains leaned against the speaker's platform and took notes while the other stood a few feet from the platform among the audience. Vallandigham concluded his speech with a call to "hurl 'King Lincoln' from his throne."[29] As a result of the captains' reports, Vallandigham was arrested in his home at Dayton, on Burnside's orders, early after midnight on May 5 and escorted to Kemper Barracks, the military prison in Cincinnati. On May 6 and 7, he was tried by a military commission convened by General Burnside, found guilty of violation of General Order No. 38, and sentenced to imprisonment for the duration of the war.[30]

On the first day of his imprisonment, Vallandigham smuggled out a message, "To the Democracy of Ohio," in which he protested that his arrest was illegal and triggered by no offense other than an expression of his "political opinion." He urged his fellow Democrats to "be firm" and assured them: "As for myself, I adhere to every principle, and will make good, through imprisonment and life itself, every pledge and declaration which I ever made, uttered or maintained from the beginning."[31] Vallandigham's counsel applied to the United States circuit court, sitting at Cincinnati, for a writ of *habeas corpus*, which was denied. This time, unlike *Merryman*, the circuit court agreed with the suspension.[32] An application was made later for a writ of *certiorari* to bring the proceedings of the military commission for review before the Supreme Court of the United States.

This application was denied on the ground that the Supreme Court had no jurisdiction over a military tribunal.[33]

General Burnside approved the finding and the sentence of the military commission and made plans to send Vallandigham to Fort Warren, Boston Harbor, for imprisonment. Before these plans could be carried out, however, President Lincoln telegraphed an order that commuted the sentence to banishment from Union territory.

Vallandigham was then conducted by way of Louisville, Kentucky, and Murfreesboro, Tennessee, into Confederate lines. He reached the headquarters of General Braxton Bragg on May 25.[34] But before the federal officers left him, Vallandigham announced defiantly: "I am a citizen of Ohio, and of the United States. I am here within your lines by force and against my will. I therefore surrender myself to you as a prisoner of war."[35] Vallandigham subsequently found his way to the Confederate capital of Richmond, where he was received indifferently by the Confederate authorities, although he maintained the fiction that he was a Confederate prisoner of war. Having resolved before leaving Cincinnati to endeavor to go to Canada, Vallandigham, without interference, took passage on June 17 on the blockade runner *Cornubia* of Wilmington bound for Bermuda, arriving on June 20. After ten days in Bermuda, he traveled by steamer to Halifax, Canada, arriving there on July 5. He then found his way to Niagara Falls, Canada, and then settled at Windsor, opposite Detroit, where he remained until he returned to Ohio on June 15, 1864.[36]

The arrest, military trial, conviction, and sentence of Vallandigham aroused excitement throughout the country. The public roundly criticized Burnside for the issuance of General Order No. 38 and for its use against the Ohio Copperhead. President Lincoln also endured severe criticism for commuting instead of countermanding Vallandigham's sentence. The general dissatisfaction with the case was not confined to radical Copperheads. The outcome also disturbed many conservative Democrats who were otherwise loyal government supporters in the prosecution of the war. Many Republican newspapers joined in questioning the action, and public meetings of protest were organized in several cities. The Democrats of Albany hosted one of the most dignified and impressive protest meetings on Saturday evening, May 16, 1863, three days before Lincoln altered Burnside's sentence of imprisonment and ordered that Vallandigham be sent beyond federal lines. Staged in the park in front of the state capitol, it was presided over by Erastus Corning, a distinguished congressman from the city. Democratic governor Horatio Seymour, though unable to attend, endorsed the meeting in a letter, which was also published by nearly every Democratic newspaper in the North. The question posed in that letter, and indeed on the minds of all Democrats in attendance, was whether "the war was being waged to put down rebellion in the South or 'to destroy free institutions at the North.'"[37]

At the rally, fiery speeches criticized Burnside for his action against Vallandigham. Orator after orator expressed outrage against the allegedly arbitrary action of the Administration in suppressing the liberty of speech and of the press, the right of trial by jury, the law of evidence, and the right of *habeas corpus*, and, in general, its assertion of the supremacy of military over civil law. The attendees adopted a series of resolutions by acclamation and ordered that a copy of these resolutions be transmitted "to his Excellency the President of the United States, with the assurance of this meeting of their hearty and earnest desire to support the existing Rebellion." Three days later, Corning addressed the resolutions to the president and sent them along with a brief note signed by himself, as president of the assemblage, and by its vice presidents and secretaries. Though couched in dignified and respectful language, the resolutions clearly articulated the position of those attending the meeting—they regarded the arrest and imprisonment of Vallandigham illegal and constitutional, and deplored the alleged usurpation of personal rights by the Administration.[38]

On May 28, 1863, the president acknowledged receipt of the resolutions in a note addressed to "Hon. Erastus Corning," promising to "give the resolutions . . . consideration" and "to find time, and make a respectful response."[39]

There is no record that Lincoln was consulted by General Burnside in advance of the issuance of General Order No. 38, or over the arrest, trial, and sentence of Vallandigham. Indeed, Lincoln knew of Vallandigham only what he read in the newspaper. Lincoln was, of course, thoroughly familiar with Vallandigham as leader of the Copperhead critics of his Administration, but Vallandigham, after being rejected by Democratic party leaders in his 1863 bid for Ohio governor, apparently decided to become "a martyr to the cause [and] have himself arrested."[40] If left to his discretion alone, Lincoln would probably have counseled that Vallandigham be allowed to talk himself to death politically.

Yet on June 12, 1863, the president sent a studied reply to the Albany Democrats addressed to "Hon. Erastus Corning & others." In a closely reasoned document of more than 3,000 words, constructed in lawyer-like fashion, Lincoln justified the action of the Administration in the arrest, trial, imprisonment, and banishment of Vallandigham and elaborated on his view that certain proceedings are constitutional "when, in cases of rebellion or Invasion, the public Safety requires them, which would not be constitutional when, in [the] absence of rebellion or invasion, the public Safety does not require them." The president defended the action not on free speech grounds but on the effects of such speech. The political instincts of the lawyer-president emerged in Lincoln's reply when he said:

> In giving the resolutions that earnest consideration which
> you request of me, I can not overlook the fact that the meeting speak as "Democrats." Nor can I, with full respect
> for their known intelligence, and the fairly presumed
> deliberation with which they prepared their resolutions, be

permitted to suppose that this occurred by accident, or in any way other than that they preferred to designate themselves "democrats" rather than "American citizens." In this time of national peril I would have preferred to meet you upon a level one step higher than any party platform.[41]

Corning referred Lincoln's response to the committee that reported the resolutions while they were widely printed in pro-Lincoln newspapers throughout the country. On July 3, Corning forwarded to the president the rejoinder of the committee, another document of some 3,000 words. This rejoinder dwelt at length upon what the committee deemed "repeated and continued" invasions of constitutional liberty and private rights by the Administration and asked anew what the justification was "for the monstrous proceeding in the case of a citizen of Ohio." The rejoinder, drawn mainly by a former justice of Ohio's Court of Appeals, did not maintain the evenhanded dignity of the original resolutions, charging Lincoln with "pretensions to more than regal authority," and insisted that he had used "misty and cloudy forms of expression" in setting forth his pretensions. The committee was especially sensitive to Lincoln's argument that the resolutions were presented by "Democrats" instead of by "American citizens" and sought to portray the president as a usurper of constitutional liberties: The president was too busy with countless other issues to engage in prolonged debate. He had his say in his reply to the initial resolutions, ignored the rebuttal and turned to other matters.

Almost simultaneously, Lincoln found himself engaged in a similar encounter with Democrats in Ohio. The Ohio Democratic State Convention held at Columbus on June 11, 1863, nominated Vallandigham for governor by acclamation while he was still within the Confederate lines. George E. Pugh, Vallandigham's lawyer in the *habeas corpus* proceedings, was nominated for lieutenant governor.

The convention passed a series of resolutions condemning the arrest, trial, imprisonment, and banishment of Vallandigham and appointed a committee of nineteen members to communicate with the president and to request the return of Vallandigham to Ohio. Fifteen members of the Committee of Nineteen, twelve of them either congressmen or congressmen-elect, left for Washington on June 23 to address the president.[42] The committee called on the president at the White House and filed with him its protest, including an abridged version of the resolutions adopted by the Ohio Democratic State Convention. Similar in import to those adopted by the Albany Democrats, the resolutions held that "the arrest, imprisonment, pretended trial, and actual banishment of Clement L. Vallandigham" was a "palpable" violation of the Constitution.[43] The committee went on to elaborate its view that the Constitution is no different in time of insurrection or invasion from what it is in time of peace and public security.[44]

Reemploying the arguments he had used in his letter to the Albany Democrats, Lincoln promptly replied to the Ohio committee. He added "a word" to his Albany response:

> You claim that men may, if they choose, embarrass those
> whose duty it is, to combat a giant rebellion, and then be
> dealt with in turn, only as if there was no rebellion. The
> constitution itself rejects this view. The military arrests and
> detentions, which have been made, including those of Mr.
> V. which are not different in principle from the others, have
> been for *prevention*, and not for *punishment*—as injunctions to stay injury, as proceedings to keep the peace—. . .[45]

In concluding his reply, Lincoln introduced a new legal argument. He insisted that the attitude of the committee encouraged desertion and resistance to the draft and promised to release Vallandigham if a majority of the committee would sign and return to him a duplicate of his letter committing themselves to the following propositions:

> 1. That there is now a rebellion in the United States, the object and tendency of which is to destroy the national Union; and that in your opinion, an army and navy are constitutional means for suppressing that rebellion.
>
> 2. That no one of you will do any thing which in his own judgment, will tend to hinder the increase, or favor the decrease, or lessen the efficiency of the army or navy, while engaged in the effort to suppress that rebellion; and,
>
> 3. That each of you will, in his sphere, do all he can to have the officers, soldiers, and seamen of the army and navy, while engaged in the effort to suppress the rebellion, paid, fed, clad, and otherwise well provided and supported.[46]

Not surprisingly unconvinced, the Ohio committee spurned Lincoln's concluding proposals and demanded in its rejoinder the revocation of the order of banishment, not as a favor, but as a right, without sacrifice of dignity and self respect. Once again, Lincoln did not reply to the rejoinder of the Ohio committee.[47]

Safe in his retreat in Canada, Vallandigham accepted the nomination for governor of Ohio by the Democratic State Convention in an impassioned letter, "Address to the Democracy of Ohio." The name of Burnside, he declared, was infamous forever in the ears of all lovers of constitutional liberty and the president was guilty of "outrages upon liberty and the Constitution." Vallandigham's "opinions and convictions as to war" and his faith "as to final results from sound policy and wise statesmanship" were not only "unchanged but confirmed and strengthened."[48]

While the Democrats went on to conduct a vigorous campaign, the Republicans nominated John Brough, a former Democrat, to oppose Vallandigham. The campaign that ensued polarized the state of Ohio. There was no middle ground in the campaign— partisanism intensified among Ohioans to the point of severed social and business relations, violence among both men and women, and even bloodshed. One Ohioan, expressing a sentiment perhaps shared today, condemned Ohioans "who permitted such a convention in their midst, desecrating by its unhallowed breath the fair escutcheon of a noble state (and at a time too when thousands of her sons are writing the story of her glory in their blood)."[49]

The tone and temper of the Democratic campaign was typified by a speech at St. Mary's, Ohio, on August 15, 1863, by Pugh, the candidate for lieutenant governor. Pugh paid his "compliments" to Lincoln in language—printed in full by the Columbus *Crisis* the following month—which outdid Vallandigham:

> Beyond the limits and powers confided to him by the Constitution, he is a mere county Court lawyer, and not entitled to any obedience or respect, so help me God. [Cheers and cries of "Good."] And when he attempts to compel obedience beyond the limits of the Constitution, by bayonets and by swords, I say that he is a base and despotic usurper, whom it is your duty to resist by every possible means, and, if necessary, by force of arms. [Cheers and cries, "That's the talk."] If I must have a despot, if I must be subject to the will of any one man, for God's sake let him be a man who possesses some great civil or military virtues. Give me a man eminent in council, or eminent in the field, but, for God's sake, don't give me the miserable mountebank who at present exercises the office of President of the United States.[50]

This extreme language may well have contributed to the result of the election. The total vote in Ohio was more than 432,000. Brough received a solid majority both at home and among the soldier votes collected in the field, winning 57 percent of the vote. Brough even carried Vallandigham's home county by a slim margin.[51]

One more formal effort was made on Vallandigham's behalf. On February 29, 1864, Ohio congressman George H. Pendleton (later that year to become the Democratic candidate for vice president of the United States) offered the following resolution in the House of Representatives and moved the previous question for adoption:

> Resolved, . . . That the military arrest, without civil warrant, and trial by military commission without jury, of Clement L. Vallandigham, a citizen of Ohio, not in the land or naval forces of the United States or the militia in actual service, by order of Major General Burnside, and his subsequent banishment by order of the President, executed by military force, were acts of mere arbitrary power, in palpable violation of the Constitution and laws of the United States.

The proposed resolution was killed by a vote of seventy-seven to forty-seven.[52]

In developing his arguments for sustaining the government's actions on Vallandigham, Lincoln turned above all to the doctrine of necessity. In his view, the civil courts were powerless to deal with the insurrectionary activities of individuals.[53] As Lincoln expressed the problem:

> [H]e who dissuades one man from volunteering, or induces one soldier to desert, weakens the Union cause as much as he who kills a union soldier in battle. Yet this dissuasion, or inducement, may be so conducted as to be no defined crime of which any civil court would take cognizance.[54]

Lincoln knew, as president, he had to act to counter such subtle, and not so subtle, treasons. In his most famous passage on the subject, contained in the Corning Letter, Lincoln stated eloquently:

> Must I shoot a simple-minded soldier boy who deserts, while I must not touch a hair of a wiley agitator who induces him to desert? This is none the less injurious when effected by getting a father, or brother, or friend, into a public meeting, and there working upon his feelings, till he is persuaded to write the soldier boy, that he is fighting in a bad cause, for a wicked administration of a contemptable government, too weak to arrest and punish him if he shall desert. I think that in such a case, to silence the agitator, and save the boy, is not only constitutional, but, withal, a great mercy.[55]

In the "epilogue" to his book, *The Fate of Liberty*, historian Mark E. Neely, Jr., closes by admitting:

> If a situation were to arise again in the United States when the writ of *habeas corpus* were suspended, government would probably be as ill-prepared to define the legal situation as it was in 1861. The clearest lesson is that there is no clear lesson in the Civil War—no neat precedents, no ground rules, no map. War and its effect on civil liberties remain a frightening unknown.[56]

Neely's point is well taken today: Since September 11, 2001, many scholars and citizens have questioned what effect President Bush's reactions and actions to the problems of national security and war will have on his legacy and on civil liberties. Currently, there is much dissension among Americans over the president's motive in the war on Iraq. Surely, President Bush has not yet met the greatest challenges this war will present. Even though Lincoln improvised on civil liberties during the Civil War, he ultimately preserved the American system itself. After the Iraqi conflict ends, Bush must create a more democratic government, and reunite not only the American people, but with as many countries as he can.

Today, "alerts and precautions concerning possible saboteurs" are a "prominent feature of life," but there were terrorists even in the time of Lincoln. In 1864, Southern agents devised a plan to use arson to spread panic throughout Northern cities. Security was heightened in and around Washington to protect against the arsonists' plans. In New York, arsonists were successful and destroyed a lumberyard and some houses. While "it is encouraging to know that this nation has endured such troubles before and survived them," terrorist measures regarded as severe in Lincoln's time seem mild when compared to those of Osama Bin Laden or Saddam Hussein.[57]

After Bin Laden and his forces of Al Qaeda admitted to masterminding the destruction of the Twin Towers and the Pentagon on September 11, hundreds of suspected Al Qaeda associates were arrested and detained in Guantánamo Bay, Cuba. President Bush proposed the use of military tribunals to try foreigners charged with terrorism. With over ninety million cases in our justice system each year, proponents argued that these commissions were needed. Such commissions do not enforce national laws, but a body of international law that has evolved over the centuries.[58]

Historically, military commissions during wartime began as traveling courts when there was a need to impose quick punishment. The use of military tribunals, rather than the usual justice system, was used not only during the Civil War, but also during the Revolutionary War, Mexican War, and both World Wars. Lincoln declared martial law and authorized such forums to try guerillas or terrorists during the American Civil War because of the ability of the tribunals to act quickly, preserve and protect intelligence gathered through interrogation, and otherwise protect civilians who would have been jurors if tried in a United States district court. During the Civil War, the Union Army conducted at least 4,271 trials by military commission, which reflected the disorder of the time.

Lincoln answered his critics with a reasoned, constitutional argument. A national crisis existed and in the interest of self-preservation he had to act. At the same time he realized Congress had the ultimate responsibility to pass judgment on the measures he had taken. He found the right of self-preservation in Article II, section 1, of the Constitution, whereby the chief executive is required "to preserve, protect and defend" it, and in section 3, that he "take care that the laws be faithfully executed." All of the laws which were required to be "faithfully executed" were being resisted, and "failed of execution" in nearly one-third of the states.

Like Lincoln's critics during the Civil War, many have expressed their concern about the modern use of military tribunals.[59] Some fear that "people around the world will view the outcome as a foregone conclusion."[60] Others have questioned whether the proposed use of military tribunals would survive a court challenge, asserting that courts may not find that current circumstances justify the use of the tribunals.[61]

It is not clear whether the 9/11 terrorists and detainees, whether apprehended in the United States or abroad, are protected under America's criminal justice system. Initially, President Bush proposed that those detained as enemy combatants be protected by neither the international law of war nor the four Geneva Conventions. However, he reversed himself when many countries indicated that if detainees would not be entitled to the Geneva Convention protections, they would be hesitant to turn over any alleged terrorists in their custody. Furthermore, our own Department of Defense indicated that if this country refused to apply the international law protections, Bush would be putting troops in Afghanistan, and now Iraq, at risk if they were captured.[62] Afghanistan and other unfriendly countries would likely refuse to apply such protections as well.

To address some of the confusion, the Pentagon issued regulations to govern tribunals. Under Military Commission Order No. 1, issued in March 2002, the secretary of defense was vested with the power to "issue orders from time to time appointing one or more military commissions to try individuals subject to the President's Military Order and appointing any other personnel necessary to facilitate such trials."[63]

The commissions are to be composed of military personnel and civilians who are commissioned sitting as both trier of fact and law. Any evidence may be admitted as long as, according to a reasonable person, it will have probative value. The defendant is entitled to a presumption of innocence and must be convicted beyond a reasonable doubt. Only two-thirds of the panel, however, is needed to convict. The sentence may be reviewed by the Department of Defense and the president.

Despite efforts to clearly regulate the parameters of these tribunals, criticism has remained. A *New York Times* editorial issued after the establishment of these regulations noted that despite the fact that the idea of military tribunals for suspected terrorists is less troubling than it was at inception, "there is still no practical or legal justification for having the tribunals. The United States has a criminal justice system that is a model for the rest of the world. There is no reason to scrap it in these cases."[64]

The rebuttal to this argument has been that with over ninety million cases in our justice system each year, the federal courts may be ill-equipped to efficiently adjudicate terrorism cases. Unique issues like witness security, jury security, and preservation of intelligence have and will cause even more extraordinary delay.

So what is the best way to handle cases of those detained as enemy combatants? Who has jurisdiction over such matters—federal courts or military tribunals? Do United States citizens detained as enemy combatants warrant different protections than foreign detainees?

Legal experts have suggested that a combination of independent federal court review and military tribunal may be the answer. Harvey Rishikoff, former FBI legal counsel, suggests that, clearly, the federal court system as it now exists is ill-equipped to handle matters of domestic and international security. He suggests that "A specialized federal security court could accommodate the particular challenges of prosecuting terrorism cases without undermining constitutional principles." The "New Court for Terrorism" could "craft procedures for secret evidence gathered by sources and methods that should not be disclosed. It would have jurisdiction over matters that involve citizens and noncitizens operating in a loose network for terrorist purposes."[65]

During the 2003–4 term, the United States Supreme Court agreed to consider three cases in which jurisdiction and authority over enemy combatants were at issue.[66] The Supreme Court first considered the case of *Rasul v. Bush*, brought by foreign detainees captured abroad during the hostilities between the United States and the Taliban and detained at Guantánamo Bay, Cuba. The detainees challenged their detention by filing petitions in the District Court for the District of Columbia. The District Court determined that because the petitioners were held outside of the United States, it did not have jurisdiction to hear their petitions.[67] The Court of Appeals affirmed. The United States Supreme Court granted petitioners' writ of *certiorari*. After hearing arguments, the Court opined that because petitioners were being held at an American Naval Base over which the United States exercises "complete jurisdiction and control," "aliens held at the base . . . are entitled to invoke the federal courts' authority."[68] The Supreme Court remanded the case to the district court, based on their finding that the district court did indeed have jurisdiction over challenges made by foreigners to their indefinite detention in a facility under United States control.

The Court next heard arguments in *Hamdi v. Rumsfeld*. Unlike the petitioners in *Rasul*, Yassar Hamdi was an American citizen. He was fighting with the Taliban in Afghanistan in 2001 when his unit surrendered to the Northern Alliance, with which American forces were aligned. He was held at a military brig in Charleston, South Carolina, for two years without being formally charged. In his appeal to the Supreme Court, Hamdi challenged the government's treatment of him as an "enemy combatant." The Supreme Court held that due process requires that United States citizens detained in the United States be given a meaningful opportunity to contest their detention before a "neutral decisionmaker."[69]

The Court stated that the "neutral decisionmaker" could be either the federal judicial system or a military tribunal, provided such tribunal allows the detainee to challenge the factual basis for his detention. The burden is initially on the detainee. Hamdi had also asked the Supreme Court to find that the lower court erred by denying him immediate access to counsel after his detention and by disposing of the case without the benefit of counsel. The justices found that because counsel had been appointed since their granting of *certiorari*, there was no need to decide the issue.[70]

Finally, the Court was presented with *Rumsfeld v. Padilla*. The petitioner, José Padilla, was a United States citizen detained as an enemy combatant in a military brig in Charleston, South Carolina. The threshold questions raised by the *Padilla* case were: (1) whether he properly filed his petition in the appropriate court and (2) whether the president possessed the authority to militarily detain him. Because the United States Supreme Court ruled that Padilla improperly named Donald Rumsfeld and filed his petition in the wrong jurisdiction, it did not reach the second issue regarding the president's authority over this United States citizen.[71]

The decisions made by President Bush are increasingly coming under attack, and even after the Supreme Court's decisions in *Hamdi* and *Rasul*, the legal waters remain murky regarding the president's authority over citizens and noncitizens detained as enemy combatants.[72] What is clear, however, is that our nation is engaged in another conflict that may be as difficult as it is different from the Civil War. It is a war waged against us by an almost unknown and indiscernible enemy.

Some urge us to proclaim the war over with a single victory in Afghanistan. Even our strongest allies and some of our fellow citizens cannot understand why President Bush should continue the war against terrorists by going after them rather than just being reactive. Shouldn't we be satisfied with one victory? Why must we identify other sources of danger and prepare to act against them?

The Corning episode suggests that the argument over Lincoln and civil liberties was as robust in his own time as in ours (ironic in itself since part of the historical argument is that Lincoln suppressed criticism), and deserves a careful reexamination by modern historians. That Lincoln emerges from the perennial controversy that afflicted his Administration over civil liberties with a reputation for statesmanship may be the most powerful argument for his judicious application of executive authority during a national emergency.

Whether President Bush will emerge similarly unscathed is yet to be determined. Approximately nine months after September 11, 2001, two-thirds of Americans supported President Bush's creation of a Homeland Security department, and his overall approval rating was seventy-seven percent.[73] But since attention has turned to Iraq, Bush has spent much of his time attempting to persuade the American public that a war against Iraq is necessary to suppress future September 11–scale terrorism. He proposes that a war can be waged with minimal effort, "but the gods of war have always demanded sacrifice."[74]

When the government of a democratic nation imposes harsh methods to sustain itself, sincere protest and criticism will undoubtedly follow, along with slurs on democracy itself. This criticism secures the future of constitutional liberties if the nation survives; but suppose it does not survive? Suppose it fails because of internal division, dissension, or treason? In such cases, there will be greater criticism, stressing the weakness and inadequacy alleged to be characteristics of a democratic nation in an emergency.

As historian Don E. Fehrenbacher has noted, "Although Lincoln, in a general sense, proved to be right, the history of the United States in the twentieth century suggests that he brushed aside too lightly the problem of the example that he might be setting for future presidents."[75] The full impact of Lincoln's legacy on President Bush is yet to be realized. In Lincoln's words, the United States was "the last best hope of earth," and it still is for survival of democracy in the world.[76]

CHAPTER 16

After Lincoln's Reelection: Foreign Complications

William C. Harris

UNTIL RECENTLY, HISTORIANS LIKE JAMES G. RANDALL AND Allan Nevins have written that the presidential election of 1864 was significant only because it demonstrated the strength of democratic institutions in the midst of a gigantic rebellion. They claimed that the results of the war would have been the same had George B. McClellan and the Democrats won.[1] Abraham Lincoln gave credence to this historical explanation when, in a moment of exhilaration after the election, he announced that the contest had "demonstrated that a people's government can sustain a national election, in the midst of a great civil war. Until now it has not been known to the world that this was a possibility."[2] But during the campaign itself, Lincoln had a different view of the election's importance. At that time, he concluded, the stakes in the election involved nothing less than the success of the Union in the war and the end of slavery. He wrote in late July: "The present presidential contest will almost certainly be no other than a contest between a Union and a Disunion candidate, disunion certainly following the success of the latter. The issue is a mighty one for all people and all time," he contended.[3] Lincoln believed that the Democratic party, controlled by the peace wing or Copperhead faction, was giving aid and comfort to the rebels, despite a post-nomination statement by McClellan supporting the war.

Recent historians like David Long and Mark Neely have described the bitter political divisions in the North during the summer and fall of 1864, and have persuasively challenged the earlier interpretation of the relative unimportance of Lincoln's reelection. Gabor Boritt, in his presentation to the Forum, has just added to this new stream of historical studies on the 1864 election. In my book, *Lincoln's Last Months*, I attempt to build on these accounts and give the reasons the election's outcome made such a tremendous difference in American history.

What, then, did Lincoln's reelection mean? In answering this question, it should be remembered that, before the dramatic Union military successes at Mobile Bay and Atlanta, Lincoln appeared destined to lose the election. Union or Republican victory in November meant the success of the party's firm war policy in contrast to the weak and vacillating approach of McClellan and the Democrats. The Democratic platform, drafted by such distinguished Copperhead lights as Clement Vallandigham, pronounced the war a failure and called for a cease-fire preparatory to a convention of the states to restore the Union with all of their rights guaranteed, including slavery. Jefferson Davis could have written the platform because an armistice would probably have sapped the will of the North to continue the war. The Davis administration was not about to agree on a peace short of independence and thus, after a cease-fire, would have shunned a convention to negotiate the restoration of the Southern states to the Union. A Lincoln defeat at least would have led to confusion in Washington on how the war should end and prolonged the battlefield carnage and all the social and political disorders associated with the conflict. Though slavery was perhaps too far gone to survive very long, a Democratic victory would have continued indefinitely the life of the institution and placed the adoption of the Thirteenth Amendment in jeopardy. A McClellan victory would have emboldened conservatives in Congress, and, though short of a majority, changed the course of reconstruction, federal support for blacks, and the wartime financial measures. Furthermore, a Lincoln defeat would have diminished his reputation in history and short-circuited his apotheosis as America's greatest statesman and folk hero.

After the election, Lincoln's main concern was ending the war as soon as possible on his terms—the disbandment of Confederate armies, the restoration of the Union, and emancipation. These were hardly revolutionary terms in his mind. Other issues also needed attention, including the flare-up of Indian-settler conflict in the West, the illicit trade in the South, the war debt, sensitive patronage matters, including the appointment of a new chief justice of the U.S. Supreme Court, and, by no means the least important, foreign affairs.

Troubles with Great Britain and France in late 1864 and early 1865, after a two-year period of relative quiet, raised the specter of an American armed conflict with one or both of these European powers. Controversies flared up with Britain over Confederate raids from sanctuaries in Canada and with France over that country's intervention in Mexico. Furthermore, as Union victory appeared imminent, many Northerners began to demand retribution against the French and especially the British for the aid that they had given to the Southern rebellion. It was no secret that the leadership class and merchants in these two nations had believed that the South would win its independence and hopefully divide upstart America into two less potent nations. A Confederate victory would also administer a blow to the revolutionary doctrine of republicanism in the Western world. In the 1864 election, much of the European press and the elite, with exceptions like John Bright in Parliament and republicans in France, favored McClellan because they expected him to agree on a compromise peace that would increase the political and sectional divisions in America.[4] The strongly pro-Confederate *Times* (of London), on the other hand, expressed the view that Lincoln's reelection would further the disintegration of the Union by pledging "the nation to a steady continuance in its suicidal policy" of suppression.[5] Lincoln's triumph in November produced a remarkable change in European opinion regarding the outcome of the war. Many in the British and French leadership class now expected that not only would the United States be soon reunited but it also would use its expanding military power against them to seek restitution for their alleged unneutral acts during the Civil War. In late 1864 and early 1865, these leaders feared that, unless the Civil War issues were settled, American intervention in Canada and in Mexico would occur. An armed Anglo-French alliance against the United States would then become a necessity to protect their possessions and interests in North America.

Much of the credit for preventing events from cascading out of control should go to President Lincoln and Secretary of State William H. Seward. Some credit also should be given to British Prime Minister Henry John Temple Palmerston and French Foreign Minister Edouard Drouyn de Lhuys, who foresaw the serious consequences of an American war for their countries and rejected actions that could have easily led to war. The working relationship between the president and his secretary of state had improved dramatically since 1861 when Lincoln had made it clear to Seward who was the boss. During the war Lincoln stood by Seward when Radical Republicans, believing that the secretary was the evil genius in the administration, demanded his removal as the price for their support. Lincoln did not accommodate them. Seward reciprocated the president's loyalty and predicted after his reelection that "henceforth all men will come to see him [as] a true, loyal, patient, patriotic, and benevolent man [who] will take his place with Washington and Franklin, and Jefferson, and Adams among the benefactors of the country and of the human race."[6]

Historians have generally attributed American foreign policy decisions during the war to Seward, except for Lincoln's important role in the settlement of the *Trent* affair in late 1861.[7] However, Lincoln and Seward often consulted on a variety of matters pertaining to the war. It is reasonable to assume that in these conversations issues relating to foreign affairs were discussed. It is also reasonable to conclude that Seward secured the approval of Lincoln before acting or sending instructions to American ministers in Europe. Indeed, his dispatches to American foreign representatives were replete with references to the wishes or instructions of the president on policies and issues.[8] At no time was this truer than in the late-war controversies with Great Britain and France.

Confederate operations out of British-controlled Canada in late 1864 created a greater and more immediate concern for Lincoln than the French imperial adventure in Mexico. Rebel activities based in Canada included financial support to Copperhead candidates in the fall mid-western elections and raids to free Confederate prisoners in the Great Lakes region. In September, Confederate raiders operating from Windsor, Canada, attempted to seize the U.S.S. gunboat *Michigan* at Sandusky, Ohio, and free Southern prisoners held on nearby Johnson's Island. The raiders, led by John Yates Beall, a former Confederate army officer who had been granted a naval commission by Richmond to engage in privateering, failed to capture the warship. But they seized two steamers on Lake Erie, took some of the property to Canada, and scuttled one of the vessels at Windsor, reportedly while British Canadian officials watched. In December, Beall crossed the border into New York to continue his effort to free Confederate prisoners. His luck soon ran out. Federal authorities captured him and a military commission, appointed by General John A. Dix in New York, sentenced him to death for spying and conducting "irregular and unlawful warfare as a guerrilla." Several leading Republicans, including crusty old Thaddeus Stevens, who had no love for rebels, pleaded with Lincoln to commute Beall's sentence to imprisonment on the ground that he was a naval officer pursuing military operations. Even Beall's sister came to the White House and begged for his life, but Lincoln, despite his well-deserved reputation for clemency, refused to intervene. The president's decision probably hinged on his erroneous belief that Beall had been involved in the plot to burn New York hotels and other buildings at the time of the November election.[9]

The incendiary attack on New York City by Confederates based in Canada, following rumors of other rebel plots to disrupt the 1864 election, created fears in the North and added to Northern hostility against the British. According to Captain Robert C. Kennedy, one of the eight raiders, the plan was to set fire to thirty-two buildings, but the phosphorus for igniting the fires was not ready and the attempt was postponed until November 25. The purpose was no longer to disrupt the election; it was, Kennedy declared, to retaliate for General Philip H. Sheridan's "atrocities in the Shenandoah Valley . . . [and] let the people of the North understand . . . that they can't be rolling in wealth and comfort while we at the South are bearing all the hardships and privations" of the war. Ten hotels and Barnum's Museum were only slightly damaged in the attack, and no one died or received serious injuries in the fires. The raiders easily escaped to Canada. However, Kennedy was captured when he crossed the border seeking to return to the South. He was tried and sentenced to be hanged by another of General Dix's military commissions, a fate that the New York Times and fearful New Yorkers demanded for him. In his case, no Northerners pleaded with Lincoln for his life, and on March 25, 1865, Kennedy, defiant to the end, went to the gallows.[10]

Northerners believed, with some justification, that British and Canadian authorities were doing little or nothing to break up the nests of Confederate plotters on their soil. Montreal was the base for most of the rebel agents: there, Jacob Thompson, a former member of President Buchanan's Cabinet, and former U.S. Senator Clement C. Clay, were directing operations across the border while many sympathetic Canadians looked the other way. The threat of an armed American intervention to suppress Confederate activities in lower Canada increased dramatically when, after a bold rebel raid on St. Albans, Vermont, in late 1864, the raiders escaped across the border and Canadian officials refused to hand them over to American authorities.[11]

When Justice Charles Coursol, a Montreal police magistrate, released the prisoners on a technicality along with the money they had seized in Vermont, Northern anger reached a fever pitch. Some powerful Republicans in states bordering on Canada saw the St. Albans affair as part of a larger picture of British hostility toward the Union that needed to be redressed. Senator Zachariah Chandler of Michigan wrote a New England friend that the United States should punish "John Bull for his insolence, impertinence and criminality" during the war; if not, "we deserve the contempt of the world." Chandler declared that the Lincoln administration should act now when American forces were "strong and battle-tested." The *New York Times* called for intervention in Canada, admitting that it might "lead to war with England. But if it must come, let it come. . . . We were never in better condition for a war with England" than now, the *Times* announced. Democrats and self-styled independents like James Gordon Bennett of the *New York Herald* joined the Republicans in demanding that the United States, as the *Herald* expressed it, take Canada by the throat and throttle her "as a St. Bernard would throttle a poodle pup."[12] Secretary of Navy Gideon Welles called Coursol's release of the raiders "an outrage that cannot be acquiesced in," and Secretary of State Seward wrote to Charles Francis Adams, the American minister in London, that "there is imminent danger of a war" over the border incidents.[13]

General Dix, commanding in New York, did not wait for instructions from Washington on the crisis. He issued an order on December 14 for his troops to pursue rebel raiders across the border into Canada and, when captured, "under no circumstances" turn them over to British Canadian authorities.[14] The order, if implemented, could have meant war with Britain.

Lincoln, who had adopted a policy of one war at a time as long as American sovereignty was not threatened or egregious violations of neutral rights did not occur, recognized the danger in Dix's directive. The next day he had Secretary of War Edwin M. Stanton revoke the order, explaining that "the act of invading neutral territory by military commanders is . . . too grave and serious to be left to the discretion or will of subordinate commanders." Nevertheless, Lincoln promised to give the authority for military commanders to cross the border if circumstances required it in order "to pursue marauders, thieves, or murderers of any description."[15]

Lincoln did not sit idly by waiting for British Canadian officials to overrule Coursol's decision and demonstrate their determination to put an end to rebel incursions into the United States. He took measures that he hoped would prompt Canadian authorities to comply with American demands and thus forestall the necessity for armed intervention. The president announced that because of "recent assaults and depredations committed by inimical and desperate persons, who are harbored [in Canada], it has been thought proper to give notice," as required by the Rush-Bagot agreement of 1817, "that after the expiration of six months, . . . the United States must hold themselves at liberty to increase their naval armament upon the [Great] lakes." He threatened to end the reciprocal trade treaty of 1854 if Canadian officials did not act to prevent rebel raids. Through Secretary of State Seward, the president directed that passports be required of all foreigners entering the United States except bona fide immigrants. To soften his actions and keep the door open for a peaceful resolution of the crisis, Lincoln added that "the Colonial authorities of Canada are not deemed to be intentionally unjust or unfriendly towards the United States; but, on the contrary, there is every reason to expect that, with the approval of the [British] imperial government, they will take the necessary measures to prevent new incursions across the border."[16] The Senate supported Lincoln and, outraged by the release of the St. Albans raiders, unilaterally abrogated the reciprocal trade accord of 1854 with Canada. At the same time it gave the required six months' notice for the termination of the Rush-Bagot demilitarization agreement.[17]

The prospect of war spread fear on the Canadian side of the border; and across the Atlantic, Britons fully expected that Lincoln, pressured by Northern opinion, would invade Canada. Prime Minister Palmerston concluded that the United States was preparing for war with Britain, but it would not strike until after the defeat of the Confederate States. In the interval, he promised Queen Victoria that he would attempt to prepare Canadian defenses for the anticipated invasion. From London, Charles Francis Adams wrote Seward on February 23 that "the impression is now very general that peace and restoration [of the Union] are synonymous with war with this country."[18]

But there would be no war between the two Atlantic powers. Neither Palmerston, nor Lincoln, nor Canadian authorities wanted war. Palmerston knew that if war occurred, Canada and the maritime provinces would be lost and British commerce would be seriously crippled. Lincoln had no desire to launch the United States into an international war when he was on the verge of realizing his longing for peace at home and for the restoration of the Union. Indeed, he understood that a war with Britain, perhaps joined by France, could permit the Southern rebels to snatch victory from the jaws of defeat. Faced with ruin if an invasion occurred, Canadian Prime Minister John A. Macdonald and British Governor General Stanley Monck moved in early 1865 to defuse the border crisis.

Monck secured the rearrest of nine of the St. Albans raiders. (However, the prisoners were not extradited to the United States but held for trials in Canada; they ultimately received no punishment.) Meanwhile, Macdonald began militia patrols on the border and took action to eliminate the nests of Confederate agents in Montreal and elsewhere in Canada.[19]

Lincoln, who characteristically had displayed patience during the crisis, accepted the British Canadian show of good will and rescinded the passport order. In early March, he informed the British that the Rush-Bagot disarmament agreement would "remain practically in force," since no more rebel raids from Canada were anticipated.[20] On March 23, Palmerston told Parliament that "there is no danger of war with America. Nothing that has recently passed indicates any hostile disposition on the part of the United States toward us."[21] At the same time the British press, which had been generally hostile to Lincoln, began to convey a favorable view of the backwoods president. Even the pro-Confederate *Times* of London reported on the changing tone in Britain toward the American president. *The Spectator* (London), greatly impressed by Lincoln's second inaugural address, told its readers, "Mr. Lincoln has persevered through all," including foreign difficulties, "without ever giving way to anger, or despondency, or exultation, or popular arrogance, or sectarian fanaticism, or caste prejudice, visibly growing in force of character, in self-possession, and in magnanimity." *The Spectator* admitted that "we can detect no longer the rude and illiterate mould of a village lawyer's thought, but find it replaced by a grasp of principle, a dignity of manner, and a solemnity of purpose" rarely found in political leaders.[22]

Still, the British felt uneasy about what might happen after the Civil War when the United States was almost certain to press compensation claims for damages caused by Confederate sea raiders built in Britain and for other presumed violations of neutral rights. At General Ulysses S. Grant's headquarters in Virginia in late March

1865, Lincoln seemed to favor retribution against the British, though he stopped short of threatening war. According to Horace Porter (Grant's aide-de-camp), the president, while sitting around the campfire, exclaimed: "England will live to regret her inimical attitude toward us. After the collapse of the rebellion, John Bull will find that he has injured himself much more seriously than us." Lincoln particularly expressed his resentment toward Britain for his having to surrender rebel emissaries John Slidell and James M. Mason after their seizure from the *Trent* in 1861. He told Grant and his officers that "it was a pretty bitter pill to swallow, but I contented myself with believing that England's triumph in the matter would be short-lived, and that after ending our war successfully, we would be so powerful that we could call her to account for all the embarrassments she had inflicted upon us."[23] Though Porter might not have quoted Lincoln precisely, the president's bellicosity on this occasion could have been triggered by a visit earlier in the day to the Petersburg battlefield, where he saw the bloody results of a failed Confederate attempt to breach the Federal lines. Like most Northerners, Lincoln partly blamed British aid to the rebels for the prolongation of such carnage.

Seward agreed that the British should have to pay for having "lavishly contributed material support to the insurgents and employ[ing] every moral engine to aid them in overthrowing the government of the United States." Though "demands for redress are very apt to culminate in schemes of conquest. This, however, is not the policy of the President," he wrote Charles Francis Adams. Lincoln "deems conquests unnecessary, demoralizing, and injurious to the republic; . . . unworthy the character of a great nation. . . . The President does not for a moment think of sending armies or navies with such a purpose or upon such motives as have been indicated" in Europe "into Canada, or the West Indies, or Mexico."[24] What steps Lincoln would have taken after the war to secure redress for British wrongs at sea and elsewhere cannot be known. During

Andrew Johnson's presidency, Seward played a leading role in seeking compensation from the British in the so-called *Alabama Claims* negotiations; however, it was not until after he had left the State Department that an agreement was reached which only partly met American demands. But the settlement cleared the way for better Anglo-American relations that would reach fruition in the early twentieth century.

The controversy over the French in Mexico and Napoleon III's installation of Maximilian of Hapsburg as emperor in 1864 became acute after Lincoln's reelection and with the impending success of the Union in the Civil War. Parallel to the winter crisis with Britain over Canada, the Mexican conflict threatened to escalate into an armed confrontation between the two powers. The French intervention in Mexico had clearly violated the Monroe Doctrine. Though Lincoln, Secretary of State Seward, and the American people may only have speculated on Napoleon's intentions in the Western Hemisphere, the French emperor had outlined a Grand Design, as it was called, for North America that included the reorganization of the United States, the Confederate States, and Mexico into a confederation similar to that of the German states.[25]

Napoleon had some trouble taking the Monroe Doctrine seriously, perhaps because Seward, in his communications with France, had avoided mentioning this important American foreign policy statement lest it irritate Napoleon and prompt him to recognize the Confederacy. Lincoln himself seemed less concerned about the issue of the Monroe Doctrine than about the imposition of a nonrepublican, imperial government on the Mexican people. He believed that the success of the French in Mexico would be a disturbing setback for the progress of republicanism and self-government in the Western Hemisphere. The president also feared that French forces might link up with the Confederates in Texas and provide critical material support for the continuation of the Southern rebellion. Already, as the French moved northward, the border was becoming a sieve for supplies for General Kirby Smith's trans-Mississippi army. Union General Nathaniel P. Banks' Red River campaign of 1864, which ended in disaster, had been launched partly to counter the French threat in the Southwest and to cut off material support for the Confederacy. Still, even as Maximilian consolidated his position, Lincoln and Seward assured the French government that the United States had no hostile intentions toward France or its puppet regime. In his annual message to Congress in December 1864, Lincoln referred to Mexico as "a theatre of civil war," avoiding any public suggestion of French imperialism. He also announced that the United States had strictly maintained neutrality between the hostile forces in Mexico.[26] Technically, Lincoln was correct; however, agents of Benito Juarez and American sympathizers operated with virtual impunity in procuring arms and recruits for the Mexican cause in New York, San Francisco, and Union-occupied New Orleans.[27] Furthermore, Lincoln recognized the Juarez government, despite the fact that by late 1864 its rag-tag forces had lost the Mexican heartland to the French.

Republicans in Congress, joined by minority Democrats whose party had actively supported southward expansion before the war, were furious with the Lincoln administration for ignoring the French violation of the Monroe Doctrine. Earlier in 1864, the House of Representatives had unanimously adopted a resolution, introduced by Henry Winter Davis, chair of the Committee on Foreign Affairs, asserting that its members

> were unwilling by silence, to leave the nations of the world under the impression that they are indifferent spectators of the deplorable events now transpiring in the Republic of Mexico; and they therefore think fit to declare that it does not accord with the policy of the United States to acknowl-edge a monarchial government, existing on the ruins of any

republican government in [North] America, under the aus-
pices of any European power.

With the critical 1864 election approaching, the Republican-domi-
nated Senate failed to approve the Davis resolution. Still, Seward,
speaking for Lincoln, reassured the French that the resolution did
not reflect any change in American policy toward the conflict in
Mexico, though he admitted that it "truly interprets the unanimous
sentiment of the people of the United States in regard to Mexico."
He also informed the French that the matter of foreign affairs "is
a practical and purely Executive [power], and the decision of its
constitutionality belongs not to the House of Representatives, nor
even to Congress, but to the President of the United States."[28]

When Congress met in December, the brilliant Henry Winter
Davis, livid at the Lincoln administration's effort to undercut the
House action, introduced a resolution asserting the constitutional
right of Congress to have "an authoritative voice in . . . prescribing
the foreign policy of the United States, as well as in the recognition
of new [governments]." In the afterglow of Lincoln's victory at the
polls, the House tabled the resolution, only to revive it after Davis
made a passionate speech attacking Seward, not Lincoln, and resigning as chairman of the House Committee on Foreign Affairs.
The resolution then passed the House.[29]

Davis's success, however, was brief. Republican newspapers denounced the House's action, charging that the resolution had more
to do with Radical Republican and Democratic hostility toward Lincoln and Seward than the conduct of foreign affairs. The *New York
Times* declared that "the House of Representatives has no right" to
dictate to the president "upon any subject foreign or domestic; and
any attempt to do so is simply an assumption of power with which
it is not clothed." The *Times*, whose main editor was Henry J. Raymond, chair of the national Republican committee, maintained that

Lincoln had repeatedly warned the French against its imperialism in Mexico and that its continuance would inevitably "involve the two countries in war."[30] The *Times* was wrong; Lincoln had not threatened war against the French. Senators, led by Charles Sumner, chair of the Foreign Relations Committee, despite their dislike of Seward and the administration's appeasement policy toward the French, sensed public opposition and refused to challenge Lincoln's control of foreign relations. The Senate did not consider the House resolution.

But the issue of the French in Mexico did not go away; it only intensified in early 1865. The *New York Herald*, reputedly the newspaper with the largest circulation in America, repeatedly demanded the enforcement of the Monroe Doctrine not only in Mexico but everywhere in Latin America. Now was the time to act, the *Herald* exclaimed on January 25: "We are now more powerful than we ever were before, and in every way prepared to wage war on a vast and expensive scale." James Gordon Bennett, the influential proprietor of the *Herald*, even had a plan to end the Civil War and reunite the country by having Confederate veterans join Union troops in a campaign to expel the French and Maximilian from Mexico.[31] Francis P. Blair, Sr., sought to give practical effect to this plan when he met with Jefferson Davis at Richmond in January. Davis seemed to agree with the plan, believing that it would mean an armistice, followed by Confederate independence and not reunion. With this in mind, Davis appointed three peace commissioners to negotiate with Lincoln and Seward at Hampton Roads, Virginia.[32]

News of Lincoln's willingness to meet with the Confederates in early February sent shock waves through the diplomatic corps in Washington. Louis de Geofroy, the French chargé d'affaires in Washington, excitedly reported to Paris that plans were afoot to combine the two armies for an assault on both Mexico and Canada. He indicated that Seward opposed such a venture, but he claimed that Lincoln "affects a great independence from the members of his cabinet and would be perfectly capable of making some great decision without consulting his advisors."[33]

Actually, at Hampton Roads, Lincoln rejected out of hand any discussion of the Bennett-Blair scheme when the Confederate commissioners raised the question and Seward indicated a wish to hear it explained. A French visitor in Washington who was frequently in the company of the president also downplayed the idea of a joint Northern-Southern intervention. He wrote to his wife that, though "Lincoln clearly saw that America was in a position which allowed her to speak firmly" to France, he wanted no war over Mexico.[34] But Napoleon was convinced that an armed conflict with the United States would occur after the Civil War. He directed his Minister of Marine to report on the means of transporting 100,000 troops to Mexico to counter the anticipated American invasion. A commission of officers reported in March that such a large expedition could not be accomplished unless assisted by the British navy. But Prime Minister Palmerston refused to agree to an alliance with France against the United States for what in today's language would be called a "preemptive strike" against a foe. By this time, the crisis over the Canadian border had subsided, and Palmerston refused to be drawn into a war that surely would have meant an American invasion of Canada. Napoleon reluctantly dropped the plan, though reportedly he defiantly declared that "the honor of France was engaged in the support of Maximilian."[35]

Meanwhile, French Foreign Minister Drouyn worked to defuse the Mexican controversy. The foreign minister, evidently without the emperor's approval, told Seward that French forces would be withdrawn from Mexico as soon as possible. On his part, Seward informed the French that Lincoln's nonintervention policy remained unchanged and all "collateral questions arising out of the war [will be] left by us to the arbitrament of reason under the mutations of time." Seward confidently predicted that once the wartime passions against Europe had passed, the American people would support Lincoln in this policy.[36] As is well-known, after the Civil War Napoleon, prompted by the American decision to dispatch troops to the border, saw the handwriting on the wall for his imperialistic adventure in Mexico; he withdrew his troops and Maximilian went to his fate—a Mexican firing squad—in 1867.

In conclusion, Lincoln's determination to avoid a foreign war was severely tested during the winter of 1864–1865. Despite violations of American neutral rights and public pressure for the administration to act in a forceful manner, Lincoln persevered in his policy of avoiding war with powerful foreign nations. At the same time, he insisted that the European governments respect American sovereign rights, though he did not quibble over minor issues or demand satisfaction over British violations that could be settled after the Civil War. Still, Lincoln found distasteful if not abhorrent the presence of nonrepublican regimes or European colonies in the Americas. He believed that a French success in installing a permanent imperial government in Mexico would deal a serious blow to the progress of democracy and republican liberty in the world, which, according to his view, was the fundamental cause for which the Union fought the Civil War. After the Civil War, Secretary of State Seward continued the martyred president's foreign policy and eventually it succeeded in resolving the critical issues with Great Britain and France that the conflict had spawned.

CHAPTER 17

Henry Adams on Lincoln
Garry Wills

HENRY ADAMS RARELY REFERRED TO ABRAHAM LINCOLN IN his public writings, and then equivocally. He was in Rome when news reached him of the president's assassination, and his attitude was distant, hardly grief-stricken. He advised a friend to take with equanimity the fact that the nation's enemies did not express sorrow:

> If other people don't feel as we do about it, we might be disgusted, but that they should is so much a matter of course that I should never have doubted it. But as for the nation, pity is wasted. I am much too strong an American to have thought for a moment that we are going to be shaken by a murder.[1]

His literal distance in Rome seemed to give him an emotional distance as well, as if looking down from a great height at what was distressing others. He wrote his brother Charles Francis Adams, Jr.:

I have already buried Mr Lincoln under the ruins of the
Capitol, along with Caesar, and this I don't mean merely as
a phrase. We must have our wars, it appears, and our crimes,
as well as other countries. I think Abraham Lincoln is rather
to be envied in his death, as in his life somewhat; and if he
wasn't as great as Caesar, he shares the same sort of tomb.
History repeats itself, and if we are to imitate the atrocities
of Rome, I find a certain amusement in conducting my private funeral service over the victims, on the ground that is
most suitable for such associations, of any in the world.[2]

Adams must have been one of very few Americans able to find "a
certain amusement" in the obsequies.

This coldness is especially puzzling because Adams had many
reasons for being attentive to Lincoln. In his early twenties, he
served in the president's administration, though in a subsidiary role.
When Lincoln sent his father as minister to England, Henry went
along as Charles Francis Adams's secretary and was received at
Court as such. Later in his life, his best friend was Lincoln's secretary, admirer, and biographer, John Hay. It seems odd for Adams to
have remained so aloof from Lincoln in these circumstances.

But a careful reading of his whole work, private as well as public,
shows that Adams did have an initial hostility to Lincoln, one not
entirely dispelled by the time of his assassination, though he gradually softened and altered his view after that. He did not mark the
stages of this development, partly because he did not want to rehash
his own first views, and partly because he did not want to quarrel
openly with his father and older brother, who retained their animus
against Lincoln.

Adams liked to say in later life that he came back from Europe,
at twenty-two, to cast his first presidential vote for Lincoln.[3] But
while still traveling abroad in 1860, he had been deeply upset when
he learned that Lincoln won the Republican nomination. He was a

supporter of William Henry Seward, as were his father and brothers at home. At the beginning of the election process, he wrote from Dresden: "The day that I hear that Seward is quietly elected President of the United States, will be a great relief to me for I honestly believe that that and only that can carry us through, even if that can."[4] He and some American friends in Dresden determined to do anything possible to elect Seward,[5] as he told his brother Charles:

> You just mark what Seward says; he's the man of the age and the nation; he knows more in politics than a heap; he's a far-sighted man and yet he's got eyes for what's near, too. I aspire to know him some day. Pray tell him so if you ever lack matter of conversation. Keep him allied with papa, the nearer the better. If he comes in as President in that case, we shall see fun.[6]

When Seward, having lost the nomination, agreed to campaign for the Republican ticket in the general election, he was plotting how he could manipulate Lincoln after his election. The Adams family joined in this endeavor. Henry's brother Charles went out on a campaign swing with Seward, and the two met Lincoln for the first time at Springfield. This Seward-Adams team was acting under the instructions of Seward's political mentor, Thurlow Weed.

After Lincoln won, Weed himself went to Springfield. He meant to convince the president-elect that he should let the better known and better connected Seward form his cabinet. Seward was expected to be secretary of state, but this was not sufficient, said Weed. He hinted that his associate would not accept the post unless his wishes for other cabinet members were honored. Lincoln kept his own counsel, and let Seward, from his Senate seat in Washington, promote efforts to keep the border states from seceding. Seward came up with a series of last-minute deals. With the help of Congressman Adams, he backed an offer suggested by Maryland

Congressman Winter Davis—to admit New Mexico as a slave state. Seward also organized a closed-door peace conference with Southern representatives.

Henry Adams, writing anonymously in the Boston *Daily Advertiser*, enthusiastically backed all of Seward's initiatives. He was smitten with Seward: "From the first sight, he loved the Governor [Seward], who, though sixty years old had the youth of his sympathies."[7] After Seward's first appearance at the Adams home, Henry wrote Charles:

> I sat and watched the old fellow with his big nose and his wire hair and grizzly eyebrows and miserable dress, and listened to him rolling out his grand, broad ideas that would inspire a cow with statesmanship if she understood our language. There's no shake in him. He talks square up to the mark and something beyond it.[8]

Henry was flattered by Seward's confidences in him. "The old file [rascal] has taken a great shine to my cigars and we smoke our good papa perfectly dry after dinner."[9] The most cited physical description of Seward is Adams's from the *Education*: "a head like a wise macaw" and so on.[10] But an even more vivid one is in a letter to his brother Charles:

> I have excited immense delight among some young ladies here by a very brilliant proposition which I made to dye the old sinner's hair bright crimson, paint his face the most brilliant green and his nose yellow, and then to make an exhibition of him as the sage parrot; a bird he wonderfully resembles in manner and profile. If I had a knack at drawing, I would make some such sketch for *Vanity Fair*.[11]

The Adamses shared with Seward an impression that Lincoln had surrendered the management of things to Seward's better-skilled hands. Henry told his brother that Seward was the "virtual ruler of this country."[12] "Lincoln is all right" because he is following Seward's lead.[13] Seward "has arranged or is arranging everything with Lincoln through Thurlow Weed."[14] One of the things he was supposed to be arranging was the appointment of Charles Francis Adams as secretary of the treasury.

What Adams at first read as Lincoln's tacit support for Seward turned into resentment when, as Seward labored in what Adams took to be the good fight, the tacit support began to look like quiet sabotage. Why did Lincoln not throw his weight behind what Seward was doing? His brother Charles, who was now in Washington with Henry, would later be scathing about Lincoln's inactivity during the transition. When Lincoln at last traveled in a leisurely way toward Washington, Charles described him as "perambulating the country, kissing little girls and growing whiskers!"[15] Henry was not quite as outspoken as this, but he made his judgment clear in a major essay he wrote during this period, "The Great Secession Winter," an essay (fortunately for him at the time) not published for almost half a century. There he wrote of the attempts to conciliate the South:

> Mr. Seward, Mr. Winter Davis and the southern Whigs, Mr. Adams, Mr. Sherman and a large share of the best ability of the party, exhausted their influence in advocating these measures, and still the mass of the party hesitated, and turned for the decisive word to the final authority at Springfield. The word did not come. In its stead came doubtful rumors tending to distract public opinion still more. In spite of the assertions of newspapers and to the surprise of the country it became more and more evident that there was

no concerted action between the President-elect and the Republicans at Washington, and that Mr. Seward had acted all winter on his own responsibility. The effect of this discovery was soon evident in the gradual destruction of party discipline in Congress, where every man began to follow an independent course, or commit himself against the measures proposed, from an idea that the President was against them.[16]

When Lincoln reached Washington, the Adamses's coldness to him was not thawed. Seward tried to make Charles Francis Adams the secretary of the treasury. When Lincoln refused his request, Seward promoted Adams for the far inferior reward of appointment as minister to England. Lincoln agreed to this, and Charles Francis accepted. But when Charles Francis went to thank Lincoln, he was expecting serious conversation about his duties. He did not realize that Seward had taken him into Lincoln's office, unexpected and unannounced, during a conversation Lincoln was having with an Illinois congressman about an appointment in his state. This confirmed Charles Francis's opinion that Lincoln was interested in nothing but grubby patronage aspects of the presidency. Charles Francis registered his disgust with the interview in his diary (March 28, 1861). Charles Francis, Jr., repeated his father's account in his own autobiography, and Ernest Samuels accepted this version of events in his influential biography of Henry.[17] Thus was established the attitude of the whole Adams family toward Lincoln. But Mark Neely explains how the Adamses, predisposed to dislike Lincoln, misinterpreted what had happened at the interview, where Lincoln intended no discourtesy.[18] Henry never mentioned the interview in his public or private writings, and we shall see that he departed from the views of his father and brother.

But this would not happen for a while. He and his father continued in London to think that Lincoln was handling the war badly, and they kept looking to Seward for guidance, despite Seward's own erratic ways as secretary of state. They did this even after an initial and temporary disillusionment with Seward. A mere month after his arrival, Charles Francis received an instruction (Dispatch No. 10) from Seward that seemed mad. The minister was told to deliver this message to the Foreign Office: If Great Britain recognized the South as belligerents, accepted diplomatic emissaries from the Confederacy, or failed to honor the North's blockade of the South, the United States will "become once more, as we have twice before been forced to be, enemies of Great Britain."[19] Henry wrote to his brother:

> A despatch arrived yesterday from Seward, so arrogant in tone and so extraordinary and unparalleled in its demands that it leaves no doubt in my mind that our government wishes to force a war with Europe. . . . I have said already that I thought such a policy shallow madness, whether it comes from Seward or from any one else. It is not only a crime, it's a blunder.[20]

Henry's father could not believe that Seward would invent a scheme so foolish. He wrote in his diary (June 10, 1861) that demented men in the cabinet must have forced it on the "calm and wise" secretary of state.

The Adamses in London did not realize that this was just one in a series of irresponsible acts tumbling out of Seward after the inauguration of Lincoln. After months when Seward thought that he and he alone could save the nation, he refused to assume the subordinate place Lincoln had assigned him. Seward strove to maintain his policy of conciliation toward the South. He said that Fort Sumter, in Charleston harbor, should be abandoned, since it was a provocation to the South. When Lincoln overruled him, Seward tried to sabotage the flotilla being sent to resupply the Fort—he not only leaked details of the mission to the press, but redirected the lead ship to a different objective.[21] On the same day this last ploy was attempted, he sent Lincoln "Some Thoughts for the Consideration of the President," arguing that the nation was adrift—there was no policy; the conflict over slavery was irresolvable—and therefore Lincoln should "CHANGE THE QUESTION" (his capital letters). He must demand an assurance from the European powers that they are not interfering in the American hemisphere, and—should that not be forthcoming—must "convene Congress and declare war against them." This would reunite the North and the South, who would be fighting a common enemy—and forgetting, in the process, the subject of slavery.

Seward explained that this course would have to be pursued full time by one man, and since the president had other duties to keep him from such concentration, "I neither seek to evade nor assume responsibility" for doing it. He was asking to be made a war czar. The document is so weird that it is known to historians by its date, the April Fool's Letter. Henry would not have been puzzled by the later Dispatch No. 10 if he had known of these preambles to it. His brother Charles, who had not yet gone into the army, watched incredulously what Seward was doing in Washington. Like all the family, he had revered Seward—he campaigned with him, remember, the year before. But drawing on his diary notes from 1867, he later wrote: "Seward lost his head. He found himself fairly beyond his depth, and he plunged! The foreign-war panacea took possession of him."[22]

Lincoln had softened Dispatch No. 10 before he let Seward send it. The president offered it only for the minister's consideration, not for presentation to the British. Charles Francis accordingly muted and disguised its message when dealing with the Foreign Office. But rumors of this and other aberrations of Seward were relayed to London by the British minister in Washington, Lord Lyons. To them were added speeches in which Seward had talked of the inevitability of Canada someday becoming part of the United States—which was interpreted, along with his other bellicosities, to mean he wanted war with England in order to gain Canada. Charles Francis Adams had to cope with a belief (which even Henry shared) that Seward was maneuvering toward a foreign war.

Because Henry now suspected Seward of wanting to provoke war, he thought the *Trent* affair—the Union capture of Confederate agents, James Mason and John Slidell, off a British ship—was an aggression authorized by Washington, and therefore despaired of his father's task in keeping England from an alliance with the South. He wrote to his brother:

> I consider we are dished, and that our position is hopeless. . . . It is our ruin. . . . Now all the fat's in the fire, and I feel like going off and taking up my old German life again as a permanency. It is devilish disagreeable to act the part of Sisyphus, especially when it is our own friends who are trying to crush us under the rock. . . . This nation [England] means to make war. Do not doubt it. What Seward means is more than I can guess. But if he means war also, or to run as close as he can without touching, then I say that Mr Seward is the greatest criminal we've had yet.[23]

Henry described the British anger over the capture of Mason and Slidell: "The phlegmatic and dogmatic Englishman has been dragged into a state of literal madness, and though not actually riotous, he has lost all his power of self-control."[24] That passion on one side of the Atlantic was matched with an equal frenzy on the other side. American crowds rejoiced at the imprisonment of Mason and Slidell, and wanted them tried for treason—or not, at any rate, released with an apology. The British and American governments tried to control these emotions, vacillating between compromise and ultimatum. The negotiations went on for three months.

Dumbfounded earlier by Seward's "Thoughts" on making himself a war czar, Lincoln called in the chairman of the Senate Committee on Foreign Relations, and quietly made him a consultant, his own confidential anti-Seward. Having read Seward's April Fool's Letter, Sumner backed Lincoln's softening of it, and warned Lincoln against letting such gasconading get out of hand. David Donald claims that, as a result, "Lincoln gave Sumner a virtual veto over foreign policy."[25] Sumner and Seward thus performed a neat dos-a-dos. In the secession winter, Sumner had been intransigent toward the South while Seward was yielding. Now, toward other nations, Seward was the hardliner and Sumner the accommodator. Sumner did not hide his new access, which made him the rallying point for all anti-Seward sentiment, especially in the diplomatic corps.

When it became known that Sumner was, in effect, setting up his own state department at the opposite end of Pennsylvania Avenue, his presence at diplomatic dinners and soirées became as indispensable as that of Seward. Visiting foreigners in Washington, like Prince Napoleon, a cousin of Napoleon III, naturally enough sought out Sumner, for this and more: He was the only senator who spoke fluent French, he had such a wide acquaintance abroad, and he exercised power.[26]

Sumner was on very good terms with the British minister in Washington, Lord Lyons, and he assured him that Seward's hard line should not be taken as the policy of the whole government. This message, sent back to England, only partially eased misgivings there since Seward was still seen as hostile. But Lyons could at least convey the impression that Lincoln had room to maneuver between Seward and Sumner. Meanwhile, Sumner used his English friends to warn the president against intransigence over the *Trent*. During his time in London, Sumner had become close to the liberal reformers John Bright and Richard Cobden, letters from whom he showed to Lincoln, confiding that retention of Mason and Slidell would surely lead to war. Bright recommended submission of the problem to mediators. Lincoln seriously considered this recommendation, backed by Sumner.[27] Having established that as a working option in the cabinet, he then moved beyond it by deciding that the mediation process would take too long—a quicker way of releasing the men should be found. The idea of invoking a procedural error was actually suggested by Charles Francis Adams in a letter to Seward.[28]

No wonder Henry thought Seward's resulting paper brilliant.[29] He and his father still thought Lincoln incapable of real statesmanship, and were not yet aware of Sumner's role in the matter, so they attributed the outcome to "Mr. Seward's good sense"[30] and "Seward's skill."[31] Henry was still complaining in May of 1862: "How do you suppose we can shut people's eyes to the incompetence of Lincoln?"[32] They undoubtedly heard something of Sumner's intervention from his friends Cobden and Bright, who were the Adamses's own London allies in promoting American interests,[33] but they thought that Sumner, when writing to the British reformers, was just expressing his personal jealousy of Seward. Thurlow Weed, Seward's old political manager, wrote to confirm their suspicions of Sumner.[34]

Weed had learned of the British distrust of Seward, and he suggested that Seward send him as a personal emissary to England. Normally, American diplomats on the scene would resent an informal intruder, especially if it were known that the newcomer had closer personal ties with the secretary of state than did the minister. Nor did it help matters that Weed's reputation as a party boss had preceded him to England. But the Adamses welcomed Weed, and watched him work his political magic even on the British.[35] As a newspaper editor himself, Weed was able to deal with British journalists and convince at least some of them that they had misjudged his close friend Seward. Henry, still in his hero-worshiping days, even conceived a "sympathy and affection" for the old political fixer and followed him around "much like a little dog."[36] The more Seward was accepted, the Adamses felt, the easier their tasks would be.

But Weed promoted Seward by attacking Sumner, deepening the Adamses's disaffection with the latter.

Charles Francis Adams was entirely won back to Seward, though the seeds of doubt had been planted in Henry's more probing mind. The father would continue to say that Lincoln should never have been elected. In his 1873 eulogy to Seward, he described the candidate from Illinois (now eight years dead) this way:

> [He was] a person selected partly on account of the absence of positive qualities, so far as was known to the public, and absolutely without the advantage of any experience in national affairs, beyond the little that can be learned by an occupation for two years of a seat in the House of Representatives.

Charles Francis was still rebuking Lincoln for not lending aid to the compromise efforts of Seward:

> His mind had not even opened to the nature of the crisis. From his secluded abode in the heart of Illinois, he was only taking the measure of geographical relations and party services, and beginning his operations where others commonly leave off.[37]

The fact that Henry no longer agreed with this accusation is proved from the *Education*, where he completely rewrote the history of the 1860–1861 transition, claiming, against the evidence of his own writings at the time, that Lincoln and Seward had acted in perfect accord throughout it. He was erasing the grounds for his early criticism of Lincoln.

> Rightly or wrongly the new President and his chief advisers in Washington decided that, before they could administer the government, they must make sure of a government to

administer, and that this chance depended on the action of
Virginia. The whole ascendancy of the winter wavered between the effort of the cotton states to drag Virginia out,
and the effort of the new President to keep Virginia in. . . .
As far as a private secretary knew, the party united on its
tactics.[38]

This was a tacit reversal. The closest he came to an overt one in the
Education was the oblique admission that he might not have been
qualified to judge Lincoln in 1860. After noting that Lincoln at the
inaugural ball showed "above all a lack of apparent force," he
admits: "Had young Adams been told that his life was to hang on
the correctness of his estimate of the new President, he would have
lost."[39]

Adams's final view of Lincoln must be pieced out between his
continuing to distance himself from his family's condemnations and
his praise and recommendation of Hay's Lincoln biography. He had
learned by 1869 to admire the Gettysburg Address and the Second
Inaugural, which he urged his closest British friend to include in an
anthology of American literature.[40] He read Hay's "great work" on
Lincoln while it was being written, and declared it "very good" on
the eve of publication.[41] He declared that Hay and his coauthor
John Nicolay "have done a work the equal of which I know not in
any literature." Reflecting on what he considered the poor quality
of honorarees getting Harvard degrees that year (1890), he told an
editor: "If Harvard College had any literary (or other) sense, it
would have crowned that work by giving every possible distinction
to its authors, instead of doing—what it does."[42]

Adams's desire for Hay to receive an honorary degree was
proven no idle thought when, in 1892, Adams was offered that distinction himself, and explained why he declined it:

No work of mine warrants it in itself; and still less when
compared with other contemporary work. Indeed, in my

opinion, the College should long ago have conferred degrees on the authors of what I consider far the first work on American history in popular and political importance that has appeared in my time; I mean the Life of Lincoln. If I am in error, you can correct me, but as far as my literary knowledge goes, no great man of any time in any country has ever had from his contemporaries a biography that will compare with this whether in scope, taste or literary execution. Nothing that I have ever done, or ever shall do, will hold its own beside portions of the Lincoln, as for example the account of Gettysburg. The admirable character of the work, which raises it above all books of the kind; the subject, peculiarly interesting to Harvard College; the opportunity to testify respect for the fame and character of Lincoln; the chance for once to escape from the circle of University limitations, and to take a lead in guiding popular impressions; all these motives struck me as overwhelming in dictating recognition of the history. I could not without positive shame put myself in a position where I should seem to countenance the idea that any work of mine compared in importance either of purpose, of moral value, or of public interest to the singularly noble and American character of this monument to the greatest man of our time.[43]

There it is at last, the tribute Adams had been avoiding so long, the recognition that Lincoln was "the greatest man of our time." His brother Charles was upset that Henry would turn Harvard down, partly perhaps because he was proffering the Lincoln book as his reason—Charles still thought Lincoln was second-rate. Adams's act was, I like to think, not only a tribute to his friend Hay but a long-delayed act of retribution for the underestimation of Lincoln. He had at last come to terms with the greatness he almost missed.

CHAPTER 18

Lincoln's Assassination and John Wilkes Booth's Confederate Connection

Edward Steers, Jr.

ON READING THE NEWS OF ABRAHAM LINCOLN'S DEATH, A young South Carolina girl wrote in her diary, "Hurrah! Old Abe Lincoln has been assassinated! . . . our hated enemy has met the just reward of his life."[1] While these words clearly reflect the sentiment of the young girl, we are told they represent a misguided view. Popular history has taught us to believe that the South, like the North, viewed Lincoln's death as a great tragedy.

To the people in the North, a great leader was struck down at the very moment of his triumph. Like Moses, Lincoln had led his people to the Promised Land only to be denied entry for himself. The tragedy of Lincoln's death gripped the North like no other event in the Nation's young history. His funeral lasted for three weeks and was repeated in twelve major cities including the capitals of five states. In all, Lincoln's body traveled over 1,600 miles and was witnessed by nearly seven million people or nearly one in every five Americans before reaching home.

Lincoln's apotheosis in the North was immediate following word of his death. Printmakers rushed to bring the eager public scenes of an ascending Lincoln being welcomed into heaven by George Washington. The Founder of the Nation was now welcoming the Savior of the Nation into Heavenly bliss. While Northerners had lost the man who saved their country, Southerners had lost their only hope for a just and magnanimous peace. Lincoln's death was as tragic for the defeated South as it was for the victorious North—or so we are told.

But like so much of the story of Lincoln's assassination, this view of his death is a myth—a myth that has been manufactured. In reality, the great majority of people throughout the South rejoiced at the news of Lincoln's assassination. Contrary to the popular myth that Lincoln's death was a national tragedy, Southerners saw Lincoln's death as tyrannicide—the killing of a great tyrant.

The editor of the *Texas Republican* spoke for most Southerners when he wrote: "It is certainly a matter of great joy and congratulations that Lincoln is dead, because the world is happily rid of a monster that disgraced the form of all humanity."[2] The editor of the *Galveston Daily News* pointed out to his readers that Lincoln's death was ordained, writing in his editorial column: "God Almighty ordered this wondrous event or it could never have taken place."[3]

Many Southerners viewed John Wilkes Booth, as he believed he would be, as a liberator. The young girl who rejoiced on hearing the news of Lincoln's death was saddened to hear of Booth's: "Poor Booth, to think that he fell at last. Many a true heart in the South now weeps for his death."[4] Another Southern editor agreed, writing: "There is no reason to believe that Booth was actuated by malice or vulgar ambition. He slew Lincoln as a tyrant, and the enemy of our country—therefore, we honor his deed. Booth will surely be placed among the heroic benefactors of all mankind."[5]

The passing of time, however, has seen a twisting of history's take on Lincoln's murder as viewed by many Southerners. We have come to accept a simplistic view of Lincoln's death for no other reason than it has been repeated so many times that any attempt to revise it is considered no better than the numerous conspiracy myths that claim "Stanton did it" or "Booth escaped."

In a review of *Blood on the Moon* appearing in the *Washington Post* the reviewer admonished me for writing that the Confederacy rejoiced in Lincoln's death. He wrote "thoughtful Southerners knew that Lincoln's death was a catastrophe for them as for the nation." Booth, the reviewer wrote, was simply a "mama's boy" who grew into a "puerile fanatic" acting on his own. His plot, in the reviewer's words, was "shabby and ineffectual."

The reviewer went on to write,

> The weakest feature of Steers's book is a muddled and inde-
> cisive treatment of the long-exploded canard that high Con-
> federate officials were in on the assassination plot, . . . The
> libel, however, has never been officially expunged, although
> *the standard accounts* (emphasis added) unequivocally
> absolve Davis. Steers surely knows it. . . . Pending the dis-
> covery of reputable evidence, the speculation about the cul-
> pability of high Confederates (or even members of Lincoln's
> own cabinet) in the assassination plot may confidently be
> relegated to the trash heap of pseudo-history.[6]

The reviewer hedged his criticism by introducing the word "high" before "Confederates" leaving the reader to conclude that I accuse Jefferson Davis and members of his cabinet with ordering Lincoln's assassination. I do no such thing. What I do claim is that Confederate officials (whether they are "high" officials depends on your definition of "high") were closely involved with Booth from the outset of his plot to remove Lincoln as president and commander in chief of the military. Confederate agents who worked for Judah P. Benjamin, Confederate Secretary of State, provided key contacts to Booth along with financial assistance to help carry out his opera-tion. For the reviewer to cite "standard accounts" in support of his own view of Lincoln's assassination is the very problem with this

important part of our history. It is the "standard accounts" that fail
to consider important evidence found in the primary record involving Confederate officials.[7]

The *Post* reviewer went on to support his position exonerating
Confederate officials by quoting the Radical Republican Thaddeus
Stevens: "While the Confederate leaders were enemies of the country, they were not assassins, these men were gentlemen." Both
Stevens and the reviewer were apparently unaware that these "gentlemen" adopted a policy of no quarter in taking Black soldiers as
prisoners[8] and that all captured Union officers in command of
United States Colored Troops would be turned over to the authorities in those states where they were captured to be prosecuted
under the laws that dealt with inciting slave uprisings—laws that
uniformly carried the death penalty.[9]

These "gentlemen" sanctioned acts of terror that included a plan
to poison the Croton reservoir that provided the drinking water to
the people of New York City[10]—noncombatants that included
women and children. These "gentlemen" approved the burning of
the cities of New York, Boston, Chicago, and Cincinnati, a confla-
gration that would have killed thousands of civilians had it been
successful.[11] Its failure was not for any lack of effort, but was due to
faulty execution. And most diabolical, these "gentlemen" instituted
a plan of germ warfare aimed at infecting civilian populations in the
North with yellow fever and smallpox.[12]

Such acts, however, were not restricted to the South. "Black
Flag Warfare," as it was unofficially called, occurred on both sides
of the conflict—North and South. The incidents I just mentioned
form a part of the Confederate context leading up to Lincoln's assassination. But there is a Union context as well. Let me give you
two examples that I feel are important to understanding the context
of Lincoln's assassination.

In May 1863, Robert E. Lee drained Richmond of most of its
defenders to strengthen his army during the battle of Chancellors-
ville. On May 3, a brigade of Union cavalry under Judson Kilpatrick

came within two miles of breaching Richmond's weak defenses and entering the city. The residents of Richmond prepared for the worst. But Kilpatrick, meeting unexpected resistance, suddenly broke away and headed north back to his base on the Rappahannock River. President Lincoln, in a telegram dated May 8, 1863, to Joseph Hooker, then commander of the Army of the Potomac, wrote: ". . . there was not a sound pair of legs in Richmond, and that our men, had they known it, could have safely gone in and burnt every thing & brought us Jeff. Davis."[13]

The wording of this telegram is disturbing. Think of what Lincoln is saying—burn everything—and bring us Jeff Davis! The civilian casualties of such a burning could have been horrific, and could Davis have been captured and carried away to Washington without the death of many of those around him?

The telegram is of considerable importance in giving us insight into Lincoln's thinking at the time, thinking that recognizes the burning of a city filled with civilians and the targeting of Davis as legitimate military acts. And yet, while this telegram appears in *The Collected Works of Abraham Lincoln* and in the *Official Records* of the Union Army, it is absent from every study of Lincoln's assassination.

The telegram is associated with a second incident that bears on the context of Lincoln's assassination. Within a few weeks after his aborted raid, Kilpatrick was called to Washington, where he met with Lincoln and Secretary of War Edwin M. Stanton. Shortly after his meeting, Kilpatrick drew up plans for yet another raid; this time designed to attack Richmond from two points simultaneously. Kilpatrick would take a force of approximately 2,500 men and enter Richmond from the north while a separate detachment of 500 cavalrymen under command of Colonel Ulric Dahlgren would swing south of the city, free the Union prisoners held on Belle Isle in the James River and enter Richmond from the south.

Kilpatrick once again met stiff resistance and, fearing his plan had been tipped off to Confederates, turned back. Dahlgren, unable to free the prisoners on Belle Isle, attempted to flee by heading east toward Butler's main army on the Peninsula. Dahlgren and his men were ambushed by a contingent of Confederate cavalry and Dahlgren killed. On Dahlgren's body were several documents that influenced the thinking of the South in fighting the war. The papers, like Lincoln's earlier telegram to Hooker, spoke of freeing the prisoners held at Belle Isle and turning them loose in Richmond armed with "oakum and turpentine" and exhorting them "to destroy and burn the hateful city," and that, "Jeff. Davis and his cabinet must be killed on the spot."[14]

While there is no evidence to directly link the documents found on Dahlgren's body to Lincoln, the Confederate leadership had no doubts that Lincoln had sanctioned them. The Southern reaction to the papers was outrage. Braxton Bragg, military advisor to Davis, urged Davis to execute Dahlgren's men immediately and release the text of Dahlgren's papers as justification for the execution. Secretary of War James A. Seddon agreed: "General Bragg's views coincide with my own on this subject."[15] Before acting on Bragg's and Seddon's recommendation Davis turned to Lee, asking Lee's opinion. Lee wrote to Davis: "I presume that the blood boils with indignation in the veins of every officer and man as they read the account of the barbarous and inhuman plot." Lee then answered Davis's question: "Nor do I think that under present circumstances policy dictates the executions of these men. It would produce retaliation."[16] At the time of Lee's response his son, Rooney Lee, was a Union prisoner and Lee was rightfully concerned with the possibility of retaliation.

Although debate continues among historians whether Lincoln targeted Davis, it is a debate that misses the point. Whether the papers reflected orders from Lincoln or were the unilateral act of a zealous cavalryman, the Confederate leadership in Richmond believed the papers to be authentic and the plot to kill Davis and his cabinet real. Perception, after all, is reality, and the perception throughout the South was that Lincoln had sanctioned the burning of Richmond and the assassination of Davis and his cabinet.

Like the telegram that Lincoln sent to Hooker in May 1863, the Dahlgren affair, as it came to be known, has failed to find its way into the influential Civil War histories. Where it does appear, it is simply described without analysis. While many authors appear unimpressed with the implications of the Dahlgren affair, Davis was not. In his memoir Davis wrote, "The enormity of his offense was not forgotten!"[17] If not forgotten, what, then was the Confederate response to "the enormity of his offense" that Davis refers to?

Targeting the political leaders of a country for assassination was considered outside the rules of civilized warfare—it was a violation of the Union's own General Order Number 100.[18] General Order Number 100 was intended to restate in a concise form, the international laws and customs of land warfare as recognized by the United States in the middle of the nineteenth century.[19] While assassination was unlawful, retaliation was permissible under Section I of General Order Number 100. Retaliation not for revenge, but as a means of protective retribution. If Davis was a legitimate target, so was Lincoln according to his own rules of warfare.

Clearly, actions such as the Dahlgren Raid and the Confederate reaction to it indicate a change on both sides as the war dragged on. By the spring of 1864, Davis had decided to establish a major clandestine operation in Canada for the purpose of carrying out attacks against the North. He chose an old friend from Mississippi, Jacob Thompson, to head the operation. The purpose of the Canadian-based operation was severalfold: 1. to attempt to free Confederate prisoners held at Johnson's Island and Camp Douglas; 2. to disrupt the U.S. fishing fleet operating off the coast of Canada and the United States; and 3. to initiate a series of actions aimed at the Northern population with the ultimate goal of demoralizing that population, thereby collapsing support for Lincoln in his reelection bid in November of 1864. It is in this latter purpose that the concept of Black Flag Warfare became a reality.

Among the actions undertaken was an effort to infect Northern cities with yellow fever, a plot that also targeted Lincoln by preparing a special valise containing expensive dress shirts believed contaminated with the deadly yellow fever. The shirts were to be delivered to Lincoln in the White House with the purpose of infecting Lincoln with the deadly disease.[20]

While several of these projects were attempted, none succeeded, but they illustrate the level the war had reached, as hopes for Southern independence grew dim. It was at the time these very plots were actively being planned that Booth first began his conspiracy to capture Lincoln and turn him over to Confederate leaders in Richmond.

Booth appears to have first begun putting his conspiracy together during the second week of August in 1864—less than five months after the Dahlgren Raid and at the same time the Confederate operation in Canada was plotting actions against Northern cities. During that second week in August, Booth visited Baltimore. At the time of his visit Booth's career as a dramatic actor had taken a marked turn downward.

Booth was a highly accomplished individual whose success on the American stage had covered him with considerable fame. Handsome and debonair, Booth was both respected and well-loved by all that knew him. The Ford brothers considered him a close friend. Those that knew him best had nothing but praise for him. One friend said of Booth: "John cast a spell over most men. As he talked he threw himself into his words,—brilliant, witty, enthusiastic. He could hold a group spellbound by the hour with the force and fire and beauty that was within him." The *New York World* described him as "a star of the greatest magnitude." Booth agreed with the *New York World*'s assessment, writing to a friend: "My goose does indeed hang high (long may she wave)."[21]

In May of 1864, Booth's star burned out, and it was at his own doing. Booth appeared in his last paid performance as an actor on May 23. From June 1864 until the night of April 14, eleven months later, Booth would appear in only three more stage performances and all three would be benefits without pay. Booth's lucrative source of income ended abruptly early in 1864.

During the same period, his large investment in an oil well in northwestern Pennsylvania went bust with Booth losing over $6,000.[22] A few weeks after Booth lost his oil investment he transferred all of his remaining assets to his mother Mary Ann Booth and older brother, Junius, Jr., and sister Rosalie. By August 1864 when Booth met with Samuel Arnold and Michael O'Laughlen he was out of work and out of assets he had so carefully accumulated over his short, but brilliant acting career. On paper, at least, Booth was without any resources or visible means of support, and it was the result of his own doing. Clearly, something was up.

Joe Simonds, Booth's partner in his oil venture in Pennsylvania, noticed a marked change in his good friend's behavior. In a letter to Booth that same winter, Simonds wrote, "I hardly know what to make of you . . . so different from your usual self. Have you lost all your ambition or what is the matter."[23] The matter was Booth's decision that "something great and decisive" must be done if his beloved Confederacy was to have any chance at surviving. That something was Booth's plan to capture Lincoln and take him to Richmond where he would be used as a bargaining chip in gaining the release of desperately needed Confederate soldiers being held in Northern prison camps.

The plan was not as unrealistic as some people have claimed. Beginning in the fall of 1862 and continuing through the fall of 1864, there were at least three separate plots by Confederate officials to kidnap Lincoln and carry him to Richmond, and one of these plots was undertaken with the help and funding of Seddon, the Confederate Secretary of War at the time.[24]

When Booth returned to Baltimore in August 1864, he sent for two friends from his childhood days: Arnold and O'Laughlen. Arnold had attended school with Booth at St. Timothy's Hall in Catonsville, Maryland, and the O'Laughlen family lived across the street from the Booth home on Exeter Street. Both Arnold and O'Laughlen had served in the Confederate army before returning to their homes and civilian life in Baltimore. Booth knew this and decided to seek their help.

Years later Arnold described his meeting with Booth in a memoir and acknowledged that Booth recruited both himself and O'Laughlen into a plan to capture Lincoln and carry him to Richmond.[25] Both men agreed to help.

Having recruited Arnold and O'Laughlen, Booth next turned to the logistics of his plan. If he were going to successfully capture Lincoln and carry him south to Richmond, he would need a safe avenue of escape. Much of the area between Washington and Richmond was occupied by Union troops and posed a serious threat to an escape party. Therefore Booth would need help. And he would need guidance along the way and safe harbors in which to stay.

Southern Maryland was the obvious choice for an escape route. The area was teeming with Confederate sympathizers and Confederate agents who had successfully avoided Union authorities for three years while providing support to Richmond's war effort. It contained two major routes, referred to as "mail lines," that Confederate agents used throughout the war to move people and material between various points in the North and Richmond. One of these routes was an obvious choice to carry a captured Lincoln south.

But, if Booth were to successfully enlist the aid of cohorts in southern Maryland, he would need an introduction of some sort. In searching for that introduction, Booth did not look south to southern Maryland, but, surprisingly, looked north to Montreal, Canada. Montreal was a major site for Confederate agents operating out of

Canada. The city had earned the title of "Little Richmond" because of all of the Confederate agents that had located there and all of the Confederate gold deposited in her banks.

On October 16, eight weeks after meeting with Arnold and O'Laughlen, Booth crossed over the border into Canada.[26] On October 18, he registered at St. Lawrence Hall, a hotel in Montreal that served as headquarters to several Confederate agents including a man by the name of Patrick Charles Martin.[27] Prior to Davis's sending Thompson and his assistants to Canada, Martin had been in charge of Confederate operations in Montreal. Among his many schemes was a plan to capture the *U.S.S. Michigan* and use the Union warship to free the 2,600 Confederate prisoners held on Johnson's Island located in Lake Erie.[28]

Booth was in Montreal a total of ten days, from October 18 to October 27. During those ten days he was seen on at least two occasions meeting with Martin. At least one of those meetings between Booth and Martin occurred in the Ontario Bank of Montreal, where Booth purchased a bank draft for sixty-one pounds Canadian (the equivalent of $7,700 U.S. dollars in today's market), a substantial amount of money at a time when Booth was without any source of income. According to the bank teller's later testimony at the conspiracy trial, Booth purchased the draft using three hundred dollars in gold.[29]

At the same time Booth purchased the draft for sixty-one pounds, he opened an account with the Ontario Bank for $455. The head teller testified that Booth had come to the bank with Martin and had opened the account using ten twenty-dollar Montreal bills and a check for $255 from a man by the name of Davis drawn on the Merchants Bank. The teller identified Mr. Davis as a broker from Richmond who established his money exchange opposite St. Lawrence Hall.[30]

The draft for sixty-one pounds was recovered from Booth's body at the Garrett farm[31] and Booth's Ontario Bank book showing $455 was found at the Kirkwood House in George Atzerodt's room where Atzerodt had registered on the morning of April 14—the day of the assassination, linking the two men.[32]

On his return to Washington from Montreal, Booth opened still another account, this one in Jay Cooke's Washington bank where he deposited $1,750. Booth dispersed all of these funds between December 20 and March 16, a period of three months immediately prior to the assassination.[33]

Between October 27 and November 16, Booth entered into financial transactions involving $2,815, all at a time when he was without any known source of income and during the height of his recruitment activity. The source of this money is unclear at present but offers interesting possibilities. The fact that part of the funds deposited in the Ontario Bank can be directly traced to "Mr. Davis," a Confederate money broker from Richmond, suggests that Booth was receiving financial aid from Confederate officials in Canada with the sanction of those in Richmond.

In addition to Booth's financial transactions, a close reading of the investigative reports and trial transcript show one other important piece of evidence involving Martin. When Booth left Montreal on October 27, he carried an important document. It was a letter of introduction that Martin prepared for Booth. The letter was directed to two men living in Charles County, Maryland: Dr. William Queen and Dr. Samuel Mudd. The letter supports the thesis that Booth's trip to Charles County in 1864 was facilitated by the Confederate operation in Canada. Booth's trip was, in essence, arranged such that Booth would be put in contact with key people in southern Maryland who could help with his capture plan.

The statement that Booth carried a letter of introduction from a Confederate agent in Montreal introducing him to Mudd runs counter to everything we have heard about Mudd and his alleged innocence. The letter suggests that Mudd was known to Martin, and, was, in Martin's opinion, an important contact for Booth to make—hence the need for the letter. The letter is a direct link between Booth, Mudd, and Confederate agents in Canada, and ties all three together in the fall of 1864.

The importance of the letter is obvious and yet it cannot be found in the several biographies of Mudd. The evidence for the letter's existence is not cryptic. It can be found in the primary records in the National Archives pertaining to the trial of the Lincoln conspirators. The existence of the letter became a part of the trial record. How did knowledge of its existence come about? The answer follows.

Two days after Lincoln's death, on Monday morning, April 17, two detectives from the Provost Marshal's office in Baltimore arrested Arnold at Fortress Monroe, where Arnold was working as a clerk. After taking Arnold into custody one of the two arresting officers, Eaton Horner, began questioning Arnold about his relationship with Booth. Horner was later called as a prosecution witness at the conspiracy trial. When asked about his interrogation of Arnold, Horner made the important revelation about the letter. While on the witness stand, he testified that Arnold had told him that Booth first visited Charles County in southern Maryland in the fall of 1864, and that he did so carrying a letter of introduction to Mudd.[34] When questioned by Mudd's attorney as to whether Arnold had really stated the letters were to Dr. Queen *or* Dr. Mudd, Horner replied "*and* Dr. Mudd" (emphasis in original transcript).[35] While Arnold said he did not know who wrote the letter of introduction, we again turn to the trial transcript for the answer.

A man by the name of John Thompson, the son-in-law of Dr. Queen, the other correspondent of the letter, was put on the witness stand where he testified that he had actually read the letter Booth carried naming Queen and Mudd as correspondents, and said that it was "from a man named Martin."[36]

Horner's testimony does not stand alone. It is corroborated by another of Booth's co-conspirators, Atzerodt, the man assigned by

324   EDWARD STEERS, JR.

Booth to kill Vice President Andrew Johnson. Shortly before Atzerodt was hanged, the *Baltimore American* published a statement by him that was described as a "confession." The newspaper stated: "Atzerodt said Booth was well acquainted with Dr. Mudd, and carried a letter of introduction to him from Canada when he first visited him in November." The newspaper went on to further state: "Atzerodt also said that Booth told him two weeks before the murder that Booth had sent provisions and liquor to Dr. Mudd's house for supplying the escape party on their way to Richmond with the President."[37]

Booth's visit to Canada suggests that he was seeking aid. Without the help of Martin and Mudd, Booth could never have put together his team of cohorts or his avenue of escape through southern Maryland. It was Mudd who later arranged two separate meetings where he introduced two Confederate agents, Thomas Harbin and John Surratt, to Booth.[38] As a result of these meetings, both Harbin and Surratt agreed to help Booth with his capture plan. It was Surratt who later recruited Atzerodt, Lewis Powell, and Davy Herold into the fold.

Thus, Surratt, Harbin, Atzerodt, Powell, and Herold can all be traced to Mudd, and Booth's introduction to Mudd can be traced to Martin in Montreal. Mudd was, in fact, the key conspirator in helping Booth assemble his team and it was Martin who sent Booth to Mudd.

And yet the public's view of Dr. Mudd and his relationship to Lincoln's assassination remains that of a simple country doctor who became the unexpected victim of a vengeful government for simply following his Hippocratic Oath.

The evidence linking Booth to Mudd through Martin and the Confederate operation in Montreal seems sure. The evidence linking Booth to Confederate funds in Montreal is less sure, but Booth was clearly drawing considerable funds from someone. If not the Confederate operation in Canada, where was Booth getting his money?

Booth's meeting with Martin, his financial dealings with the Ontario Bank facilitated by Martin and Davis, and Martin's letter of introduction to Drs. Queen and Mudd all link Booth to the Confederate operation in Canada. While the link may be circumstantial, it surely is not without credible evidence.

Notes

1. Lincoln's Political Faith in the Peoria Address
JOSEPH R. FORNIERI

1. *The Collected Works of Abraham Lincoln*, 9 vols., ed. Roy P. Basler et al. (New Brunswick, N.J.: Rutgers University Press, 1953–55), 2:275.

2. Joseph R. Fornieri, *Abraham Lincoln's Political Faith* (DeKalb, Ill.: Northern Illinois University Press, 2003), 92–132.

3. *Collected Works of Lincoln*, 3:462.

4. "Inauguration Address, March 4, 1801," in *The Life and Selected Writings of Thomas Jefferson*, ed. Adrienne Koch and William Peden (New York: Modern Library, 1944), 324–25 (emphasis added).

5. *Collected Works of Lincoln*, 3:375.

6. Ibid.

7. Ibid., 2:240 (emphasis added).

8. Joseph R. Fornieri, "Lincoln, the Natural Law and Prudence," in *The Language of Liberty: The Political Speeches and Writings of Abraham Lincoln*, ed. Joseph R. Fornieri (Washington D.C.: Eagle Publishing Company, 2003), xix–lxiii; Richard A. Horsley, "The Law of Nature in Philo and Cicero," *The Harvard Theological Review* 71, 1–2 (January–April 1978): 35–39; Harry V. Jaffa, *A New Birth of Freedom* (Lanham, Md.: Rowman & Littlefield, 2000), 509.

9. Fornieri, *Abraham Lincoln's Political Faith*, 70–91.

10. Fornieri, *Abraham Lincoln's Political Faith*.

11. *Collected Works of Lincoln*, 2:272.

12. Adams quoted in Michael Novak, *On Two Wings: Humble Faith and Common Sense at the American Founding* (San Francisco: Encounter Books, 2002), 35, 37.

13. Harry V. Jaffa, *The Conditions of Freedom: Essays in Political Philosophy* (Baltimore: John Hopkins University Press, 1975), 149–60.

14. *Collected Works of Lincoln*, 2:264, 281.

15. Ibid., 2:265–66.

16. Ibid., 2:266.

17. Ibid., 2:271; Fornieri, *Abraham Lincoln's Political Faith*, 133–41.

18. *Collected Works of Lincoln*, 2:255.

19. Ibid., 2:281–82.

20. Ibid., 2:275.

21. Ibid., 2:271.

22. Ibid., 2:265.

23. Ibid., 2:278.

24. Ibid.

25. Ibid., 2:276.

26. Ibid.

27. Ibid., 5:419–20.

28. See A. James Reichley, *Religion in American Public Life* (Washington, D.C.: Brookings Institution, 1985); Richard John Neuhaus, *The Naked Public Square: Religion and Democracy in America* (Grand Rapids, Mich.: W. B. Eerdmans, 1984).

29. Alexis de Tocqueville, *Democracy in America*, trans. George Lawrence and ed. J. P. Mayer (New York: Doubleday, 1969), 292–93.

30. Novak, *On Two Wings*.

2. *Lincoln's Political Religion and Religious Politics*
LUCAS E. MOREL

1. First Debate with Stephen A. Douglas at Ottawa, Illinois, August 21, 1858, in *The Collected Works of Abraham Lincoln*, 9 vols., ed. Roy P. Basler et al. (New Brunswick, N.J.: Rutgers University Press, 1953–55), 3:27.

2. Cited from *Life and Times of Frederick Douglass* in *Frederick Douglass: Autobiographies*, ed. Henry Louis Gates (New York: Library of America, 1994), 801, 804.

3. Address Before the Young Men's Lyceum of Springfield, Illinois, January 27, 1838, in *Collected Works of Lincoln*, 1:112.

4. For an interpretation of Lincoln's religious development as it influenced his politics that emphasizes his early devotion to "republican ideals" instead of "God or scripture," see Nicholas Parrillo, "Lincoln's Calvinist Transformation," *Civil War History* 46, no. 3 (September 2000): 227–53.

5. Elton Trueblood, *Abraham Lincoln: Theologian of American Anguish* (New York: Harper & Row Publishers, 1973), 121. See also Robert N. Bellah and Phillip E. Hammond, *Varieties of Civil Religion* (San Francisco: Harper & Row, Publishers, 1980), 12, wherein Bellah states that in America "there are no official interpreters of civil theology," and yet "we did produce at a critical juncture in our history at least one great civil theologian, Abraham Lincoln." See also Robert N. Bellah, *The Broken Covenant: American Civil Religion in Time of Trial* (New York: Seabury Press, 1975), 46. Sidney E. Mead described Lincoln as, "in a real sense the spiritual center of American history." "Abraham Lincoln's 'Last, Best Hope of Earth': The American Dream of Destiny and Democracy," *Church History* 23, no. 1 (March 1954): 3.

6. In a seminal article on civil religion, Robert N. Bellah defines American civil religion as the "set of beliefs, symbols, and rituals" that form our "public religious dimension." "Civil Religion in America," *Daedalus* 96 (Winter 1967): 4.

7. Cf. John G. West, Jr., *The Politics of Revelation and Reason: Religion and Civic Life in the New Nation* (Lawrence: University Press of Kansas, 1996). West shows that some evangelical reform movements—in particular, those addressing the Sunday mails and the Cherokee removal controversies—made their social and political appeals not merely on religious grounds but on the basis of human reason:

> Because government authority would be kept separate from ecclesiastical authority, churches now could be trusted to create—and defend—civic morality. Stripped of any pretensions that might have made them dangerous to republicanism, churches were free to reform society according to the moral law held in common by both revelation and reason. (West, *The Politics of Revelation and Reason*, 210)

Robert N. Bellah observes that the more moderate wing of abolitionism, led by Theodore Dwight Weld, sought reform by calling for greater enforcement of the U.S. Constitution:

Weld and his associates developed a constitutional argument that even as early as 1835 described the treatment in the North of free Negroes and abolitionists as "denials of rights to the equal protection of the laws, the safeguards of due process, and the privileges and immunities of citizens," . . . Unlike Garrison the group around Weld believed that emancipation was implicit in the Constitution and that what that document needed was not burning [as Garrison did] but clarification and enforcement. (Bellah, *The Broken Covenant*, 52)

8. See Mark A. Noll, "'Both . . . Pray to the Same God': The Singularity of Lincoln's Faith in the Era of the Civil War," *Journal of the Abraham Lincoln Association* 18, no. 1 (Winter 1997): 1–26.

9. Address Before the Young Men's Lyceum of Springfield, Illinois, January 27, 1838, in *Collected Works of Lincoln*, 1:114.

10. Ibid., 112.

11. An exhortation to law-abidingness can be found in the Bible in 1 Timothy 2:1–4, among other places, which gives Christians the hope that their obedience to the government will produce both peace for them and salvation for others:

I exhort therefore, that, first of all, supplications, prayers, intercessions, and giving of thanks, be made for all men; For kings, and for all that are in authority; that we may lead a quiet and peaceable life in all godliness and honesty. For this is good and acceptable in the sight of God our Saviour; Who will have all men to be saved, and to come unto the knowledge of the truth.

12. Address before the Young Men's Lyceum of Springfield, Illinois, January 27, 1838, in *Collected Works of Lincoln*, 1:112.

13. Wayne C. Temple, *Abraham Lincoln: From Skeptic to Prophet* (Mahomet, Ill.: Mayhaven Publishing, 1995), 23.

14. Cf. William S. Corlett, Jr., "The Availability of Lincoln's Political Religion," *Political Theory* 10, no. 4 (November 1982): 520–40, which presents Lincoln's "political religion" as an expression of a "civic humanism" having nothing to do with revealed religion.

15. One is reminded of a similar discussion of the necessity of "veneration" for "stability" in even "the wisest and freest governments" in *Federalist* No. 49. James Madison writes:

In a nation of philosophers, . . . reverence for the laws, would be sufficiently inculcated by the voice of enlightened reason. But a nation of philosophers is as little to be expected as the philosophical race of kings wished for by Plato. And in every other nation, the most rational government will not find it a superfluous advantage, to have the prejudices of the community on its side. (*The Federalist*, ed. Jacob E. Cooke [Middletown, Conn.: Wesleyan University Press, 1961], 340)

16. Address Before the Young Men's Lyceum of Springfield, Illinois, January 27, 1838, in *Collected Works of Lincoln*, 1:115.

17. Joshua F. Speed, *Reminiscences of Abraham Lincoln and Notes of a Visit to California* (Louisville, Ky.: John P. Morton and Company, 1884), 32–33. Don E. Fehrenbacher and Virginia Fehrenbacher, in their compilation of recollected Lincoln utterances, rank this story a "C" on a scale of "A" to "E" for reliability. ("A" denotes a Lincoln quotation recorded by the auditor within days of hearing it, and "E" denotes a quotation that "is probably not authentic.") "C" is a quotation "recorded noncontemporaneously." In Speed's case, his published account of his encounter came twenty years after the fact (*Recollected Words of Abraham Lincoln* [Stanford: Stanford University Press, 1996], 414, lii–liii). According to Mary Todd Lincoln, Lincoln "read the bible a good deal about 1864." "Mary Todd Lincoln (WHH interview [September 1866])," in *Herndon's Informants: Letters, Interviews, and Statements about Abraham Lincoln*, ed. Douglas L. Wilson and Rodney O. Davis (Urbana: University of Illinois Press, 1998), 360. Temple records that Joshua F. Speed joined Trinity Methodist Church late in life (Temple, *Abraham Lincoln: From Skeptic to Prophet*, 295 n. 123). See also infra, n. 24.

18. In an 1866 letter to William Herndon, Speed commented on Lincoln's faith: "I think that when I first knew Mr L he was skeptical as to the great truths of the Christian Religion. I think that after he was elected President, he sought to become a believer—and to make the Bible a preceptor to his faith and a guide for his conduct" ("Joshua F. Speed to WHH [12 January 1866]," in *Herndon's Informants*, 156).

19. For a similar interpretation offered earlier this century, see Christopher Dawson, *Religion and the Modern State* (London: Sheed and Ward, 1938), chaps. 6, "Religion and Politics," and 7, "The Religious Solution," 102–28.

20. Mark Y. Hanley, *Beyond a Christian Commonwealth: The Protestant Quarrel with the American Republic, 1830–1860* (Chapel Hill: University of North Carolina Press, 1994), 158, 31. See also Christoph Schönborn, "The

Hope of Heaven, the Hope of Earth," *First Things* 52 (April 1995): 32–38, and George Weigel, "The Church's Political Hopes for the World; or, Diognetus Revisited," in *The Two Cities of God: The Church's Responsibility for the Earthly City*, ed. Carl E. Braaten and Robert W. Jenson (Grand Rapids, Mich.: Wm. B. Eerdmans, 1997), 59–77.

21. Lincoln to Allen N. Ford, August 11, 1846, in *Collected Works of Lincoln*, 1:383.

22. Handbill Replying to Charges of Infidelity, July 31, 1846, ibid., 382.

23. Lincoln to Mary S. Owens, May 7, 1837, ibid., 78.

24. Remarks to Baltimore Presbyterian Synod: Two Versions [No. 1], October 24, 1863, ibid., 6:535. The context for his remark, though, paints a less skeptical picture of Lincoln's faith. In the immediately preceding sentence, Lincoln states that as president he "was early brought to a living reflection that nothing in my power whatever, in others to rely upon, would succeed without the direct assistance of the Almighty, but all must fail." The sentence that follows Lincoln's wish that he was "more devout" actually affirms his piety: "Nevertheless, amid the greatest difficulties of my Administration, when I could not see any other resort, I would place my whole reliance in God, knowing that all would go well, and that He would decide for the right" (ibid., 6:535, 536). Among the earliest extant writings of Lincoln is a handwritten copybook of arithmetic, a page of which includes the following rhyme: "Abraham Lincoln / his hand and pen / he will be good but / god knows When" (Copybook Verses [1824–1826], in ibid., 1:1). Cf. the assessment by Francis B. Carpenter, a portrait painter who lived at the White House for six months in 1864 as he painted a reenactment of Lincoln's first reading of the Emancipation Proclamation: "In the ordinary acceptation of the term, I would scarcely have called Mr. Lincoln a *religious* man,—and yet I believe him to have been a sincere *Christian*" (F. B. Carpenter, *The Inner Life of Abraham Lincoln* [New York City: Hurd and Houghton, 1868; originally published in 1866 as *Six Months at the White House with Abraham Lincoln*], 185–86; emphasis in original). Biographer Ward Hill Lamon, a member of Lincoln's inner circle as president, turns Carpenter's view on its head semantically, while expressing the same sentiment: "He was not a Christian in the orthodox sense of the term, yet he was as conscientiously religious as any man" (Dorothy Lamon Teillard, ed., *Recollections of Abraham Lincoln, 1847–1865* [1895; reprint, Lincoln: University of Nebraska Press, 1994], 334). This echoes Mary Todd's statement to William H. Herndon: "he was a religious man always, as I think," but "he was not a technical Christian" ("Mary

Todd Lincoln [WHH notes on interview, September 1866]," in *Herndon's In-formants*, 360).

25. Speed, *Reminiscences of Abraham Lincoln*, 32. Cf. Douglas L. Wilson, *Honor's Voice: The Transformation of Abraham Lincoln* (New York: Alfred A. Knopf, 1998), 309–12, which argues of Lincoln: "Disguising his religious views, or construing them in a more favorable light, became necessary for an ambitious and rising man who needed the good opinion of the public to succeed" (312).

26. Speech in U.S. House of Representatives on the Presidential Question, July 27, 1848, in *Collected Works of Lincoln*, 1:503.

27. Hans J. Morgenthau, "The Mind of Abraham Lincoln: A Study in De-tachment and Practicality," in *Essays on Lincoln's Faith and Politics*, ed. Ken-neth W. Thompson (Lanham, Md.: University Press of America, 1983), 8.

28. The passage cited most often on this subject comes from a eulogy Con-gressman Henry C. Deming delivered before the General Assembly of Con-necticut in 1865: "He [Lincoln] said, he had never united himself to any church, because he found difficulty in giving his assent, without mental reservations, to the long complicated statements of Christian doctrine which characterize their Articles of Belief and Confessions of Faith" (William J. Wolf, *The Almost Cho-sen People: A Study of the Religion of Abraham Lincoln* [Garden City, N.Y.: Doubleday, 1959], 74). The Fehrenbachers rank Deming's recollection a "C" (on a scale of "A" to "E") for reliability (*Recollected Words of Abraham Lincoln*, 137).

29. Allen C. Guelzo, "Abraham Lincoln and the Doctrine of Necessity," *Journal of the Abraham Lincoln Association* 18, no. 1 (Winter 1997): 66–67; Temple, *Abraham Lincoln: From Skeptic to Prophet*, 6.

30. Lincoln to Martin S. Morris, March 26, 1843, in *Collected Works of Lin-coln*, 1:320 (emphasis added).

31. Lincoln to James Shields, September 17, 1842, in ibid., 299–300, and Memorandum of Duel Instructions to Elias H. Merryman, [September 19, 1842], in ibid., 300–2. For a brief history of Christian antagonism toward duel-ing in early America, see Anson Phelps Stokes, ed., *Church and State in the United States: Historical Development and Contemporary Problems of Religious Freedom under the Constitution*, 3 vols. (New York: Harper & Brothers, 1950), 2:5–12.

32. Communication to the People of Sangamo County, March 9, 1832, in *Collected Works of Lincoln*, 1:5 n. 1. Lincoln ran eighth out of thirteen candi-dates for four seats in the lower house of the Illinois General Assembly. Never-theless, his New Salem returns were all the more impressive given that he only

recently moved to the area six months prior to announcing his candidacy for Illinois State Representative. In addition, he interrupted the campaign for three months to lead a local militia brigade in the Black Hawk War, being elected captain by his men. Two years later, he would run second in a field of thirteen candidates for four Sangamon County seats, and poll first (out of seventeen candidates) in his next two reelection bids.

33. "Farewell Address (19 September 1796)," in *George Washington: A Collection*, ed. W. B. Allen (Indianapolis: Liberty Fund, Inc., 1988), 521. Lincoln would make explicit reference to Washington's Farewell Address in his famous Cooper Institute Address; however, the context was not religion but rather sectionalism due to the slavery controversy (Address at Cooper Institute, New York City, February 27, 1860, in *Collected Works of Lincoln*, 3:536–37).

34. "To the Annual Meeting of Quakers (September 1789)," in Allen, *George Washington: A Collection*, 533.

35. Last Public Address, April 11, 1865, in *Collected Works of Lincoln*, 8:399–400.

36. Order for Sabbath Observance, November 15, 1862, in ibid., 5:497.

37. For a close interpretation of Lincoln's Temperance Address, see Lucas E. Morel, *Lincoln's Sacred Effort: Defining Religion's Role in American Self-Government* (Lanham, Md.: Lexington Books, 2000), chap. 4.

38. For an examination of this split as it related to the political tensions of the times (slavery, in particular), see C. Bruce Staiger, "Abolitionism and the Presbyterian Schism of 1837–1838," *The Mississippi Valley Historical Review* 36 (December 1949): 391–414. See also Mitchell Snay, *Gospel of Disunion: Religion and Separatism in the Antebellum South* (Cambridge: Cambridge University Press, 1993), chap. 4, "Harbingers of Disunion: The Denominational Schisms," 113–50; Daniel G. Reid with Robert D. Linder, Bruce L. Shelley, and Harry S. Stout, eds., *Dictionary of Christianity in America* (Downers Grove, Ill.: InterVarsity Press, 1990), s.v. "New School Presbyterians," 819–20; and Charles H. Lippy and Peter W. Williams, eds., *Encyclopedia of the American Religious Experience: Studies of Traditions and Movements*, 3 vols. (New York: Charles Scribner's Sons, 1988), s.v. "Presbyterianism," by Louis Weeks, 1:502–3. The Methodists and Baptists would split in 1843 and 1845, respectively, over the issue of slavery. See Edwin S. Gaustad, ed., *A Documentary History of Religion in America: To the Civil War* (Grand Rapids, Mich.: Wm. B. Eerdmans, 1982), 491–97.

39. Staiger, "Abolitionism and the Presbyterian Schism of 1837–1838," 393.

40. For a brief history of this doctrinal development within the Presbyterian Church, see Gilbert H. Barnes, *The Antislavery Impulse, 1830–1844* (Gloucester, Mass.: Peter Smith, 1957), 3–12. See also Clifton E. Olmstead, *History of Religion in the United States* (Englewood Cliffs, N.J.: Prentice-Hall, Inc., 1960), 311–14 and 189–90, for discussion of the preceding generation's dispute over the doctrine of original sin and the free will of man.

41. Cited in Barnes, *The Antislavery Impulse*, 11.

42. Barnes lists several of the early aims of "the Great Eight" societies that would take shape under the leadership of the Great Revivalists like Charles Grandison Finney and protégé Theodore Dwight Weld: promoting home and foreign missions, distributing Bibles and tracts, funding Sunday schools, promoting temperance, and converting sailors. He notes, "the benevolent empire was dominated by 'New-School' Presbyterians, liberals of the Great Revival" (Barnes, *The Antislavery Impulse*, 17, 18). See also Staiger, "Abolitionism and the Presbyterian Schism," 397: "Although Finney devoted himself almost exclusively to revivalism, his doctrines lent themselves to a great interest in social reform. Theodore Dwight Weld, a convert of Finney's, shaped this interest into another revival, one in which slaveholding was identical with sin." Weld would go on to become the great temperance speaker of frontier America, as well as write *Slavery As It Is*, an 1839 book from which Harriet Beecher Stowe mined details for her 1852 literary bombshell, *Uncle Tom's Cabin*. See Joan D. Hedrick, *Harriet Beecher Stowe: A Life* (New York: Oxford University Press, 1994), 230.

43. For derivation of the "hard shell" label and its theological import, see "Baptist Churches in U.S.A." and "Primitive Baptists" descriptions in the *Dictionary of Christianity in America*, 110–11 and 940, respectively, and "Primitive Baptist," in *Handbook of Denominations in the United States*, 9th ed., ed. Frank S. Mead and rev. ed. Samuel S. Hill (Nashville: Abingdon Press, 1985), 51–52.

44. Temperance Address, February 22, 1842, in *Collected Works of Lincoln*, 1:279.

45. Cf. the namesake of the Washingtonian Society. In his "General Orders" of April 18, 1783, which called for a cessation of hostilities between the United States and Great Britain, George Washington concluded with a call to toast the successful termination of the Revolutionary War: "An extra ration of liquor to be issued to *every* man tomorrow, to drink Perpetual Peace, Independence and Happiness to the United States of America" (Allen, *George Washington: A Collection*, 238).

46. Lincoln probably added the phrase "under God" on the platform as he listened to Edward Everett's oration. Lincoln's famous last line reads: "that this nation, under God, shall have a new birth of freedom—and that government of the people, by the people, for the people, shall not perish from the earth" (Address Delivered at the Dedication of the Cemetery at Gettysburg, November 19, 1863, in *Collected Works of Lincoln*, 7:23 and 7:19–20 n.19). Cf. Garry Wills, *Lincoln at Gettysburg: The Words That Remade America* (New York: Simon & Schuster, 1992), 194, 198, and 261: "that the nation shall, under God, have a new birth of freedom, and that the government of the people, by the people, and for the people, shall not perish from the earth."

47. See Morel, *Lincoln's Sacred Effort*, chap. 5.

48. But as David W. Blight argues in *Race and Reunion: The Civil War in American Memory* (Cambridge, Mass.: The Belknap Press of Harvard University Press, 2001), national unity would soon come at the expense of black Americans.

49. All quotations from Lincoln's Second Inaugural Address are from Second Inaugural Address, March 4, 1865, in *Collected Works of Lincoln*, 8:332–33.

50. Cf. Andrew Jackson, "Second Inaugural Address (4 March 1833)," in *A Compilation of the Messages and Papers of the Presidents: 1787–1897*, 20 vols., ed. James D. Richardson (Washington, D.C.: Government Printing Office, 1896), 3:3: "To do justice to all and to submit to wrong from none has been during my Administration its governing maxim, . . ."

51. Lincoln to Thurlow Weed, March 15, 1865, in *Collected Works of Lincoln*, 8:356 (emphasis added).

52. Address to the New Jersey Senate at Trenton, New Jersey, February 21, 1861, in ibid., 4:236.

3. Lincoln, Douglas, and Popular Sovereignty: The Mormon Dimension
JOHN Y. SIMON

1. Leonard Arrington, *Brigham Young: American Moses* (New York: Alfred A. Knopf, 1985), 66.

2. Robert W. Johannsen, *Stephen A. Douglas* (New York: Oxford University Press, 1973), 16–104.

3. Robert Bruce Flanders, *Nauvoo: Kingdom on the Mississippi* (Urbana: University of Illinois Press, 1965), 96–101; Johannsen, *Douglas*, 104–7.

4. George U. Hubbard, "Abraham Lincoln as Seen by the Mormons," *Utah Historical Quarterly* 31, no. 2 (Spring 1963): 93–94.

5. Allen Johnson, *Stephen A. Douglas: A Study in American Politics* (New York: Macmillan, 1908), 59–60.

6. Flanders, *Nauvoo*, 287.

7. John E. Hallwas and Roger D. Launius, *Cultures in Conflict: A Documentary History of the Mormon War in Illinois* (Logan, Utah: Utah State University Press, 1995), 87; see also Thomas Ford, *A History of Illinois* . . . (Chicago: S. C. Griggs & Co., 1854), 318–19.

8. Robert W. Johannsen, ed., *Letters of Stephen A. Douglas* (Urbana: University of Illinois Press, 1961), 120–27.

9. Richard D. Poll, "The Mormon Question Enters National Politics, 1850–1856," *Utah Historical Quarterly* 25 (April 1957): 119.

10. Speech, June 12, 1857, *Illinois State Register*, June 18, 1857.

11. *Illinois State Journal*, June 23, 1857.

12. Speech, June 26, 1857, in *The Collected Works of Abraham Lincoln*, 9 vols., ed. Roy P. Basler et al. (New Brunswick, N.J.: Rutgers University Press, 1953–55), 2:398–99.

13. Will Bagley, *Blood of the Prophets: Brigham Young and the Massacre at Mountain Meadows* (Norman: University of Oklahoma Press, 2002), 80–81.

14. First Annual Message, December 8, 1857, in *A Compilation of the Messages and Papers of the Presidents, 1789–1902*, James D. Richardson, ed. (Washington, D.C.: Bureau of National Literature and Art, 1907), 5:454–56.

15. April 2, 1860, *Congressional Globe*, 1496.

16. April 2, 1860, *Congressional Globe*, 1515.

17. April 3, 1860, *Congressional Globe*, 1514.

18. Speech, April 10, 1860, in *Collected Works of Lincoln*, 4:41–42.

19. E. B. Long, *The Saints and the Union: Utah Territory during the Civil War* (Urbana: University of Illinois Press, 1981), 27.

20. Ibid., 61.

21. Hubbard, "Abraham Lincoln as Seen by the Mormons," 103; Long, *Saints and the Union*, 191–92.

22. John A. Jones to Lincoln, August 7, 1858, Abraham Lincoln Papers, Library of Congress.

4. The Campaign of 1860: Cooper Union, Mathew Brady, and the Campaign of Words and Images

HAROLD HOLZER

1. *Illinois Daily State Journal*, February 23, 1860.

2. *Illinois State Register*, February 23, 1860, published in the *Chicago Daily Times*, February 26, 1860.

3. Leonard W. Volk, "The Lincoln Life-Mask and How it was Made," *Century Magazine* 23 (December 1881): 223–28.

4. Andrew Freeman, *Abraham Lincoln Goes to New York* (New York: Coward-McCann, 1960), 54–55.

5. *Chicago Press and Tribune*, February 29, 1860.

6. See, for example, the daguerreotype by Polycarpus von Schneidau around the time of his 1854 Peoria address, and ambrotypes by Calvin Jackson and William Judkins Thomson during the 1858 Lincoln-Douglas debates in *Lincoln in Photographs: An Album of Every Known Pose*, rev. ed., by Charles Hamilton and Lloyd Ostendorf (Dayton, Ohio: Morningside Books, 1985), 370–71.

7. Lincoln to James F. Babcock, September 13, 1860, in *The Collected Works of Abraham Lincoln*, 9 vols., ed. Roy P. Basler et al. (New Brunswick, N.J.: Rutgers University Press, 1953–55), 4:114.

8. Roy Meredith, *Mr. Lincoln's Camera Man: Mathew B. Brady* (New York: Scribner's, 1946), 59.

9. George Alfred Townsend, "Still Taking Pictures," *New York World*, April 12, 1891, quoted in Mary Panzer, *Mathew Brady and the Image of History* (Washington, D.C.: Smithsonian Institution Press, 1997), 224.

10. Francis B. Carpenter, *Six Months at the White House with Abraham Lincoln: The Story of a Picture* (New York: Hurd & Houghton, 1866), 46–47.

11. Lincoln to Harvey G. Eastman, April 7, 1860, in *Collected Works of Lincoln*, 4:39–40.

12. *Portraits and Sketches of the Lives of All the Candidates for the Presidency and Vice-Presidency, for 1860 . . .* (New York: J. C. Buttre, 1860), 4, back cover.

5. *"I See the President": Abraham Lincoln and the Soldiers' Home*
MATTHEW PINSKER

1. *Specimen Days*, "Abraham Lincoln," No. 45 [August 12, 1863], Walt Whitman, *Prose Works* (Philadelphia: David McKay, 1892); Bartleby.com, 2000, http://www.bartleby.com/229 (accessed October 29, 2002).

2. The others were James Buchanan, Rutherford B. Hayes, and Chester Arthur. See Paul R. Goode, *The United States Soldiers' Home: A History of Its First Hundred Years* (Richmond, Va.: William Byrd Press, 1957).

3. *Washington Sunday Chronicle*, April 14, 1861.

4. Buchanan quoted in Goode, *United States Soldiers' Home*, 62; *New York Times*, March 8, 1861; *Washington Sunday Chronicle*, April 14, 1861.

5. Mary Lincoln to Hannah Shearer, Washington, July 11, 1861, reprinted in *Mary Todd Lincoln: Her Life and Letters*, ed. Justin G. Turner and Linda Levitt Turner (New York: Alfred A. Knopf, 1972), 94.

6. Mary Lincoln to George D. Ramsay [Soldiers' Home], July 20, [1864], Turner and Turner, *Mary Todd Lincoln*, 177.

7. Mary Lincoln to Elizabeth Blair Lee, Chicago, August 25, 1865, Turner and Turner, *Mary Todd Lincoln*, 267.

8. John Hay to William H. Herndon, Paris, September 5, 1866, in *Herndon's Informants: Letters, Interviews, and Statements about Abraham Lincoln*, ed. Douglas L. Wilson and Rodney O. Davis (Urbana: University of Illinois Press, 1998), 331.

9. David V. Derickson, "The President's Guard," typescript recollection courtesy of Jane Westenfeld, Ida M. Tarbell Papers, Allegheny College, Meadville, Pa.

10. Edward Dicey, *Spectator of America*, ed. Herbert Mitgang (Chicago: Quadrangle Books, 1971), 61; orig. pub. as *Six Months in the Federal States* (Macmillan & Co., 1863).

11. Aldace F. Walker to Father, Fort Massachusetts, October 8, 1862, transcripts available from Fort Ward Museum Library, Alexandria, Va.

12. George Borrett, "An Englishman in Washington in 1864," *The Magazine of History With Notes and Queries* 38 (Extra no. 149; 1929): 6–7.

13. Quoted in Allen C. Clark, "Abraham Lincoln in the National Capital," *Records of the Columbia Historical Society* 27 (1925): 89.

14. John Hay, "Life in the White House in the Time of Lincoln," *Century* 41 (November 1890): 34; John Hay to William H. Herndon, Paris, September 5, 1866, in *Herndon's Informants*, 331.

15. Quoted in Clark, "Abraham Lincoln," 90.

16. Dispatch of December 4, 1862, appearing in *Sacramento Daily Union*, December 30, 1862, in *Lincoln Observed: Civil War Dispatches of Noah Brooks*, ed. Michael Burlingame (Baltimore, Md.: Johns Hopkins University Press, 1998), 13–14.

17. F[rancis]. B. Carpenter, "Personal Impressions of Mr. Lincoln" (New York) *The Independent*, April 27, 1865, 1:2.

18. Hay, "Life in the White House," 35–36. Passage from *Richard II* 3.ii.155–60.

19. Abraham Lincoln to James H. Hackett, August 17, 1863, in *The Collected Works of Abraham Lincoln*, 9 vols., ed. Roy P. Basler et al. (New Brunswick, N.J.: Rutgers University Press, 1953–55), 6:392–93.

20. Invoices from John Alexander, upholsterer, Washington, May 21, 1864, Record Group 217, Records of the U.S. General Accounting Office (GAO), Records of the First Auditor, Audit 151.223, October 24, 1864, National Archives.

21. Borrett, "An Englishman in Washington in 1864," 2–15.

22. Leonard Swett, "The Conspiracies of the Rebellion," *North American Review* 144 (February 1887): 187–88.

23. Diary entry, Saturday, July 25, 1863, in *Inside Lincoln's White House: The Complete Civil War Diary of John Hay*, ed. Michael Burlingame and John R. Turner Ettlinger (Carbondale, Ill.: Southern Illinois University Press, 1997), 67–68.

24. Mary Lincoln to Mrs. Charles [Fanny] Eames, Soldiers' Home, July 26, [1862], in Turner and Turner, *Mary Todd Lincoln*, 130–31.

25. *Specimen Days*, "Abraham Lincoln," No. 45 [August 12, 1863], Walt Whitman, *Prose Works* (Philadelphia: David McKay, 1892); Bartleby.com, 2000, http://www.bartleby.com/229 (accessed October 29, 2002).

26. Maunsell B. Field, *Memories of Many Men And of Some Women* (New York: Harper & Brothers, 1874), 321.

27. *New York Tribune*, July 8, 1862.

28. Remarks to Delegation of Veterans of 1812, July 4, 1862, in *Collected Works of Lincoln*, 5:306.

29. *Charleston Mercury*, February 26, 1861, in *Abraham Lincoln: A Press Portrait*, by Herbert Mitgang (1956; reprint, New York: Fordham University Press, 2000), 234.

30. Willard A. Cutter to Elizabeth Cutter, Washington, D.C., March 31, 1864, Willard A. Cutter Papers, Allegheny College, Meadville, Pa.

6. *Varieties of Religious Experience: Abraham and Mary Lincoln*
JEAN BAKER

1. William James, *The Varieties of Religious Experience* (London: Longmans, Green, 1915), 31–32, 379.

2. David Herbert Donald, *Lincoln* (New York: Simon & Schuster, 1995), 33.

3. *The Collected Works of Abraham Lincoln*, 9 vols., ed. Roy P. Basler et al. (New Brunswick, N.J.: Rutgers University Press, 1953–55), 1:382.

4. Jean Baker, *Mary Todd Lincoln: A Biography* (New York: W. W. Norton, 1987), 19, 23.

5. Ibid., 23.

6. John Bayliss, *Black Slave Narratives* (New York: Macmillan, 1970), 147–52; B. A. Botkin, *Lay My Burden Down* (Chicago: University of Chicago Press, 1945), 29–41.

7. Justin G. Turner and Linda Levitt Turner, *Mary Todd Lincoln: Her Life and Letters* (New York: Alfred A. Knopf, 1972), 15–16.

8. Ibid., 86.

9. Donald, *Lincoln*, 514.

10. *Collected Works of Lincoln*, 4:226.

11. Katherine Helm, *The True Story of Mary, Wife of Lincoln* (1928; reprint, Rutland, Vt.: Academy Books, 1999), 111.

12. Baker, *Mary Todd Lincoln: A Biography*, 128.

13. Ibid., 218–22.

14. Turner and Turner, *Mary Todd Lincoln*, 256; Helm, *True Story of Mary*, 227.

15. James Moorhead, *American Apocalypse: Yankee Protestants and the Civil War, 1860–1869* (New Haven: Yale University Press, 1978), 44.

16. *Collected Works of Lincoln*, 8:333. See also Glen E. Thurow, "Abraham Lincoln and American Political Religion," in *The Historian's Lincoln: Pseudohistory, Psychohistory, and History*, ed. Gabor S. Boritt (Urbana: University of Illinois Press, 1988), 125–43; and David Hein's response, 144–47.

17. Quoted in Lucas E. Morel, *Lincoln's Sacred Effort: Defining Religion's Role in American Self-Government* (Lanham, Md.: Lexington Books, 2000), 210.

18. *Collected Works of Lincoln*, 7:535.

7. The Poet and the President: Abraham Lincoln and Walt Whitman
DANIEL MARK EPSTEIN

1. Daniel Mark Epstein, *Lincoln and Whitman: Parallel Lives in Civil War Washington* (New York: Ballantine Books, 2004).

8. 1862—A Year of Decision for President Lincoln and General Halleck
JOHN F. MARSZALEK

1. The number of books on Abraham Lincoln is staggering. The best single volume is David Herbert Donald, *Lincoln* (New York: Simon & Schuster, 1995). The standard biography of Edwin M. Stanton is Benjamin P. Thomas and Harold M. Hyman, *Stanton, the Life and Times of Lincoln's Secretary of War* (New

York: Knopf, 1962). The author of this essay has recently completed a biography of Halleck entitled *Commander of All Lincoln's Armies: A Life of General Henry W. Halleck* (Cambridge: The Belknap Press of Harvard University Press, 2004).

2. *American Heritage Dictionary*, 2nd College Edition (Boston: Houghton Mifflin, 1985).

3. Salmon P. Chase to M. D. Potter, February 17, 1862, in *The Salmon P. Chase Papers*, ed. John Niven (Kent: Kent State University, 1996), 3:135.

4. Halleck to Don Carlos Buell, February 18, 1862, Halleck to George B. McClellan, February 19, 20, 1862, in *The War of the Rebellion: A Compilation of the Official Records of the Union and Confederate Armies*, 128 vols. (Washington, D.C.: Government Printing Office, 1880–1901), ser. 1, 7:632–33, 636, 641.

5. McClellan to Halleck, February 21, 1862, Stanton to Halleck, February 21, 1862, in *Official Records*, ser. 1, 7:645, 648.

6. A source of excellent brief articles on these battles and other Civil War matters, complete with appropriate bibliography, is David S. Heidler and Jeanne T. Heidler, eds., *Encyclopedia of the American Civil War, A Political, Social and Military History*, 5 vols. (Santa Barbara, Calif.: ABC-CLIO, 2000).

7. Stanton to Halleck, June 27, 1862, Lincoln to Halleck, July 2, 1862, Halleck to Lincoln, July 2, 1862, in *Official Records*, ser. 1, 17, pt. 2:41, 63–64. These letters and others cited in this essay are available in other places in the *Official Records* too. Only one location per letter is cited in these notes. A convenient source for Lincoln letters is *The Collected Works of Abraham Lincoln*, 9 vols., ed. Roy P. Basler et al. (New Brunswick, N.J.: Rutgers University Press, 1953–55).

8. Halleck to Elizabeth Halleck, July 6, 1862, in Schoff Civil War Collection, University of Michigan. The printed, although not complete, version of this and other Halleck letters to his wife are found in Henry W. Halleck, "Letters of Gen. Henry W. Halleck, 1861–1862," *Collector* 21 (January–March, 1908): 29, 39–40, 52–53, and in James Grant Wilson, "Types and Traditions of the Old Army. II. General Halleck—A Memoir," *Journal of the Military Service Institution of the United States* 36, 37 (May–June and September–October, 1905): 537–56, 333–56.

9. Halleck to Elizabeth Halleck, July 13, 1862, in Halleck, "Letters," 39–40, and Wilson, "Types and Traditions," 556–57; Stanton to Halleck, July 11, 1862, in *Official Records*, ser. 1, 17, pt. 2:90; Lincoln to Halleck, July 14, 1862, in *Official Records*, ser. 1, 17, pt. 2:97.

10. Chase to Richard C. Parsons, July 20, 1862, in Niven, *Chase*, 3:231.

11. Theodore C. Pease and James G. Randall, eds., *The Diary of Orville Hickman Browning*, 2 vols., *Collections of the Illinois State Historical Library*, July 25, 1862, 20:563.

12. Letters and Telegrams from Headquarters of the Army, Record Book, Secretary of War Memoranda, July 27, 1862, EG, Box 23, Huntington Library; McClellan to Halleck, August 1, 1862, in *Official Records*, ser. 1, 11, pt. 3:346.

13. Halleck to Elizabeth Halleck, in Ricks Collection, Illinois State Historical Library, also in Halleck, "Letters," 40, and Wilson, "Types and Traditions," 557; Halleck to McClellan, July 30, 1862, in *Official Records*, ser. 1, 11, pt. 3:343. McClellan reprinted many letters in his *McClellan's Own Story* (New York: Charles L. Webster, 1887), 473–74. See also Stephen W. Sears, ed., *The Civil War Papers of George B. McClellan, Selected Correspondence, 1860–1865* (New York: Ticknor and Fields, 1989).

14. McClellan to Halleck, August 1, 1862, in *Official Records*, ser. 1, 11, pt. 3:345–46.

15. Stanton to Halleck, August 4, 1862, in *Official Records*, ser. 1, 12, pt. 2:8–11.

16. Halleck to Elizabeth Halleck, August 9, 1862, in Schoff Civil War Collection, University of Michigan, also in Halleck, "Letters," 52, and Wilson, "Types and Traditions," 557.

17. Halleck to McClellan, August 31, 1862, in McClellan Papers, Library of Congress; McClellan to Halleck, August 31, 1862, in *Official Records*, ser. 1, 11, pt. 1:103; Halleck to "General McClellan's Headquarters," September 1, 1862, in *Official Records*, ser. 1, 12, pt. 3:787; Pope to Halleck, August 25, September 3, 1862, in *Official Records*, ser. 1, 12, pt. 2:65–66, 19–20.

18. Excellent books on this historic pronouncement are John Hope Franklin, *The Emancipation Proclamation* (Garden City, N.Y.: Doubleday, 1963), Allen C. Guelzo, *Lincoln's Emancipation Proclamation: The End of Slavery in America* (New York: Simon and Schuster, 2004), Harold Holzer, Edna Greene Medford, and Frank J. Williams, *The Emancipation Proclamation, Three Views* (Baton Rouge: Louisiana State University Press, 2006). See also November 4, 1862, in *The Diary of Gideon Welles: Secretary of the Navy under Lincoln and Johnson*, 3 vols., ed. Howard K. Beale (New York: W. W. Norton & Co., 1960), 1:180.

19. Lincoln to Horace Greeley, August 22, 1862, in *Collected Works of Lincoln*, 5:388–89.

20. Lincoln to Halleck, Halleck to Stanton, January 1, 1863, in *Official Records*, ser. 1, 21:940.

21. Halleck to Stanton, January 1, 1863, in *Official Records*, ser. 1, 21:940–41; John Hay, *Letters of John Hay and Extracts from His Diaries* (Washington, D.C.: n.p., 1908), August 30, 1862, 1:60–63.

22. Beale, *Diary of Gideon Welles*, December 29, 1862, 1:209.

9. *"I Felt It to Be My Duty to Refuse":* *The President and the Slave Trader*
WILLIAM LEE MILLER

1. Francis B. Carpenter, *The Inner Life of Abraham Lincoln: Six Months in the White House* (1866; reprint, Lincoln: University of Nebraska Press, 1995), 68–69.

2. Docket file of the Abraham Lincoln Papers at the National Archives. Record Group 204, Stack Area 230, Row 40, Compartment 27, Shelf 2, "Docket of Pardon Cases 1853–1923, Vol. 3 of 81, PI-87 Entry 7."

3. Rhoda White to Abraham Lincoln, February 17, 1862, in Abraham Lincoln Papers at the Library of Congress. I refer to this letter throughout the essay. Materials from the Lincoln Papers are available at http://lcweb2.loc.gov/ammem/alhtml/malhome.html.

4. Petitions to the President of the United States (two), from Portland, Maine, dated December 1861. 1861 Executive Clemency files, Record A, Page 391, in Abraham Lincoln Papers at the National Archives.

5. Stay of Execution for Nathaniel Gordon, February 4, 1862, in *The Collected Works of Abraham Lincoln*, 9 vols., ed. Roy P. Basler et al. (New Brunswick, N.J.: Rutgers University Press, 1953–55), 5:128.

6. Warren S. Howard, *American Slavers and the Federal Law, 1837–1862* (Berkeley: University of California Press, 1963), chap. 13, passim.

7. Speech at Peoria, Illinois, October 16, 1854, in *Collected Works of Lincoln*, 2:264.

8. I count six full pardons in the list of criminal prosecutions under the slave trade acts 1837–1862 in Howard, *American Slavers*, appendix, 224–35. None of these of course was a capital case.

9. Don E. Fehrenbacher, *The Dred Scott Case: Its Significance in American Law and Politics* (New York City: Oxford University Press, 1978), 27.

10. Max Farrand, ed., *The Records of the Federal Convention of 1787*, 3 vols. (New Haven: Yale University Press, 1966), 2:415.

11. Speech at Peoria, Illinois, October 16, 1854, in *Collected Works of Lincoln*, 2:275.

12. Howard, *American Slavers*, 26.

13. Ibid., 11–12.

14. W. E. B. DuBois, *The Suppression of the African Slave Trade to the United States of America, 1638–1870* (1896; reprint, Baton Rouge: Louisiana State University Press, 1969), 188–91.

15. Annual Message to Congress, December 3, 1861, in *Collected Works of Lincoln*, 5:46.

16. Howard, *American Slavers*, 194.

17. Ibid., 195–96.

18. Stuart Lutz, "Lincoln Let Him Hang," *Civil War Times* 37, no. 1 (March 1998): 37.

19. Gilbert Dean to Abraham Lincoln, February 18, 1862, in Abraham Lincoln Papers at the National Archives.

20. Edward Dicey, *Spectator of America*, ed. Herbert Mitgang (Chicago: Quadrangle Books, 1971), 59.

21. Speech at Peoria, Illinois, October 16, 1854, in *Collected Works of Lincoln*, 2:267–68 (emphasis added).

22. Edward Bates to Abraham Lincoln, February 19, 1862, in Abraham Lincoln Papers at the National Archives.

23. Dicey, *Spectator of America*, 59–60.

10. Abraham Lincoln and Ulysses S. Grant
JEAN EDWARD SMITH

1. William B. Hesseltine, *Ulysses S. Grant: Politician* (New York: Dodd, Mead & Co., 1935), vii.

2. J. G. Randall, "The Unpopular Mr. Lincoln," *The Abraham Lincoln Quarterly* 2 (June 1943): 255–80.

3. Hans L. Trefousse, "Abraham Lincoln's Reputation during His Administration," in *The Lincoln Forum: Rediscovering Abraham Lincoln*, ed. John Y. Simon and Harold Holzer (New York: Fordham University Press, 2002), 187–210.

4. Wood Gray, *The Hidden Civil War: The Story of the Copperheads* (New York: Viking Press, 1942), 130.

5. *Ex Parte Merryman*, 17 Fed. Cas. 144 [No. 9487], C.C.D. Md. 1861.

6. David Herbert Donald, *Lincoln* (New York: Simon & Schuster, 1995), 424.

7. Merrill D. Peterson, *Lincoln in American Memory* (New York: Oxford University Press, 1994), 26–27.

8. March 5, 1877, James A. Garfield, in *The Diary of James A. Garfield*, 4 vols., ed. Harry J. Brown and Frederick D. Williams (East Lansing: Michigan State University Press, 1973), 3:453–54.

9. David Herbert Donald, "Introduction to the Torchbook Edition," in *Essays on the Civil War and Reconstruction*, by William A. Dunning (Gloucester, Mass.: Peter Smith, 1969), x–xi. Also see Dunning, *Reconstruction: Political and Economic, 1865–1877* (New York: Harper, 1907).

10. *United States v. Harris*, 106 U.S. 629 [1883].

11. *United States v. Cruikshank*, 2 Otto 542 [1872].

12. *United States v. Reese*, 2 Otto 214 [1872].

13. *Civil Rights Cases*, 109 U.S. 3 [1883].

14. *Plessy v. Ferguson*, 163 U.S. 537 [1896].

15. Charles Warren, *The Supreme Court in United States History*, 2 vols. (Boston: Little, Brown, 1922), 2:608.

12. Lincoln and His Admirals
CRAIG L. SYMONDS

1. T. Harry Williams, *Lincoln and His Generals* (New York: Knopf, 1952), vii.

2. Tyler Dennett, ed., *Lincoln and the Civil War in the Diaries and Letters of John Hay* (New York: Dodd, Mead, & Co., 1939), 179.

3. *The Collected Works of Abraham Lincoln*, 9 vols., ed. Roy P. Basler et al. (New Brunswick, N.J.: Rutgers University Press, 1953–55), 4:266.

4. John Niven, *Gideon Welles: Lincoln's Secretary of the Navy* (New York: Oxford University Press, 1973), 325.

5. *Collected Works of Lincoln*, 4:317–18.

6. Niven, *Welles*, 329.

7. Chester Hearn, *Admiral David Dixon Porter* (Annapolis, Md.: Naval Institute Press, 1996), 1–35.

8. David Dixon Porter, *Incidents and Anecdotes of the Civil War* (New York: D. Appleton & Co., 1885), 13–14.

9. Ibid., 14–15.

10. Lincoln to Foote, April 1, 1861, in *Official Records of the Union and Confederate Navies in the War of the Rebellion* (Washington, D.C.: Government Printing Office, 1894–1922), 4:109; hereafter cited as *ORN*.

11. Porter later claimed that Seward knew very well that the *Powhatan* was slated for the expedition to Sumter, and that the secretary of state deliberately attempted to sabotage the Fort Sumter expedition. The evidence is inconclusive, however. If Seward had known of Welles's plan for the *Powhatan*, he would have had no reason to go to the navy secretary on April 5 to ask him why he had assigned that ship to other duty. Porter, *Incidents and Anecdotes*, 15.

12. Foote to Welles, April 4, 1861, in *ORN*, 4:234.

13. Howard K. Beale, *Diary of Gideon Welles: Secretary of the Navy under Lincoln and Johnson*, 3 vols. (New York: W. W. Norton & Co., 1960), 1:24.

14. Seward to Porter and Porter to Seward, April 6, 1861, in *ORN*, 4:112.

15. Porter, *Incidents and Anecdotes*, 22.

16. Undated entry, in Beale, *Diary of Gideon Welles*, 1:25.

17. James M. Merrill, *Du Pont: The Making of An Admiral* (New York: Dodd, Mead & Co., 1986); H. A. Du Pont, *Rear-Admiral Samuel Francis Du Pont, United States Navy, A Biography* (New York: National Americana Society, 1926), chap. 1.

18. James R. Soley, *The Blockade and the Cruisers*, vol. 1 of *The Navy in the Civil War* (New York: Scribners, 1890), 29–45.

19. Fox to Du Pont, June 3, 1862, in *Samuel Francis Du Pont: A Selection from his Wartime Letters*, 3 vols., ed. John D. Hayes (Ithaca: Cornell University Press, 1969), 2:96.

20. Du Pont to Sophie Du Pont, March 27, 1863, in Hayes, *Du Pont Letters*, 2:519.

21. Du Pont to Welles, April 15, 1863, in *ORN*, 14:5–8.

22. Lincoln to Du Pont, April 13, 1863 [3:40 p.m.], in Hayes, *Du Pont Letters*, 3:25.

23. Lincoln to Du Pont and David Hunter, April 14, 1863, in *Collected Works of Lincoln*, 6:173–74; Du Pont to Welles, April 16, 1863, in *ORN*, 14:140; Du Pont to Sophie Du Pont, April 17, 1863, in Hayes, *Du Pont Letters*, 3:40.

24. Du Pont to Welles, October 22, 1863, and Welles to Du Pont, November 4, 1863, in Hayes, *Du Pont Letters*, 3:253–71.

25. Clarence E. N. Macartney, *Mr. Lincoln's Admirals* (New York: Funk and Wagnalls, 1956), 116.

26. October 31, 1863, in Beale, *Diary of Gideon Welles*, 1:477.

27. Porter to Welles, April 7, 1863, in *ORN*, 24:537.

28. Charles L. Dufour, *The Night the War was Lost* (Garden City, N.Y.: Doubleday & Co., Inc., 1960).

29. Porter to Farragut, July 3, 1862, in *ORN*, 18:641–43.

30. Welles to Porter, October 1, 1862, in *ORN*, 23:388.

31. Welles claimed that Lincoln had "not great admiration" for Porter, but that he was just the man for "rough work on the Mississippi" (October 1, 1862, in Beale, *Diary of Gideon Welles*, 1:157–58).

32. Lincoln's Message to the Senate, December 8, 1863, in *Collected Works of Lincoln*, 7:56–57.

13. *After Emancipation: Abraham Lincoln's Black Dream*
MICHAEL VORENBERG

1. Some of the ideas in this essay have been expressed or are more fully developed in Michael Vorenberg, "Slavery Reparations in Theory and Practice: Lincoln's Approach," in *White Man's President?: Abraham Lincoln and Race*, ed. Brian Dirck (DeKalb: Northern Illinois Univ. Press, forthcoming). For my earlier views on Lincoln and colonization, see Michael Vorenberg, "Abraham Lincoln and the Politics of Black Colonization," *Journal of the Abraham Lincoln Association* 14 (Summer 1993): 23–45.

2. Alexander H. Stephens, *A Constitutional View of the Late War Between the States*, 2 vols. (Philadelphia: National Publishing Company, 1868–1870), 1:611–14.

3. W. C. Bibb, "Visit of an Alabamian to Washington City in the Spring of 1865," transcription from the *Gulf Messenger* 6 (1893): 16, Carl Sandburg papers, Illinois Historical Survey, University of Illinois at Champaign-Urbana; see Carl Sandburg, *Abraham Lincoln: The War Years*, 4 vols. (New York: Harcourt, Brace & Company, 1939), 4:238–40.

4. David Herbert Donald, "Abraham Lincoln: Whig in the White House," in *Lincoln Reconsidered: Essays on the Civil War Era*, 2nd ed., by David Herbert Donald (New York: Vintage, 1961), 187–208. See Daniel Walker Howe, *The Political Culture of the American Whigs* (Chicago: University of Chicago Press, 1979).

5. Samuel L. M. Barlow to Henry Stebbins, New York, February 1, 1864, in Samuel L. M. Barlow letter books, Henry E. Huntington Library, San Marino, Calif.

6. Francis P. Blair, Sr. to William Lloyd Garrison, June 21, 1864, in Blair Family MSS., Manuscript Division, Library of Congress. Laura Giddings Julian,

wife of U.S. Representative George Julian, had a conversation with the elder Blair in early 1864 in which he said that if all the blacks were not sent to Texas they would perish like the Native Americans. "Poor old man," wrote Mrs. Julian to her sister, "[he] can never work off that colonization scheme. . . ." (Laura A. Julian to Mollie Giddings, February 27, 1864, George W. Julian MSS., Indiana State Library, Indianapolis).

7. See Sandburg, *Abraham Lincoln: The War Years*, 4:43–44. John A. Campbell, another of the commissioners at Hampton Roads, was probably the first to record Lincoln telling the story; his account is reprinted in John A. Campbell, *Reminiscences and Documents Relating to the Civil War During the Year 1865* (Baltimore: John Murphy and Co., 1887), 14. Henry J. Raymond, *The Life and Public Services of Abraham Lincoln* (New York: Derby and Miller, 1865), 745–46, has Lincoln telling Raymond that he did indeed tell the "root, hog, or die" story at Hampton Roads.

8. William Henry Herndon and Jesse William Weik, *Herndon's Life of Lincoln* (1889; reprint, New York: Da Capo Press, 1983), 1:37.

9. *The Collected Works of Abraham Lincoln*, 9 vols., ed. Roy P. Basler et al. (New Brunswick, N.J.: Rutgers University Press, 1953–55), 1:8.

10. *Collected Works of Lincoln*, 4:62. For the full text of his autobiographic sketches, see *Collected Works of Lincoln*, 3:511–12, 4:60–67.

11. See, for example, Lincoln's speech at Springfield, in *Collected Works of Lincoln*, 2:405–6; and his speech at Ottawa, August 21, 1858, in *Collected Works of Lincoln*, 3:16.

12. *Collected Works of Lincoln*, 5:372.

13. Lincoln to Banks, August 5, 1863, in *Collected Works of Lincoln*, 6:365; Proclamation of Reconstruction, December 8, 1863, in *Collected Works of Lincoln*, 7:55; Lincoln to Thomas W. Conway [General Superintendent, Freedmen, Department of the Gulf], March 1, 1865, in *Collected Works of Lincoln*, 8:325.

14. Proceedings of the American Anti-Slavery Society at its Third Decade, Held in the City of Philadelphia, December 3, 4, 1863, cited in Philip Foner, ed., *Life and Writings of Frederick Douglass*, 5 vols. (New York: International Publishers, 1952), 3:386.

15. See James M. McPherson, *The Negro's Civil War: How American Negroes Felt and Acted During the War for the Union* (1965; reprint, Urbana, Ill.: University of Illinois Press, 1982), 277–80.

16. P. J. Staudenraus, *Mr. Lincoln's Washington: Selections from the Writings of Noah Brooks, Civil War Correspondent* (New York: Thomas Yoseloff, 1967), 382–83.

17. For the phrase "ambition for education," see autobiography for Jesse W. Fell, December 20, 1859, in *Collected Works of Lincoln*, 3:511.

18. See, for example, Yaa Asantewa Nzingha, "Reparations + Education = The Pass to Freedom," in *Should America Pay?: Slavery and the Raging Debate on Reparations*, ed. Raymond A. Winbush (New York: Amistad, 2003), 299–314.

19. *Collected Works of Lincoln*, 8:333.

14. The Second Inaugural Address: The Spoken Words
RONALD C. WHITE, JR.

1. Abraham Lincoln to Thurlow Weed, March 15, 1865, in *The Collected Works of Abraham Lincoln*, 9 vols., ed. Roy P. Basler et al. (New Brunswick, N.J.: Rutgers University Press, 1953–55), 8:356. No letter from Weed has been found.

2. In Lincoln's time the old Congress ended on March 4, the date of his inauguration, but a new Congress did not convene until December.

3. *New York Times*, March 4, 1865, 4. The detailed descriptions of different aspects of the Inaugural week are taken from the accounts in numerous newspapers. The newspapers of this era were intensely political, often serving as political organs for parties or elements within parties. Their partisan points of view have been taken into account in constructing the context.

4. *Philadelphia Inquirer*, March 6, 1865.

5. Selden Connor to Mother, March 6, 1865, Selden Connor Correspondence, Lincoln Collection, John Hay Library, Brown University.

6. Maggie Lindsley, *Maggie Lindsley's Journal* (privately printed, 1977), 73.

7. *The Times* (London), March 20, 1865, 9 (Report, "From Our Correspondent," written on March 7); *New York Herald*, March 6, 1865, 4.

8. Waldo E. Martin, Jr., *The Mind of Frederick Douglass* (Chapel Hill: University of North Carolina, 1984), 63–64.

9. Michael Shiner, *Diary, 1813–1865*, 182, Library of Congress; Noah Brooks, *Washington in Lincoln's Time* (New York: Rinehart & Company, Inc., 1958), 213.

10. *New York Herald*, March 4, 1865, 4; *The Times* (London), March 17, 1865, 9.

11. The letter is quoted in *Collected Works of Lincoln*, 7:517–18; also, Francis Brown, *Raymond of the Times* (New York: Norton, 1951), 260.

12. *Collected Works of Lincoln*, 7:518.

13. Memorandum Concerning His Probable Failure of Re-election, August 23, 1864, in *Collected Works of Lincoln*, 7:514–15.

14. See the rhetorical analysis of Amy R. Slagell, "Anatomy of a Masterpiece: A Close Textual Analysis of Abraham Lincoln's Second Inaugural Address," *Communication Studies* 42, no. 2 (Summer 1991): 155–71.

15. John M. Vanderslice, *Gettysburg: A History of the Gettysburg Battlefield Memorial Association* (Philadelphia: The Memorial Association, 1897), 176.

16. The two vice presidents, John Tyler and Millard Fillmore, who acceded to office because of the death of their predecessor, did not give inaugural addresses.

17. These names for God are from *Inaugural Addresses of the Presidents of the United States from George Washington to John F. Kennedy* (Washington, D.C.: Government Printing Office, 1961): Washington, 4; Adams, 11; Jefferson, 16; Madison, 25; Monroe, 45; Jackson, 60; and Buchanan, 117.

18. Psalm 127:1, quoted ibid., 53.

19. Mark A. Noll, "The Bible and Slavery," in *Religion and the American Civil War*, ed. Randall M. Miller, Harry S. Stout, and Charles Reagan Wilson (New York: Oxford University Press, 1998), 48–49.

20. Story Written for Noah Brooks, in *Collected Works of Lincoln*, 8:154–55.

21. In the first draft he penned "four thousand years ago." In the final draft he inserted "three thousand years ago."

22. Address Delivered at the Cemetery at Gettysburg, in *Collected Works of Lincoln*, 7:23.

15. *Abraham Lincoln and Civil Liberties: Then and Now*
FRANK J. WILLIAMS

1. See, e.g., Arthur M. Schlesinger, Jr., "The Ultimate Approval Rating," *New York Times Magazine*, December 15, 1996, 48. Lincoln did well, too, in a survey of influential, if not always magnanimous, people in the second millennium. He ranks 32nd behind Gutenberg (1st) and Hitler (20th). Agnes Hooper Gottlieb et al., *1,000 Years, 1,000 People: Ranking the Men and Women who Shaped the Millennium* (New York: Kodansha International, 1998).

2. See, e.g., *New York Tribune*, June 15, 1863.

3. J. G. Randall, *Lincoln: The Liberal Statesman* (New York: Dodd, Mead & Co., 1947), 123.

4. *The Collected Works of Abraham Lincoln*, 9 vols., ed. Roy P. Basler et al. (New Brunswick, N.J.: Rutgers University Press, 1953–55), 4:332.

5. See Donald L. Robinson, "Inherent Powers," in *The Oxford Companion to the Supreme Court of the United States*, ed. Kermit L. Hall et al. (New York: Oxford University Press, 1992), 428–29.

6. *Collected Works of Lincoln*, 4:431.

7. Tyler Dennett, ed., *Lincoln and the Civil War in the Diaries and Letters of John Hay* (New York: Dodd, Mead & Co., 1939), 11.

8. *Collected Works of Lincoln*, 4:344.

9. *Ex parte* Merryman, 17 F. Cas. 144 (C.C.D. Md. 1861), (No. 9, 487).

10. *U.S. Constitution*, art. I, § 9, c. 2.

11. *Collected Works of Lincoln*, 4:430.

12. *Habeas Corpus* Act, ch. 80, 12 Stat. 755 (1863).

13. *Ex parte* Milligan, 71 U.S. (4 Wall.) 2, 120–21 (1866).

14. *Collected Works of Lincoln*, 4:429.

15. Prize Cases, 67 U.S. (2 Black) 635 (1862).

16. Charles Warren, *The Supreme Court in United States History*, 2 vols. (Boston: Little, Brown, & Co., 1922), 2:382.

17. See *Prize Cases*, 67 U.S., 669.

18. *Collected Works of Lincoln*, 5:434–45.

19. Ibid., 6:29–30.

20. Richard Hofstadter, *The American Political Tradition* (New York: Alfred A. Knopf, 1948), 131.

21. See Edna Greene Medford, "'Beckoning Them to the Dreamed Promise of Freedom': African-Americans and Lincoln's Proclamation of Emancipation," in *The Lincoln Forum: Abraham Lincoln, Gettysburg and the Civil War*, ed. John Y. Simon et al. (Mason City, Iowa: Savas Publishing Co., 1999), 51, 58.

22. *Collected Works of Lincoln*, 6:408.

23. Copperhead, a reproachful epithet, was used to denote Northerners who sided with the South in the Civil War and were therefore deemed traitors, particularly those so-named Peace Democrats who assailed the Lincoln Administration. It was borrowed from the poisonous snake of the same name that lies in hiding and strikes without warning. However, "Copperheads" regarded themselves as lovers of liberty, and some of them wore a lapel pin with the head of the Goddess of Liberty cut out of the large copper penny minted by the Federal treasury.

24. *Collected Works of Lincoln*, 6:266.

25. *Congressional Globe*, 37th Cong., 1st Sess., 57–59 (1861); see generally Frank L. Klement, *The Limits of Dissent* (Lexington: University Press of Kentucky, 1970).

26. *Congressional Globe*, 37th Cong., 3rd Sess., Appendix, 52–60 (1863).

27. See *Ex parte* Vallandigham, 68 U.S. (1 Wall.) 243, 243–44 (1864).

28. Klement, *Limits of Dissent*, 149.

29. William H. Rehnquist, *All the Laws but One* (New York: Vintage Books, 1998), 65–66.

30. See Klement, *Limits of Dissent*, 152–68.

31. See ibid., 163–64.

32. See ibid., 171.

33. See *Ex parte* Vallandigham, 68 U.S. (1 Wall.) 243, 248 (1864).

34. See Klement, *Limits of Dissent*, 171, 177, 201–2.

35. See ibid., 200.

36. See Rehnquist, *All the Laws*, 68.

37. See Klement, *Limits of Dissent*, 180–81.

38. See ibid., 181.

39. *Collected Works of Lincoln*, 6:235.

40. See Rehnquist, *All the Laws*, 65, 67.

41. See *Collected Works of Lincoln*, 6:260–69.

42. See Klement, *Limits of Dissent*, 187, 189.

43. Letter from Matthew Birchard et al., to Abraham Lincoln, June 26, 1863, available at http://memory.loc.gov/mss/mal/maltext/rtf_orig/mal054f.rtf.

44. See Klement, *Limits of Dissent*, 188.

45. *Collected Works of Lincoln*, 6:303.

46. See ibid., 305.

47. Klement, *Limits of Dissent*, 189.

48. James Laird Vallandigham, *A Life of Clement L. Vallandigham* (Baltimore: Turnbull Brothers, 1872), 320–21.

49. Klement, *Limits of Dissent*, 186, 229–30, 249–50.

50. *Crisis* (Columbus), September 9, 1863.

51. Klement, *Limits of Dissent*, 186.

52. H.R.J., 38th Cong., 1st Sess., 323–24 (1864).

53. LaWanda Cox called this "Limits of the Possible." See LaWanda Cox, "Reflections on the Limits of the Possible," in *Freedom, Racism & Reconstruction: Collected Writings of LaWanda Cox*, ed. Donald G. Nieman (Athens: University of Georgia Press, 1997), 243–78.

54. *Collected Works of Lincoln*, 6:264.

55. See ibid., 266–67.

56. Mark E. Neely, Jr., *The Fate of Liberty: Abraham Lincoln and Civil Liberties* (New York: Oxford University Press, 1991), 235.

57. John Lockwood, "We Had Terrorists Even in the Time of Lincoln," *Washington Post*, February 16, 2003, B8.

58. This international law is known as the law of war. One of its fundamental axioms is that combatants cannot target civilians.

59. Ironically, the case of those tried for Lincoln's assassination was heard by a military tribunal. Although the assassin, John Wilkes Booth, was already dead, eight defendants were put on trial. Among them was Dr. Samuel Mudd, the physician who set Booth's broken leg and sent him on his way. Dr. Mudd was accused of abetting Booth's escape. He escaped the death penalty and served four years of a life sentence. See James H. Johnston, "Swift and Terrible: A Military Tribunal Rushed to Convict after Lincoln's Murder," *Washington Post*, December 9, 2001, F1. Interestingly, Dr. Mudd's grandson brought the case before a federal appeals court in September 2002 (*Mudd v. White*, 309 F.3d 819 [D.C. Cir. 2002]). He sought to have the conviction overturned, arguing that his grandfather had only been doing his duty as a doctor. As Richard Willing stated in his article, "On its face, the Mudd appeal turns on a fairly dry point of law—whether the army's decision followed the standard of review called for by the federal Administrative Procedure Act. But underlying the dispute is a basic disagreement over how the legal system should function during wartime—during the Civil War and today" (Richard Willing, "Dr. Mudd Appeal to be Heard," *The Surratt Courier*, May 2002, 3–4). Unfortunately for Dr. Mudd's family, on November 8, 2002, the court dismissed the case. Judge Harry Edwards wrote that the law under which the Mudd family was seeking to have Samuel Mudd's conspiracy conviction expunged applied only to records involving members of the military. Although Mudd was tried by a military tribunal, he was not a member of the military (*Mudd v. White*, 309 F.3d, 824).

60. William Glaberson, "Closer Look at New Plan for Trying Terrorists," *New York Times*, November 15, 2001, B6.

61. "There certainly are precedents through history for military commissions, but that doesn't mean the president has constitutional authority to use them whenever he says there's an emergency" (ibid). However, American courts have been reluctant to second-guess the chief executive as to when commissions are justified (ibid).

62. Thom Shanker and Katharine Q. Seelye, "Behind-the-Scenes Clash Led Bush to Reverse Himself on Applying Geneva Conventions," *New York Times*,

February 22, 2002, A12. Under the Geneva Conventions, protections are afforded to members of an organized command structure with someone responsible for their actions. In contrast, those being detained as enemy combatants do not wear military uniforms (enabling the other side to spare civilians without fear of counterattacks by disguised fighters), they do not carry arms openly and they do not respect the laws of war (Geneva Convention [III] Relative to the Treatment of Prisoners of War, August 12, 1949, art. 4, T.I.A.S. 3364, 75 U.N.T.S. 135). Yoram Dinstein warns against American troops who fail to wear uniforms in combat relative to being entitled to protections under the Geneva Conventions:

> The constraints of the conditions of lawful combatancy must not . . . be seen as binding on only one Party to the conflict. . . . As the hostilities progressed, it became all too evident . . . that some American combatants . . . were not wearing uniforms while in combat. It ought to be emphasized that observance by even 99 per cent of the armed forces of a Party . . . does not absolve the remaining 1 per cent. . . . Consequently, had any American combatants in civilian clothing been captured by the enemy, they would not have been entitled to prisoners of war status any more than Taliban and Al Qaeda fighters in a similar plight. (Yoram Dinstein, *The Conduct of Hostilities under the Law of International Armed Conflict.* [Cambridge: Cambridge University Press, 2004], 50)

Dinstein also believes that "Since unlawful combatants are not entitled to prisoners of war status, most criticisms against conditions of detention in Guantánamo are beside the point. However, detention (as a purely administrative measure) of those persons who are not charged with any crime in judicial proceedings cannot go beyond the termination of hostilities: hostilities in Afghanistan in connection with Taliban personnel; hostilities in which Al Qaeda is involved in the case of its incarcerated fighters" (ibid). In *Hamdan v. Rumsfeld,* 126S.Ct. 2749 (2006), the Supreme Court indicated that article 3 of the Geneva Convention prohibits torture and requires humane treatment of U.S. detainees. The Military Commissions Act of 2006 attempts to address this.

63. Department of Defense, Military Commission Order No. 1, § 2 (March 21, 2002), available at http://www.defenselink.mil/news/Mar2002/d20020321ord.pdf.

64. "Refining Military Tribunals [Editorial]," *New York Times,* March 22, 2002, A24.

65. Harvey Rishikoff, "A New Court for Terrorism," *New York Times*, June 8, 2002, A15.

66. *Rasul v. Bush*, 124 S. Ct. 2686 (2004); *Hamdi v. Rumsfeld*, 124 S. Ct. 2633 (2004); *Rumsfeld v. Padilla*, 124 S. Ct. 2711 (2004).

67. *Rasul v. Bush*, 215 F. Supp. 2d 55, 72–73 (D.D.C. 2002). In coming to this conclusion, the district court relied on *Johnson v. Eisentrager*, which it interpreted as "broadly appl[ying] to prevent aliens detained outside the sovereign territory of the United States from invoking a petition for a writ of *habeas corpus*" (ibid., citing *Johnson v. Eisentrager*, 339 U.S. 763 [1950]). The U.S. Supreme Court distinguished *Rasul* from *Eisentrager*, stating that unlike the detainees in *Eisentrager*, the petitioners in *Rasul* were "not nationals of countries at war with the United States, and they deny that they have afforded access to any tribunal, much less charged with and convicted of wrongdoing; and for more than two years they have been imprisoned in territory over which the United States exercises exclusive jurisdiction and control" (*Rasul v. Bush*, 124 S. Ct. 2693 [2004]).

68. *Rasul v. Bush*, 124 S. Ct. 2696 (citing Lease of Lands for Coaling and Naval Stations, February 23, 1903, U.S.-Cuba, art. III, T.S. No. 418; Treaty Defining Relations with Cuba, May 29, 1934, U.S.-Cuba, art. III, 48 Stat. 1683).

69. *Hamdi v. Rumsfeld*, 124 S. Ct. 2633.

70. "Absent suspension of the writ by Congress, a citizen detained as an enemy combatant is entitled to this process" (ibid., 2650–52).

71. *Rumsfeld v. Padilla*, 124 S. Ct. 2711 (2004).

72. On June 29, 2006, the United States Supreme Court decided the case of *Hamdi v. Rumsfeld*. In this 5-to-3 decision, the Court ruled that President George W. Bush did not have the authority or power to create military tribunals in Guantánamo, Cuba, but four of the justices indicated that the Congress could so authorize the president and that is what Congress did. On October 17, 2006, President Bush signed the Military Commissions Act of 2006.

73. Gary Langer, "Terror v. Liberties: Poll: Americans Believe Stopping Terror is More Important Than Privacy," June 10, 2002, available at http://abcnews.go.com/sections/us/DailyNews/terror_poll020610.html.

74. David M. Kennedy, "What is Patriotism Without Sacrifice?" *New York Times*, February 16, 2003, WK3.

75. Don E. Fehrenbacher, *Lincoln in Text and Context: Collected Essays* (Stanford, Calif.: Stanford University Press, 1987), 139.

76. Abraham Lincoln, "Annual Message to Congress (Dec. 1, 1862)," in *Abraham Lincoln: His Speeches and Writings*, 9 vols., ed. Roy P. Basler (Cleveland: The World Publishing Co., 1946), 688.

16. After Lincoln's Reelection: Foreign Complications
WILLIAM C. HARRIS

1. J. G. Randall and Richard N. Current, *Lincoln the President: Last Full Measure* (1955; reprint, Urbana: University of Illinois Press, 1991), 263; Allan Nevins, *The War for the Union: Volume IV, The Organized War to Victory, 1864–1865* (New York: Charles Scribner's Sons, 1971), 119–20; Harold M. Hyman, "Election of 1864," in *History of American Presidential Elections, 1789–1968*, ed. Arthur M. Schlesinger, Jr. (New York: Chelsea House, 1985), 1155.

2. Response to a Serenade, November 10, 1864, in *The Collected Works of Abraham Lincoln*, 9 vols., ed. Roy P. Basler et al. (New Brunswick, N.J.: Rutgers University Press, 1953–55), 8:100–1.

3. Abraham Lincoln to Abram Wakeman, July 25, 1864, in *Collected Works of Lincoln*, 7:461.

4. For example, the French consul in New York reported during the campaign that an independence movement was underway in the west and that area's separation from the Union would be followed by other regions (Lynn M. Case and Warren F. Spencer, *The United States and France: Civil War Diplomacy* [Philadelphia: University of Pennsylvania Press, 1970], 554).

5. As quoted in Ephraim D. Adams, *Great Britain and the American Civil War*, 2 vols. (New York: Longmans, Green and Company, 1925), 2:235.

6. As quoted in Frederick W. Seward, *Seward at Washington, as Senator and Secretary of State: A Memoir of His Life, with Selections from His Letters, 1861–1872* (New York: Derby and Miller, 1891), 250.

7. For a recent challenge to the view that Lincoln played only a minor role in foreign affairs during the Civil War, see Dean B. Mahin, *One War at a Time: The International Dimensions of the American Civil War* (Washington, D.C.: Brassey's, 1999), 1–3.

8. See *Papers Relating to Foreign Affairs Accompanying the Annual Message of the President, to the First Session Thirty-Ninth Congress, 1865*, Parts 1 and 2 (Washington D.C.: Government Printing Office, 1866), passim.

9. For the Beall case, see William C. Harris, *Lincoln's Last Months* (Cambridge: The Belknap Press of Harvard University Press, 2004), 153–55. For important documents regarding the Beall case, see *Memoir of John Yates Beall: His Life; Trial; Correspondence; Diary; and Private Manuscript found among His Papers* (Montreal: J. Lovell, 1865).

10. Confession of Robert C. Kennedy, March 25, 1865 (dictated a few hours before his execution), in *The War of the Rebellion: A Compilation of the Official Records of the Union and Confederate Armies*, 128 vols. (Washington, D.C.: Government Printing Office, 1880–1901), ser. 2, 8:428–29; *New York Times*, November 26, 29, 1864; *New York Tribune*, March 27, 1865.

11. For the St. Albans raid and the failure of Canadian authorities to extradite the raiders to America, see Robin W. Winks, *Canada and the United States* (Baltimore: John Hopkins Press, 1960), 298–301; Brian Jenkins, *Britain and the War for the Union*, 2 vols. (Montreal: McGill-Queens University Press, 1974–1980), 2:357, 360–63; Reginald C. Stuart, "St. Albans, Vermont, Raid," in *Encyclopedia of the American Civil War*, 5 vols., ed. David S. Heidler and Jeanne T. Heidler (Santa Barbara, Calif.: ABC-CLIO, 2000), 4:1845–46.

12. Zachariah Chandler to John M. Forbes, December 26, 1864, Zachariah Chandler Papers, Manuscript Division, Library of Congress, Washington, D.C.; *New York Times*, December 16, 1864; *New York Herald*, December 17, 18, 1864. See also the *New York World*, December 16, 1864.

13. Entry for December 16, 1864, in *Diary of Gideon Welles: Secretary of the Navy under Lincoln and Johnson*, 3 vols., ed. Howard K. Beale (New York: W. W. Norton & Co., 1960), 2:198; William H. Seward to Charles Francis Adams, December 13, 19, 1864, in *Papers Relating to Foreign Affairs, 1865*, pt. 1, 35, 49–51.

14. General Order No. 97, December 14, 1864, Headquarters, Department of the East, in *Memoirs of John Adams Dix*, 2 vols., comp. Morgan Dix (New York: Harper and Bros., 1883), 2:112.

15. Edwin M. Stanton to General John A. Dix, December 15, 1864, in Edwin M. Stanton Papers, Manuscript Division, Library of Congress, Washington, D.C.

16. Annual Message to Congress, December 6, 1864, in *Collected Works of Lincoln*, 8:141; *Annual Cyclopedia and Register of Important Events of the Year 1864* (New York: Appleton, 1868), 361.

17. *Annual Cyclopedia, 1864*, 361; Jenkins, *Britain and the War for the Union*, 2:367; Winks, *Canada and the United States*, 323–24.

18. Jenkins, *Britain and the War for the Union*, 2:368; Charles Francis Adams to William H. Seward, February 23, 1865, in *Papers Relating to Foreign Affairs, 1865*, pt. 1, 182.

19. John G. Nicolay and John Hay, *Abraham Lincoln: A History*, 10 vols. (New York: Century Co., 1890), 8:25–26; Stuart, "St. Albans, Vermont, Raid," 1846.

20. William H. Seward to Charles Francis Adams, March 8, 20, 1865, in *Papers Relating to Foreign Affairs, 1865*, pt. 1, 197, 252.

21. *The Times* (London), March 24, 1865.

22. As quoted in Herbert Mitgang, ed., *Abraham Lincoln: A Press Portrait* (Athens, Ga., and London: University of Georgia Press, 1989), 446–47.

23. Horace Porter as quoted in *Recollected Words of Abraham Lincoln*, ed. Don E. Fehrenbacher and Virginia Fehrenbacher (Stanford, Calif.: Stanford University Press, 1996), 370.

24. William H. Seward to Charles Francis Adams, March 1, 1865, in *Papers Relating to Foreign Affairs, 1865*, pt. 1, 191.

25. For Napoleon III's Grand Design, see Alfred Jackson Hanna and Kathryn Abbey Hanna, *Napoleon III and Mexico* (Chapel Hill: University of North Carolina Press, 1971), 90. This book is still the best study of Napoleon's Mexican venture and the fate of Emperor Maximilian.

26. Annual Message to Congress, December 6, 1864, in *Collected Works of Lincoln*, 8:137.

27. Case and Spencer, *The United States and France*, chap. 15. The Union governor of occupied Louisiana reportedly made a speech announcing that he "was not afraid to mention [the Monroe] doctrine by name" and proposed that Northern and Southern troops combine to expel the French and Maximilian from Mexico (ibid., 521–22). Privately, both Lincoln and Seward were sympathetic to Juarez, an admirer of the American president (Jasper Ridley, *Maximilian and Juárez* [New York: Ticknor & Fields, 1992], 119).

28. For documents relating to the Davis resolution, see Edward McPherson, ed., *The Political History of the United States of America, During the Great Rebellion* (Washington, D.C.: Philp & Solomons, 1865), 349–54, and *Speeches and Addresses Delivered in the Congress of the United States and on Several Public Occasions, by Henry Winter Davis of Maryland* (New York: Harper and Brothers, 1867), 472–79.

29. *Congressional Globe*, 38th Cong., 2d Sess. (December 20, 1864), 50–51; McPherson, *Political History*, 600.

30. *New York Times*, December 28, 1864. See also the *Boston Daily Advertiser*, December 24, 1864.

31. *New York Herald*, January 8, 25 (quotation), February 27, 1865.

32. See William C. Harris, "The Hampton Roads Peace Conference: A Final Test of Lincoln's Presidential Leadership," *Journal of the Abraham Lincoln Association* 21 (Winter 2000): 31–61.

33. Quoted in Case and Spencer, *The United States and France*, 561. Edouard de Stoeckl, the Russian minister in Washington, believed that the Blair scheme had Lincoln's approval. He reported to his government that American armies would soon be sent into Mexico. Sir Frederick Bruce, the new British minister to the United States, on the day of Lincoln's assassination, wrote London that America planned to oust Maximilian. Both Stoeckl and Bruce were wrong (Adams, *Great Britain and the American Civil War*, 251, 255n).

34. Harris, "Hampton Roads Peace Conference," 48–49; Adolphe de Chambrun, *Impressions of Lincoln and the Civil War: A Foreigner's Account*, trans. Aldebert de Chambrun (New York: Random House, 1952), 48.

35. Case and Spencer, *The United States and France*, 563–64.

36. August Belmont to William H. Seward, March 2, 1865; John Bigelow to Seward, March 2, 1865, both in William H. Seward Papers, Rush Rhees Library, University of Rochester; Seward to Bigelow, March 6, 1865, in *Retrospections of an Active Life*, 3 vols., by John Bigelow (New York: Baker and Taylor, 1909), 2:360.

17. Henry Adams on Lincoln
GARRY WILLS

1. J. C. Levenson et al., *The Letters of Henry Adams*, 6 vols. (Cambridge, Mass.: Harvard University Press, 1982–1988), 1:493.

2. Levenson et al., *Letters*, 1:494.

3. Ernest Samuels and Jayne N. Samuels, eds., *Novels, Mont St. Michael, The Education* (New York: The Library of America, 1983), 809; Levenson et al., *Letters*, 6:365, 372.

4. Levenson et al., *Letters*, 1:67.

5. Ibid., 1:76.

6. Ibid., 1:91–92.

7. Samuels and Samuels, *Education*, 814.

8. Levenson et al., *Letters*, 1:204.

9. Ibid., 1:215.

10. Samuels and Samuels, *Education*, 814.

11. Levenson et al., *Letters*, 1:223.

12. Ibid.

13. Ibid., 1:209.

14. Ibid., 1:218.

15. Charles Francis Adams II, *An Autobiography* (Boston: Houghton Mifflin Company, 1916), 77, 82.

16. Henry Adams, "The Great Secession Winter of 1860–1861," *Proceedings of the Massachusetts Historical Society* 43 (June 1910): 681–82.

17. Ernest Samuels, *The Young Henry Adams* (Cambridge, Mass.: Harvard University Press, 1965), 95–96.

18. Mark E. Neely, Jr., "Abraham Lincoln and the Adams Family Myth," *Lincoln Lore* 1667 (January, 1977): 1–4.

19. Norman B. Ferris, *Desperate Diplomacy: William H. Seward's Foreign Policy, 1861* (Knoxville: University of Tennessee Press, 1976), 22–23.

20. Levenson et al., *Letters*, 1:239.

21. Richard N. Current, *Lincoln and the First Shot* (Philadelphia: J. B. Lippincott, 1963), 103–10.

22. Adams, *Autobiography*, 89.

23. Levenson et al., *Letters*, 1:263–64.

24. Samuels, *Young Henry Adams*, 109.

25. David Donald, *Charles Sumner and the Rights of Man* (New York: Alfred A. Knopf, 1970), 25.

26. Ibid.

27. Norman B. Ferris, *The Trent Affair: A Diplomatic Crisis* (Knoxville: University of Tennessee Press, 1977), 171–81.

28. Ibid., 184–86.

29. Levenson et al., *Letters*, 1:272.

30. Samuels and Samuels, *Education*, 830.

31. Levenson et al., *Letters*, 1:295.

32. Ibid., 1:260.

33. Samuels and Samuels, *Education*, 824.

34. Ferris, *Trent Affair*, 102.

35. Levenson et al., *Letters*, 1:268, 275.

36. Samuels and Samuels, *Education*, 853.

37. Charles Francis Adams, *An Address on the Life, Character, and Services of William Henry Seward* (Albany, N.Y.: Weed, Parsons and Company, 1873), 47, 48.

38. Samuels and Samuels, *Education*, 815–16.

39. Ibid., 817.

40. Levenson et al., *Letters*, 2:46.

41. Ibid., 3:53.

42. Ibid., 3:249.

43. Ibid., 4:21.

18. Lincoln's Assassination and John Wilkes Booth's Confederate Connection
EDWARD STEERS, JR.

1. Emma LeConte, quoted in Carolyn L. Harrell, *When the Bells Tolled for Lincoln: Southern Reaction to the Assassination* (Macon, Ga.: Mercer University Press, 1997), 59–60.

2. *Texas Republican*, April 28, 1865.

3. *Galveston Daily News*, April 27, 1865. For an excellent essay on the reaction in Texas to Lincoln's death, see John M. Barr, "The Tyrannicide's Reception: Responses in Texas to Lincoln's Assassination," *Lincoln Herald* 91, no. 2 (Summer 1989): 58–64.

4. Harrell, *When the Bells Tolled for Lincoln*, 86.

5. Barr, "The Tyrannicide's Reception," 56.

6. Edwin M. Yoder, Jr., "Booth's Conspiracy," in *Book World* (*Washington Post*), February 10, 2002, 8.

7. Only authors William A. Tidwell, James O. Hall, and David W. Gaddy in their impressive study of the Confederate Secret Service, *Come Retribution: The Confederate Secret Service and the Assassination of Lincoln* (Jackson: University Press of Mississippi, 1988), conclude that Confederate officials were involved in Booth's plot.

8. S. S. Anderson to E. Kirby Smith, June 13, 1863, quoted in H.R.C., 39th Cong., 1st Sess., doc. 104, 2.

9. Dunbar Rowland, ed., *Jefferson Davis, Constitutionalist: His Letters, Papers and Speeches* (Jackson: University of Mississippi Press, 1923), 5:409–11.

10. Nat Brandt, *The Man Who Tried to Burn New York* (Syracuse, N.Y.: Syracuse University Press, 1986), 71.

11. John W. Headley, *Confederate Operations in Canada and New York* (New York: The Neale Publishing Company, 1906), 264–73; Edward Steers, Jr., "Terror—1860s Style," *North & South* 5, no. 4 (May 2002): 12–18.

12. Edward Steers, Jr., "Risking the Wrath of God," *North & South* 3, no. 7 (September 2002): 59–70.

13. *The Collected Works of Abraham Lincoln*, 9 vols., ed. Roy P. Basler et al. (New Brunswick, N.J.: Rutgers University Press, 1953–55), 6:202–3.

14. Jefferson Davis, *The Rise and Fall of the Confederate Government*, 2 vols. (New York: D. Appleton and Company, 1881), 2:506; Duane Schultz, *The Dahlgren Affair: Terror and Conspiracy in the Civil War* (New York: W. W. Norton & Company, 1998), 156–57.

15. Quoted ibid., 160.

16. Quoted ibid., 175.

17. Jefferson Davis, *The Rise and Fall of the Confederate Government*, 2 vols. (1881; reprint, New York: Da Capo Press, 1990), 1:426.

18. General Order Number 100 can be found in Benn Pitman, *The Assassination of President Lincoln and the Trial of the Conspirators* (New York: Moore, Wilstach & Baldwin, 1865), 410–19.

19. See Burris Carnahan, "General Order Number 100," in *The Trial*, ed. Edward Steers, Jr. (Lexington: The University Press of Kentucky, 2003), xcvii.

20. Edward Steers, Jr., *Blood on the Moon: The Assassination of Abraham Lincoln* (Lexington: The University Press of Kentucky, 2001), 48–49.

21. John Wilkes Booth to Edwin Frank Keach, December 8, 1862, in *"Right or Wrong, God Judge Me": The Writings of John Wilkes Booth*, ed. John Rhodehamel and Louise Taper (Chicago: University of Illinois Press, 1997), 83.

22. Testimony of Joseph Simonds in *The Conspiracy Trial, for the Murder of the President, and the Attempt to Overthrow the Government by the Assassination of its Principal Officers*, 3 vols., by Ben. Perley Poore (1865; reprint, New York: Arno Press, 1972), 1:41.

23. Quoted in Ernest C. Miller, *John Wilkes Booth in the Pennsylvania Oil Region* (Meadville, Pa.: Crawford County Historical Society, 1987), 35.

24. Steers, *Blood on the Moon*, 56.

25. Samuel Blank Arnold, *Memoirs of a Lincoln Conspirator*, Michael W. Kauffman, ed. (Bowie, Md.: Heritage Books, Inc., 1995).

26. *New York World*, April 21, 1865.

27. Tidwell et al., *Come Retribution*, 265.

28. Ibid., 330; *Official Records of the Union and Confederate Navies in the War of the Rebellion*, 30 vols. (Washington, D.C.: Government Printing Office, 1894–1914), ser. 1, 2:822–28.

29. Testimony of Robert Anson Campbell, in Poore, *The Conspiracy Trial*, 2:83–89.

30. Poore, *The Conspiracy Trial*, 2:87.

31. Statement of Luther B. Baker, NARA, M-619, reel 455, frames 0665–0689. Statement of Everton Conger, NARA, M-619, reel 455, frames 0723–0729.

32. Testimony of John Lee, in Poore, *The Conspiracy Trial*, 1:62–69.

33. Booth made two deposits into the account, the first on November 16 ($1,500) and the second on January 5 ($250). The funds were dispersed with seven checks ranging from $25 to $750.

34. Testimony of Eaton G. Horner, in Poore, *The Conspiracy Trial*, 1:430. Horner testified that Booth had "letters of introduction to Dr. Mudd and Dr. Queen."

35. Poore, *The Conspiracy Trial*, 1:435.

36. Testimony of John C. Thompson, in Poore, *The Conspiracy Trial*, 2:269.

37. *Baltimore American*, July 10, 1865, p. 1, col. 3.

38. Steers, *Blood on the Moon*, 78–79.

Contributors

JEAN BAKER is widely considered the leading authority on the life of Mary Todd Lincoln. Her 1987 biography of the president's wife won many awards. She has also written about the origins of the Republican party and the life of Adlai E. Stevenson and recently wrote the introduction for C. A. Tripp's "intimate" biography of Lincoln. Professor Baker teaches at Goucher College in Maryland.

DANIEL MARK EPSTEIN, a poet and biographer whose earlier books include lives of Nat King Cole, Aimee Semple McPherson, and Edna St. Vincent Millay, is the author of the study *Lincoln and Whitman: Parallel Lives in Civil War Washington* (2004). His verse has appeared in the *Atlantic Monthly,* the *New Yorker,* and the *Paris Review*, among other publications.

JOSEPH R. FORNIERI, associate professor of political science at Rochester Institute of Technology (RIT), won his school's 2001–2002 Provost's Award for excellence in teaching. He is the author of *Abraham Lincoln's Political Faith* (2005) and editor of *The Language of Liberty: The Political Speeches and Writings of Abraham Lincoln* (2003). Most recently, he coedited *Lincoln's American Dream: Clashing Political Perspectives* (2005).

William C. Harris is the author of *Lincoln's Last Months* (2004) and *With Charity for All: Lincoln and the Restoration of the Union* (1999), which won a Lincoln Prize. David Herbert Donald called his most recent work "one of the half-dozen books on Lincoln published in the last decade that must be read by every student of the American Civil War." Harris serves as professor emeritus of history at North Carolina State University.

Harold Holzer, senior vice president for external affairs at The Metropolitan Museum of Art, serves also as cochairman of the U.S. Lincoln Bicentennial Commission, vice chairman of the New York State Bicentennial Commission, and vice chairman of The Lincoln Forum. His twenty-eight books include *Lincoln at Cooper Union: The Speech That Made Abraham Lincoln President* (2005), which won a Lincoln Prize.

John F. Marszalek is the recently retired W. L. Giles Distinguished Professor of History Emeritus at Mississippi State University, and his most recent book is *Commander of All Lincoln's Armies: A Life of General Henry W. Halleck* (2004). His other books include *Sherman: A Soldier's Passion for Order* (1993) and the definitive story of the general and the press, *Sherman's Other War* (1999).

William Lee Miller is the author of the widely admired book, *Lincoln's Virtues: An Ethical Biography* (2002). Now serving as the Miller Center of Public Affairs Scholar in Ethics and Institutions at the University of Virginia, he is the author of many other studies, including *Arguing About Slavery: The Great Battle in the United States Congress* (1996), which won the D. B. Hardeman Prize for the best book on Congress.

Lucas E. Morel, who is associate professor of politics at Washington and Lee University in Lexington, Virginia, is the author of *Lincoln's Sacred Effort: Defining Religion's Role in American Self Government* (2000). Morel has made several appearances at The Lincoln Forum.

Geoffrey Perret, who has written critically praised best-sellers about Ulysses S. Grant, Dwight David Eisenhower, Douglas MacArthur, and John F. Kennedy, is the author of *Lincoln's War: The Untold Story of America's Greatest President as Commander in Chief* (2004). His many other books include *America in the Twenties: A History* (1983), *There's a War to Be Won: The United States Army in World War II* (1997), and *Winged Victory: The Army Air Forces in World War II* (1997).

Matthew Pinsker made a mark in the Lincoln field with *Lincoln's Sanctuary: Abraham Lincoln and the Soldiers' Home* (2003), a now-classic study of the sixteenth president and his country retreat. Pinsker, who teaches at Dickinson College in Pennsylvania, previously wrote the biography *Abraham Lincoln* (2002) for the American Presidents Reference Series.

John Y. Simon won a Lincoln Prize for his inspired editing of the twenty-eight-volume (to date) *Papers of Ulysses S. Grant,* considered both a model of documentary editing and a landmark in the study of the Civil War. A professor of history at Southern Illinois University Carbondale, Simon has written widely on Lincoln and Grant, and serves as executive director of the Ulysses S. Grant Association.

JEAN EDWARD SMITH is the author of *Grant* (2001). Currently the John Marshall Professor of Political Science at Marshall University, Smith's many other works of history and biography include *John Marshall: Definer of a Nation* (1998) and *Lucius D. Clay: An American Life* (1992).

EDWARD STEERS, JR., is widely acknowledged as the nation's leading expert on the assassination of Abraham Lincoln. His widely praised book, *Blood on the Moon: The Assassination of Abraham Lincoln* (2001) is considered the classic in the field, and his many other works on the subject include the recent volume *The Trial: The Assassination of President Lincoln and the Trial of the Conspirators* (2003).

CRAIG L. SYMONDS, recently retired as professor of history at the U.S. Naval Academy at Annapolis, now serves as chief historian of the *U.S.S. Monitor* Center at the Mariners' Museum in Newport News. His many books include acclaimed biographies of Patrick Cleburne, Franklin Buchanan, and Joseph E. Johnston, and his most recent work is *Decision at Sea: Five Naval Battles That Shaped American History* (2005).

MICHAEL VORENBERG, associate professor of history at Brown University, is the author of the book *Final Freedom: The Civil War, the Abolition of Slavery, and the Thirteenth Amendment* (2001).

RONALD C. WHITE, JR., has written seven books, including *Lincoln's Greatest Speech: The Second Inaugural* (2002) and *The Eloquent President: A Portrait of Lincoln Through His Words* (2005). Currently working on a full-length Lincoln biography, Dr. White is a professor of American Intellectual and Religious History at San Francisco Theological Seminary and a Fellow of the Huntington Library.

FRANK J. WILLIAMS, founding chairman of The Lincoln Forum, is chief justice of the Supreme Court of Rhode Island. A leading Lincoln collector, he also served as longtime president of the Lincoln Group of Boston and the Abraham Lincoln Association, and continues to serve as president of the Ulysses S. Grant Association. A member of the U.S. Lincoln Bicentennial Commission, his books include *Judging Lincoln* (2002).

GARRY WILLS, the Pulitzer Prize–winning author of *Lincoln at Gettysburg: The Words That Remade America* (1992), has written acclaimed books on a breathtaking variety of subjects, ranging from the cultural impact of George Washington to the meaning of Catholicism to the films of John Wayne. He has also written on modern leaders—Nixon, Reagan, and Kennedy. His most recent book is *Henry Adams and the Making of America* (2005).

The Lincoln Forum

www.thelincolnforum.org